Jan Harder

# Software Clones
Guilty Until Proven Innocent?

Bibliographic information published by the Deutsche Nationalbibliothek

The Deutsche Nationalbibliothek lists this publication in the Deutsche Nationalbibliografie; detailed bibliographic data are available on the Internet at http://dnb.d-nb.de .

ISBN 978-3-8325-4588-8

Logos Verlag Berlin GmbH
Comeniushof, Gubener Str. 47,
10243 Berlin
Tel.: +49 (0)30 42 85 10 90
Fax: +49 (0)30 42 85 10 92
INTERNET: http://www.logos-verlag.de

# Software Clones
## Guilty Until Proven Innocent?

Dissertation

Submitted by
## Jan Harder

on
## April 12, 2017

to the
## University of Bremen
*Faculty of Mathematics and Computer Science*

in partial fulfillment of the requirements for the degree of
## Doktor der Ingenieurwissenschaften

Defended
## October 20, 2017

Supervised by
## Prof. Dr. rer. nat. Rainer Koschke
*University of Bremen, Germany*

and
## Dr. rer. nat. Jens Krinke
*University College London, United Kingdom*

*To my parents.*

# Acknowledgments

I would like to express my sincere gratitude to my advisor Rainer Koschke for his endless patience, scientific advice, the freedom he allowed for my research, and the many opportunities he made possible to travel around the world and get in touch with so many other scientists. I also heartily thank my co-supervisor Jens Krinke for his valuable and extensive feedback, but also for lying the scientific groundwork for part of my research.

Thanks to my colleagues from the *Software Engineering Group* at the *University of Bremen*, especially to Nils Göde, with whom I co-authored so many papers, and to Rebecca Tiarks, who helped me to conduct sound human-based studies. I would also like to thank my student assistants Carsten Berje, Marcel Steinbeck, and Ole Riemann for helping me with the technical realization of all the processes and computations required for the extensive studies.

Everyone who participated in my experiments deserves thanks, as well as Debarshi Chatterji, Jeffery Carver, and Nicholas Kraft from the *University of Alabama*, who instantly volunteered to replicate my work and helped to generate significant results.

I thank my beloved wife Isabell for being so compassionate when she, yet again, had to spend a weekend alone, because I was busy working on this thesis. Last but not least, I thank my parents for their true and unwavering support, motivation, and faith.

*Jan Harder, April 2017*

# Abstract

Software systems contain redundant code that originated from the use of copy and paste. While such cloning may be beneficial in the short term as it accelerates development, it is frequently despised as a risk to maintainability and quality in the long term. Code clones are said to cause extra change effort, because changes have to be propagated to all copies. They are also suspected to cause bugs when the copied code fragments are changed inconsistently.

These accusations may be plausible but are not based on empirical facts. Indeed, they are prejudice. In the recent past, science has started the endeavor to find empirical evidence to support the alleged effects of clones.

In this thesis, we analyze the effects of clones from three different perspectives. First, we investigate whether clones do indeed increase the maintenance effort in real and long lived software systems. Second, we analyze potential reasons for the cases where clones do cause bugs. Third, we take a new perspective to the problem by measuring the effects of clones in a controlled experiment. This allows us to gather new insights by observing software developers during their work, whereas previous studies were based on historical data.

With our work we aim to empirically find advice for practitioners how to deal with clones and, if necessary, to provide an empirical basis for tools that help developers to manage clones.

# Table of Contents

# Part I

# Prelude

# Chapter 1

# Introduction

Creating software is probably one of the most complex tasks in modern engineering. Authoring its essence—the source code—is a creative and iterative process. Although the source code is a formal description of the program's behavior, it is created similarly to text writing. Programmers outline, experiment, and develop the final answer to the problem they are facing while they program. They do not have the final solution in mind when they start writing code. Proper abstractions emerge while they explore the problem in many iterations with small increments to their solution. This creative end of making software is opposed by the requirement to engineer software, that is, first of all, to develop software cost-effective and to reuse existing parts.

Both worlds benefit from a powerful tool of modern editing: *copy and paste*. It allows quick restructuring and replication of existing parts of the code and helps to accelerate the creation of new code. The use of copy and paste is a matter of course in a programmer's daily life. Its short-term benefits come along with a possible debt in the middle and long term. Changes to redundant parts of a software system may need to be repeated for all copies, making changes more expensive. Moreover, in such changes some or all copies may be overlooked. The consequences may be inconsistent behavior, incompletely fixed bugs, or even new bugs.

The assumption that redundancies in the code—which are called clones—cause harm in software is widespread. Its most popular advocates are Martin Fowler and Kent Beck who made clones the number one in their famous *stink parade of bad smells* [50]. The fear of clone-related bugs and the aim to reduce maintenance costs by removing redundancies initiated the field of code clone research. Many techniques and tools to detect clones have been proposed and developed, some of which are even commercially marketed. Methods have already been proposed for clone management in order to prevent the creation of clones or to mitigate their alleged hazards.

But what exactly is the problem these techniques try to solve? It seems natural that redundancy should be avoided, but at the same time the adoption of clone detection techniques in industry goes ahead slowly [34]. Recent research casts doubt on the conviction of clones. Cases exist where cloning is a reasonable means in software development [94] and some recent empirical results even suggest that clones are less costly to maintain than the code that is not cloned [112]. All this does not necessarily mean that cloning should be encouraged. Nevertheless, we need to learn whether and to which extent the frequently voiced negative effects of clones do actually exist. If they exist, we need to differentiate under which circumstances clones do harm, because not all of them may be bad. All measures to prevent clones or to assist programmers to handle them come at a cost. In order to bring clone detection and management into use, we need to understand the effects they aim to prevent, first.

## 1.1   Contributions

Other than most work in this field, we solely focus on the effects clones have on program correctness, changeability, and comprehension. Instead of presenting new or improved techniques to detect or manage clones, we use existing ones to improve the understanding of how clones affect software quality aspects. Understanding the effects of clones is the key to future clone detection and clone management techniques. That is, reasonable strategies to handle clones can only be justified with empirical knowledge on the effects clones have on software systems.

Research in this area is not entirely new. Others have pioneered this area of clone research and it advanced while this work was created. In this thesis we analyze the effects of clones from three different perspectives. First, we aim to continue initial research results, which are controversial and need further validation. To this end, we replicate and extend existing work, which still happens rarely. Second, with the first controlled experiment in the field of software clones we pioneer a new and yet missing methodology, which, in the meantime, has been continued by others. Third, we investigate how different code authors influence the effects of clones, which adds a new perspective to the discussion.

The remainder of this section summarizes our contributions for the three perspectives of the research subject.

### 1.1.1   Clone Stability

The first perspective of our research is how clones affect the changeability of software programs. We replicate and continue research that has been initiated by Jens Krinke and produced controversial results that suggest that clones may positively affect changeability [112]. In our research, we do not only validate Krinke's surprising findings, we also largely extend the investigation to different subject systems from different domains that are written in different languages. We also investigate whether different kinds of clones lead to different results. That is, we aim to validate and generalize Krinke's findings.

Our results give important insights about the amount of change that appears in cloned code compared to non-cloned code. These are required to determine if and when clone management activity is worthwhile.

We manually inspect how the stability of clones changes over time and what drives these changes. The results of this part contribute to the understanding how clones are created and maintained. Our results provides foundations to decide which situations should be supported by clone management tools.

### 1.1.2 Clone Authorship

The second perspective is how multiple software developers affect the maintainability of clones. We contribute a first empirical study that is solely dedicated to the question how the co-work of multiple developers in the creation and maintenance of clones affects the changeability and correctness of the software. We provide insight how developers interrelate in the creation and maintenance of clones. Our results provide empirical data to answer the questions whether multiple authors are a cause for inconsistent changes to clones that cause bugs, whether such clones are more likely to be changed inconsistently, and whether such clones cause higher maintenance costs through more frequent changes.

Our results give advice for clone management whether co-working developers must be assisted when maintaining cloned code and whether the number of authors, who are involved changing a clone, can be used to assess the risk of clones and to prioritize them for management activity.

We also present a new technique to track the authorship of source code on a fine-grained level that can be used for other research questions, too.

### 1.1.3 Clones and Programmer Performance

The third perspective is the effect clones have on the performance of programmers when they perform maintenance tasks. We conduct the first controlled experiment with programmers in the field of clone detection to analyze the effects of clones. So far, all research on the effects of clones was based only on archived data of past projects. Our results provide insight into how the performance of programmers is affected according to correctness and time by the presence of clones. As this is the first study of this kind, we provide all data required to replicate our study and report on the results of existing replication efforts.

## 1.2 Previously Published Content

Most of the contents of this thesis have been published previously in the proceedings of scientific conferences or journals. These publications are listed in this section along with the chapters where their contents are used.

- Nils Göde and Jan Harder.
  **Clone Stability**,
  *Proceedings of the 15th European Conference on Software Maintenance and Reengineering,*
  pages 65–74, 2011,
  Chapter 6

- Jan Harder and Nils Göde.
  **Cloned Code: Stable Code,**
  *Journal of Software: Evolution and Process,*
  25(10):1063–1088, 2012,
  Chapter 6

- Jan Harder and Rebecca Tiarks.
  **A Controlled Experiment on Software Clones,**
  *Proceedings of the 20th International Conference on Program Comprehension,*
  pages 219–228, 2012,
  Chapter 8

- Jan Harder.
  **How Multiple Developers Affect the Evolution of Code Clones,**
  *Proceedings of the 29th International Conference on Software Maintenance,*
  pages 30–39, 2013,
  Chapter 7

- Debarshi Chatterji, Jeffrey C. Carver, Nicholas A. Kraft, and Jan Harder.
  **Effects of Cloned Code on Software Maintainability: A Replicated Developer Study,**
  *Proceedings of the 20th Working Conference on Reverse Engineering,*
  pages 112–121, 2013,
  Replication results reported in Chapter 8

## 1.3   Thesis Outline

This thesis is organized into three parts. Part I contains this introduction. It is followed by Part II, which explains the fundamentals of software clones and the work of others that is related to this thesis. Chapter 2 gives an overview of software clones in general and introduces the definition and terminology we use in this thesis. How clones can be detected is discussed in Chapter 3. Chapter 4 discusses how clones relate to software engineering. That is, how clones are caused and how they effect the quality of software and its creation process. Since this thesis is dedicated to the effects of clones, we will derive our three research perspectives from the previous work in this area. Part II closes with Chapter 5, which gives an overview of the techniques that have been proposed to manage clones.

Part III is dedicated to the empirical studies. Each chapter presents research questions, methodology, and results for one of our three research perspectives. In Chapter 6 we investigate how clones affect the changeability of programs by comparing the amount of change in different software systems of different domains and under different measurement conditions. Chapter 7 focuses on the question whether the involvement of more than one programmer in the creation and maintenance of clones is a reason why clones are more difficult to maintain or cause bugs through inconsistent changes. Our third perspective is how the presence of clones affects the performance of programmers in terms of time and correctness when they perform maintenance tasks. We conducted a controlled experiment to pursue this question, which we describe in Chapter 8.

This thesis closes with Part IV in which we conclude our research and discuss future directions in Chapter 9.

# Part II

# Software Clones

# Chapter 2

# Definition and Terminology

As software engineers our aim is to create effective and efficient software systems in a quality that prevents errors and allows future change, as the surrounding world evolves. But it is not only the creation of such systems we strive for. Our goal is to constantly improve the way software is created to make it more effective and less error-prone.

It belongs to the nature of the field of software engineering to seek for practices that require improvement. A common belief is that software clones are one of such. When, for some reason, a piece of the software appears redundantly in more than one place, it is widely assumed that this will cause problems in the future. It seems natural that cloned software artifacts need to be maintained together. That is, if one clone instance needs to change, the others probably need to change, too. On the one hand, this causes additional effort. On the other hand, changes to clones always come with the risk that one copy is overlooked and not changed. Inconsistent behavior and even program errors could be the consequence. Besides that, duplications cause a larger code base which could be more difficult to understand for the programmer.

Although clones are only one of many 'bad practices', they are often believed to be the worst. When Kent Beck and Martin Fowler composed their famous *Stink Parade of Bad Smells* [50]—their personal compilation of the worst practices in programming— they did not define a ranking. Except for one smell, which they put on top of the list: duplicated code. They even concluded that if there is a way to remove the clone then, in any case, it will be beneficial to remove it.

This strong belief in the relevance of clones is reflected in a large research community, exclusively dedicated to software clones. It started more than two decades ago and is still growing as can be seen by annual meetings and the publication statistics Roy and colleagues presented recently [154].

Although the evil of software clones seems plausible and not deniable in the first place, the verdict is rather based on gut feelings than on empirical knowledge. As scientists and engineers we are obliged to verify the assumption before we plan measures and take action. Ever since Kapser and Godfrey presented a collection of scenarios in which cloning is a reasonable strategy [94], it is clear that a differentiated view on clones is required.

The remainder of this chapter will discuss two essential questions of software clones. The first is whether and how clones can be defined, which is a controversy. The second question is how clones are defined for the purpose of this thesis. A general overview of the field is given in the surveys by Koschke [104], Roy and colleagues [153], as well as Rattan and colleagues [147].

## 2.1   Definition

Clones may appear in different kinds of software artifacts. Besides in source code, there may also be clones in other software artifacts, such as requirement specifications [87] and models [4, 78, 143, 163]. Since this thesis is directed to the question how clones effect the maintainability of program source code, it will exclusively focus on source code clones.

The question, what makes a piece of source code a *clone*, is more difficult to answer than it may seem in the first place. The most generic definition is attributed to Ira Baxter—one of the pioneers in clone detection.

> *Clones are segments of code that are similar according to some definition of similarity.*

> — Ira Baxter

Attempts to find a more precise definition, which can be agreed upon, were not successful [93]. This leaves us with Baxter's generic interpretation, which is unsatisfying for practitioners. Often software engineers are not in particular interested into some code because it is *similar* to other code. They will be interested in code that *requires improvement* because it causes avoidable extra costs. The reason for the lack of an agreeable, more precise definition is probably that the effect of clones cannot be assessed before they can be found. Code clone research started with the technical challenge of detecting clones based on similarity. Thus, in the first place, clones were defined by what could be detected, not by what matters in practice. The definition of the term clone has been an ongoing discussion among tool developers and empirical researchers ever since.

Kapser and colleagues let experts evaluate clone candidates that were detected by different detection tools [93]. The experts were asked whether, in their opinion, a candidate is a clone or not. Only half of the 20 clones that were presented got a positive agreement of at least 80% of the experts. For some experts the similarity of code and structure was a main characteristic for clones while the judgment of others was dependent on semantics, the cause of the clone, or whether refactoring was possible. In some cases the experts even came to a different judgment because of the same argument: The fact that some clones contained idiomatic code, such as common call sequences of API methods, was named as a characteristic and an exclusion criterion for being a clone.

Despite being an eight year old discussion this disagreement still illustrates the dissent that can still be observed at recent community meetings. The definition of code clones may be based on some kind of similarity, the detection technique, their cause,

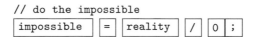

**Figure 2.1** – Tokens in source code.

their effect, or possible countermeasures. This implies that a universal definition of code clones does not exist. How they are defined depends on the respective task someone wants to achieve. Understanding cloning, refactoring existing ones and improving library interfaces are three examples for tasks that require a different definition of clones.

## 2.2  Terminology

The lack of a sound and precise definition of clones presents us with a chicken-and-egg problem. In this thesis we will analyze the effect of clones on maintainability. At present, there are no clone detectors that find clones that are relevant because of their effect on maintainability, though. Building such a clone detector would ultimately require us to understand the effects clones have on maintainability. This understanding is what we aim to achieve with our work. To gather it, we instead start our research with a technically inspired definition of clones, because only these can be detected by tools, today. That is, the terminology described in the following serves as a working definition for this thesis.

In the following we will give a generic definition of the terms but also relate each of them to token based clone detection. This is the kind of clone detection we will use throughout this thesis. The reasons for this choice will be explained in Chapter 3. All upcoming definitions have been developed and used together with the other researchers in the *Software Engineering Group* at the *University of Bremen*, where this thesis was created. Consequently, it matches the terminology frequently used by Bazrafshan, Falke, Göde, and Koschke. Since part of this work has been done in close cooperation with Nils Göde the following part closely resembles the previously published part on clone terminology in his thesis [56].

### Token

A token is the smallest meaningful unit in the source code of a program. It represents a sequence of characters that have a collective meaning [3]. The term is known from the field of language grammars and compilers. Elements such as identifiers, literals or control characters, are represented by one token. Comments and whitespace characters do not represent tokens in our definition. Figure 2.1 shows tokens in one statement.

Since source code consists of tokens, code clones are also sequences of tokens. Tokens are sequences of characters with a collective meaning [3]. Each token has a type and may have a value. The type defines a token's category, such as a literal, a specific keyword or a specific operator. Token types that have a value are identifiers and literals. Here the value is the actual character sequence that appears in the code, for instance a variable name. Token types without a value are for example keywords or braces.

## Clone Fragment

A clone fragment is a continuous code passage that appears cloned to some degree of similarity in another location of the source code. Depending on the clone type, which we will discuss in Section 2.2, clone fragments may contain gaps, that are not part of the other cloned fragment.

In the terms of token based clone detection a clone fragment $f(file, s, l)$ is a continuous sequence of tokens within one code file, which itself is a stream of tokens. A fragment starts at index $s$ of the stream and has a length of $l$ tokens. Code clones consist of at least two code fragments that are similar.

## Clone Pair

When two fragments are clones of each other according to some degree of similarity they represent a *clone pair*. The clone pair representation has the disadvantage that it causes a high volume of data, because every pair is reported as a distinct entity. The number of clone pair relations needed to represent the clone pairs created when a fragment $f$ is copied $n$ times grows quadratically with $n$. This is the case because every fragment $f_i$ is part of a clone pair with all the other fragments $f_{i+1}, ..., f_n$. The number of clone pairs can be computed using an adaption of Gauss' sum formula for integers: $\frac{n^2-n}{2}$.[1]

Although the information represented by clone pairs is precise, it is not suitable for studies as we conduct in this thesis. Besides the sheer amount of reported clone pairs, another problem is the lack of grouping. A fragment that was copied four times will be reported as six separate clone pairs. This makes it impractical to infer higher relationships form the data.

In the terms of our token based clone detection a clone pair is a triple $cp(t, f_n, f_m)$ where $f_n$ and $f_m$ are the two cloned code fragments. The type $t$ of the clone relation expresses the degree of similarity of $f_n$ and $f_n$ and is further explained in Section 2.2. If a fragment appears exactly cloned (type 1) in three locations $f_1$, $f_2$, and $f_3$ there are three clone pairs $cp_1(1, f_1, f_2)$, $cp_1(1, f_1, f_3)$, $cp_1(1, f_2, f_3)$. Among clone pairs of the types 1 and 2 (see Section 2.2) the clone pair relation is transitive $(cp_i(t_x, f_n, f_m) \land cp_j(t_x, f_m, f_o) \Rightarrow cp_k(t_x, f_n, f_o))$. It is also symmetrical $(cp_i(t_x, f_n, f_m) = cp_j(t_x, f_m, f_n))$. By our definition a clone detector will never report both versions of a symmetrical relation, but only one. The clone pair relation is irreflexive, that is, a fragment will never be a clone of its own.

---

[1]Gauss' original formula $\frac{n^2+n}{2}$ sums all integers from 1 to $n$. Compared with this, we sum only 1 to $n-1$, because the first fragment is not a clone of its own.

**Clone Class**

A *clone class* is a set of two or more code fragments that are clones of each other according to some degree of similarity. Every fragment in a clone class forms a clone pair with each other fragment in the class according to the chosen degree of similarity.

The clone class representation is more compact because it requires less relations than clone pairs, if the number of fragments is larger than two. When clone classes have more than two fragments, which often is the case, the lower volume of data clone classes create makes it easier to inspect and analyze clone reports.

In the terms of our token based clone detection a clone class represents the transitive closure over clone pair relations. A clone class is defined as $cc(t, f_1, ..., f_n)$ where, again, $t$ is the type of the clone class relation, $f_1$ to $f_n$ are the fragments that are cloned, and $n$ is the number of clone fragments with $n > 1$. Again, lets assume a fragment $f$ was copied three times without modifications (type 1). The fragments $f_1$, $f_2$, and $f_3$ form one clone class $cc(1, f_1, f_2, f_3)$. In this thesis we will only use clone classes of type 1 and type 2. We allow type-2 classes, which must contain at least one type-2 clone pair, to also contain type-1 clone pairs.

**Clone Type**

As noted before, clone definitions are generally based on some notion of similarity. Davey and colleagues proposed a categorization of the possible differences between clone fragments into four types [38]. Today, this definition is widely accepted as a least common denominator for clone classification [154].

**Type 1.** This type of clones is also commonly referred to as *exact clones*. In a type-1 clone all fragments are identical according to the detection approach. Such clones will often be identical in their textual representation, however, some detection techniques ignore whitespace or semantically irrelevant ordering of keywords and will report type-1 clones if only such differences are present.

In the terms of our token based clone detection all fragments of type-1 clone relations consist of identical token sequences. The type and the value of all tokens are identical. That is, a type-1 clone is the immediate consequence of a copy and paste action. When the fragments are changed inconsistently afterwards, they will not be type-1 clones anymore. Figure 2.2 on the next page shows a type-1 clone pair of Java methods that implement Gauss' sum for integers in a naïve fashion.

**Type 2.** The fragments of type-2 clones may differ in their identifier names and literals. Koschke and Bazrafshan also allow type-2 clones to use different operators [107]. If not by accident, such clones come to existence when code is copied and identifiers or literals are modified. Figure 2.3 on the following page shows a type-2 clone based on our previous example. The differences between the fragments are highlighted.

Sometimes type-2 clones are further classified into *consistently renamed* and *inconsistently renamed* [8]. Figure 2.3 on the next page shows a consistently renamed type-2 clone, because all occurrences of one name or value have been consistently changed into the same value. Inconsistent renaming is seen as a possible indicator for a programming mistake.

```
public int gaussIntegers(int n) {          public int gaussIntegers(int n) {
    int result = 0;                            int result = 0;
    for (int i = 1; i <= n; i++) {             for (int i = 1; i <= n; i++) {
        result = result + n;                       result = result + n;
    }                                          }
    return result;                             return result;
}                                          }
```

       **(a)** Fragment $f_1$                             **(b)** *Fragment $f_2$*

**Figure 2.2** – A type-1 clone pair

In the terms of our token based clone detection type-2 clones are token sequences where the token types are identical, but the identifier and literal tokens may have different token values. In clone classes we allow type-2 clone classes to contain type-1 clone relations as well. Let be $cc(2, f_1, f_2, f_3)$ a type-2 clone class. In this case it is possible that it consists of the clone pairs $cp_1(1, f_1, f_2)$, $cp_2(2, f_2, f_3)$, and $cp_3(2, f_1, f_3)$. In words, fragments $f_1$ and $f_2$ are exact clones of each other, while they are type-2 clones with $f_3$, which has been modified. A clone class that contains at least one type-2 clone pair and no type-3 clone pairs will be regarded as a type-2 clone class.

```
public int  gaussIntegers (int n) {        public int  sumIntegers (int n) {
    int  result  = 0;                          int  count  = 0;
    for (int i = 1; i <= n; i++) {             for (int i = 1; i <= n; i++) {
         result  =  result  + n;                    count  =  count  + n;
    }                                          }
    return  result ;                           return  count ;
}                                          }
```

       **(a)** Fragment $f_1$                             **(b)** *Fragment $f_2$*

**Figure 2.3** – A type-2 clone pair

**Type 3.** In type-3 clone relations a fragment contains gaps compared with the other. Such clones come to existence when code is added, removed, or moved inconsistently to at least one fragment, so that a *gap* appears. Type-3 clone pairs may have one or more of such differences.

In the terms of our token based clone detection the token sequences may differ between the fragments. These differences may be caused by inconsistent modifications of the fragments. Tokens may be added, removed or replaced. Figure 2.4 on the facing page shows a type-3 clone pair of our continued example. It shows two typical causes of type-3 cloning. First, the type of the method argument has been changed from a primitive type (`int`) to a class type (`Integer`) in $f_2$. While `int` is a keyword which has its own token type, `Integer` is represented by a different token type: *identifier*. This already makes the clone a type-3. But also the other adaptations, which are necessary because of the type change, are type-3 differences. Instead of using n directly its integer value must be obtained from a method. This method call has been added in two places. Furthermore, the assignment operator has been changed to the shortcut form +=, which is also a change in the token stream.

Bazrafshan defines type-3 clone classes which differ from type-1 and type-2 classes in not being transitive [20].

```
public int gaussIntegers( int  n) {
    int result = 0;
    for (int i = 1; i <= n; i++) {
      result  = result +  n;
    }
    return result;
}
```

(a) Fragment $f_1$

```
public int gaussIntegers( Integer  n) {
    int result = 0;
    for (int i = 1; i <= n .intValue() ; i++) {
      result  +=  n .intValue() ;
    }
    return result;
}
```

(b) *Fragment $f_2$*

**Figure 2.4** – A type-3 clone pair

**Type 4.** These are clones that implement *identical functionality* [38] or the *same computations* [153], but do not need to be syntactically similar. In contrast to the other types, type-4 clones cannot be defined on tokens in a meaningful way. Figure 2.5 on the next page shows an example of a type-4 clone pair. While $f_1$ implements a naïve approach to calculate the result, $f_2$ uses Gauss' formula. Both methods produce the same result, while being syntactically different.

As of today, there is no reliable way to detect such clones. This is caused by the fact that there is no way of representing and inferring the semantics of a code fragment. Thus, there is no way of comparing fragments by these means. For these reasons type-4 clones are not defined in more detail.

Juergens and colleagues conducted a small experiment in which they attempted to detect type-4 clones with conventional clone detectors [88]. They let students implement the same functionality independently and applied conventional clone detection on the solutions. Almost no clones where found, although each implementation was a type-

4 clone of all the others. They conclude that type-4 clones cannot be detected with existing tools.

```
public int gaussIntegers(int n) {
    int result = 0;
    for (int i = 1; i <= n; i++) {
      result = result + n;
    }
    return result;
}
```

(a) Fragment $f_1$

```
public double gaussQuick(double n) {
    return (Math.pow(n,2) + n) / 2;
}
```

(b) *Fragment $f_2$*

**Figure 2.5** – A type-4 clone pair

## Clone Ratio

A metric to express the degree of cloning in a software system is its *clone ratio*. It describes the percentage of code that is part of at least one clone fragment of a code base. It is also referred to as *clone coverage*. In our experiments with token based clone detection we calculate the clone ratio as the number of cloned tokens divided by the number of all tokens.

## Clone Genealogy

A clone genealogy establishes the relationship of clones across versions of the code. It is used to track individual clone classes or clone fragments over time. This kind of representation is needed to evaluate how clones change over time and how long they exist. Different definitions and extraction methods exist, which will be discussed in detail in Section 3.2.

Figure 2.6 on the facing page shows a clone genealogy based on Göde's visualization [56]. Each horizontal line represents one version of the software. Clone fragments are shown as circles which are grouped into clone classes, shown as surrounding rectangles. The lines from top to bottom connect occurrences of the same fragments in consecutive versions. Changed clone classes are highlighted. This kind of visualization is particularly useful to inspect the evolution of clones.

## Consistent and Inconsistent Changes

The fragments of clone classes or clone pairs may change from one version to the next. A *consistent change* takes place, when all fragments in a clone class or clone pair are

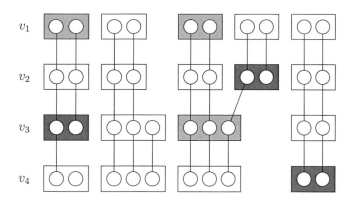

**Figure 2.6** – Göde's clone genealogy visualization [61].

changed in the same way. If the fragments are changed differently, an *inconsistent change* took place. Such changes result in type-2 or type-3 clones or let the clone disappear because the code is not similar enough to be detected as a clone anymore.

In the terms of our token based clone detection a consistent change means that the same addition, removal or replacement of tokens has been applied to all fragments. If the changes differ, an inconsistent change took place.

# Conclusion

This concludes our discussion on the definition of software clones and the essential terminology that is required to understand the following chapters. In the next chapter we will give an overview how such clones can be detected.

# Chapter 3

# Detecting Clones

The research on code clones started with the exploration of techniques to find them in the source code of computer programs. This task requires automation, because a manual search would not be practicable. Any part of a program, be it a module, procedure or just an arbitrary sequence of code, may be cloned with any other part. Hence, everything has to be compared with everything else to find all existing clones. Obviously, this problem has an inherent quadratic complexity, which also causes automated tools that use naïve approaches to deliver bad performance—even for smaller programs.

The first approaches where designed to find clones in one version of a program. The frequently assumed negative effects of clones, however, are often related to changes to clones. Inconsistent changes to the fragments of a clone class are such an example. Consequently, further techniques have been developed to track clones between the versions of the source code and to identify change patterns that may indicate problems.

This chapter first discusses the various techniques that have been proposed for clone detection. Second, existing approaches to track the evolution of clones will be discussed. Finally, an overview of clone evolution patterns is given.

## 3.1   Detection

Various techniques to detect clones in a single version of a program have been published and successfully applied to detect clones in even large-scale software systems. Today, nearly as many different approaches exist as there are definitions for what is a clone. How clones are detected depends on the definition of similarity used and the technical approach to tackle the complexity. This section gives an overview of the common techniques published in literature, ordered by the technical approach. A more detailed overview can be found in the surveys by Koschke [104], Roy and colleagues [153], and Rattan and colleagues [147].

Given the lack of an universal definition of software clones, it is difficult to compare the performance of the different approaches. The selection of the right technique depends on the software that shall be analyzed, the quality of the data, the required result data, and possibly the history that needs to be analyzed. Bellon and colleagues compared different techniques with each other regarding their precision, recall, and efficiency in terms of space and time [23]. They detected clones with different techniques and benchmarked them against a data set that was assessed by a human expert. The quality of the techniques was measured in terms of precision and recall against the reference data set.

### 3.1.1 Textual Comparison

A straightforward approach to clone detection is to search for repetitions in the program's textual representation. This is usually a two-step process. First, the text is split into smaller chunks, which are then compared in some way to find repeating text chunks. Johnson compares sets of consecutive code lines, which he groups into chunks using a sliding window technique [84, 85]. As a next step hashing is used to create a fingerprint for each chunk. Two chunks with the same fingerprint are clones of each other and can be found using common hash based data structures. Manber suggests to either generate a fingerprint for each 50 character subsequence in the program text or to generate fingerprints only at pre-defined starting points, such as method signatures [123]. Roy and Cordy combine a light-weight syntax analysis with textual comparison. First, syntactic blocks are detected which then serve as chunks for the textual comparison [151, 152]. An essential characteristic of fingerprinting is that it finds exact matches only.

Ducasse, Rieger, and Demeyer compare all code lines using hashing [44]. A result they retrieve pairs of cloned lines, which provides a very detailed view of the redundancy in a program. Hence, they use a dot plot visualization to manually identify longer clone sequences. Wettel and Marinescu presented a technique to find type-3 clones with Ducasse's approach by analyzing the dot plot matrices automatically for gaps in the sequences of cloned lines [175].

Cordy and colleagues applied a text-based clone detection approach to find similar files in web-sites. They compare lines with the Unix tool `diff` and then aggregate the number of identical lines on the file level [35].

#### Strengths

The strength of these approaches lies in their universality. They may be applied to any kind of program because they usually do not depend on specific programming languages. This also makes textual comparison a feasible technique to detect clones in incomplete or syntactically incorrect code because no further analysis of syntax or semantics is required.

#### Weaknesses

Text-based approaches are sensitive to code layout. If the only differences of two fragments are in their whitespace, line breaks, or comments, they will be represented by different strings. Although being semantically identical, string comparisons and fingerprints will only find partial matches, or no match at all because of the different textual representation. Such effects can be reduced by removing whitespace characters during hashing or by normalizing the code with pretty printers, which can add or reorder tokens. For example, they insert braces that were omitted in if blocks with only one statement or reorder method modifiers in Java. Removing comments prior to clone detection is another way to improve detection results. These measures, however, add extra effort to the detection procedure.

Grouping characters or lines into chunks to limit the number of required comparisons prevents the detection of clones that are shorter than the chunk size and, hence, reduces the recall of these techniques. Furthermore, exact string matching on a line or chunk basis is not suited to find type-2 clones.

## 3.1.2 Token Comparison

To circumvent the shortcomings of text-based techniques the program's source code can be decomposed into its smallest meaningful units. These are its tokens, which were already explained in Chapter 2. Since tokens abstract from whitespace, line breaks and comments, token-based clone detection techniques are immune to these.

Baker was the first to present an approach to clone detection utilizing tokens [7, 8]. She utilized and extended suffix trees, an existing search structure for strings. To create a suffix tree, first, all suffixes the string that will be searched are created. Second they are encoded into the tree using a construction algorithm [127, 168]. Tree construction can be achieved in linear time and space. Given the example string *abbabbab* one would add an artificial end token $ so that the list of all suffixes would be:

1. *abbabbab$*

2. *bbabbab$*

3. *babbab$*

4. *abbab$*

5. *bbab$*

6. *bab$*

7. *ab$*

8. *b$*

The tree is composed from all these suffixes. Figure 3.1 on the next page shows the resulting tree for our example. In the tree common prefixes of the suffixes are represented by the same incoming edge. All the outgoing edges from a node start with a different token. Each suffix is represented by one path from the root to a leaf. The leafs are numbered by their suffixes, according to the listing above.

The inner nodes of the suffix tree represent clones in the string. For instance the substring *abbab*, which appears twice in Figure 3.1 on the following page. This can be seen by the two paths from the root node to the leafs 1 and 4, that share the same inner

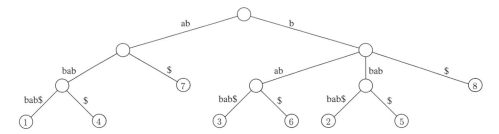

**Figure 3.1** – Suffix tree for the sequence *abbabbab$*

nodes. The start and end index of the fragments can be inferred from the leaf nodes. In this case *abbab* appears at the indices 0 and 3 of the original string, assuming that the first token has index 0. According to our definitions the *bbab* is also represented as a clone with the leaf nodes 2 and 5. To eliminate such artifacts Baker's algorithm extracts maximal clones from the tree.

Baker applied the suffix tree search for clone detection. She transforms the source code of all the program's source files into a continuous token stream —just as a compiler would do. This token stream is used to build the suffix tree. Baker inserts unique delimiter tokens at the end of each file's token stream to prevent clones that overlap file boundaries. Other approaches have adapted suffix trees for clone detection [46, 89, 92]. An alternative data structure to suffix trees are suffix arrays [17, 95].

Another approach to detect clones based on tokens was proposed by Li and colleagues who use the data-mining technique of *frequent subsequence mining* to identify recurring token sequences [120].

Token-based clone detection can be used to detect type-1, type-2, and type-3 clones. While type-1 detection is straightforward, type-2 detection can be achieved in different ways. One way is to compare the tokens only by type in the first place. In a second step type-1 and type-2 clones can be distinguished by comparing the token's literal values.

Baker proposed a method to find consistently renamed type-2 clones directly by extending suffix trees to *parameterized suffix trees* that are build of *parameterized strings*, or in short: *p-strings* [7]. Another approach is to first detect small type-1 clones and then join neighboring clones that are only gapped by an identifier or literal to longer type-2 clones [56, 167]. If one allows the gaps to contain tokens of differing token type, type-3 clones can be detected likewise [120, 167].

**Strengths**

Bellon and colleagues compare Baker's and Kamiya's token based approaches with other techniques and attest them a higher recall [23].

Building the token representation of the source code is fast. Token-based clone detection is also robust against syntactical errors in a program. That is, it can analyze source code that will not compile and it may even detect clones in languages of which the grammar is not available. A common case where this robustness is useful are sources that need pre-processing prior to compilation, such as many C and C++ programs.

Unprocessed code that contains pre-processor directives cannot be parsed, however, it can be transformed into tokens. Robustness is also important when many versions need to be analyzed, as we will do in the case studies of this thesis. Not all available versions may be free of syntactical errors. A third benefit is the possibility to analyze code snippets that do not form complete syntactical units, which is useful in scenarios where code templates have to be analyzed.

The runtime performance of these techniques benefits form the fact that no syntactic analysis is required, which most other techniques need. The suffix tree can be constructed and searched in linear space and time in respect to the length of the token stream. These approaches have been successfully used to analyze large code bases of several million lines of code quickly [59, 89, 92, 120]. The runtime performance can be further improved by parallelizing the detection process [121]. Clones may also be detected across software systems using token-based techniques. Koschke combines suffix-tree based clone detection with hashing to find redundancies between one program and a known corpus of reference programs [105]. This was used to find license violations in open-source software [70].

**Weaknesses**

According to Bellon and colleagues the good recall comes at the cost of a lower precision compared with techniques using syntax or metric comparison [23].

The abstraction from the language's syntax is a shortcoming at the same moment as it is a strength. The techniques will find any matching sequences regardless of syntactic boundaries. The reported clones will often overlap syntactic regions such as methods, classes, or any other syntactic block. One common example is that token-based clone detection will often find cloned fragments that only consist of the end of one method and the signature of the next. Such clones cannot be removed and, hence, are usually not relevant. This problem can be circumvented to some extend by inserting artificial delimiter tokens between methods, which we have done in the studies presented in this thesis. This, however, does not solve the problem that clones may overlap syntactic blocks within a method. Riemann presented a technique to use robust parsing to identify syntactic boundaries within the clones detected with token-based techniques [148].

Token-based clone detection is also sensitive to alternative representations of the same semantics. Java, for example, allows the programmer to omit braces around an `if`-statement's body if it contains only one statement. If the braces are omitted in one copy but present in another one, their token streams will differ. Token-based clone detection may find these copies as a clone when it is capable of type-3 detection. This effect can be lessened by pretty-printing the code prior to analysis.

## 3.1.3  Syntactical Comparison

The discussion on textual and token-based approaches has revealed that code layout and concrete syntax make it difficult to detect similarities. Moreover, these approaches ignore the syntax, which provides valuable information on the code's structure and logical boundaries, such as functions.

Syntactical approaches to clone detection take advantage of the program syntax by converting the code into an *abstract syntax tree* (AST) using the same mechanisms compilers work with. ASTs abstract from all representational information such as layout, braces, or keywords. The tree only contains the program structure and the ordered logical elements needed to execute it. Therefore, clone detection becomes a problem of comparing subtrees of the programs AST.

Similar to the aforementioned techniques, most AST-based clone detection first split the trees into smaller units, which then are compared in a second step. Baxter and colleagues find clones in ASTs by first creating hash codes of all subtrees and, second, comparing these hash codes with each other [19]. Wahler and his colleagues instead use *frequent itemset mining*, a technique from the discipline of data mining, to find statement-level subtrees that occur together [169]. Further comparison techniques include dynamic programming [179], structural abstraction [45], and anti-unification [27]. Multiple authors used tree similarity measures to identify similar subtrees [83, 109, 136, 155]. Lee and colleagues extended this idea with an index-based technique to find similar metric vectors. [117]. Koschke, Falke and Frenzel transformed the tree comparison problem into a search problem on sequences. They use a traversal to serialize the AST into a sequence of tree nodes that can then be analyzed for clones using suffix trees [46, 108]. Their approach combines the advantages of token based and syntax based techniques. Tairas published a similar technique [164].

### Strengths

AST-based approaches take advantage of the syntax instead of ignoring it. Knowing the structure and the syntactic meaning of code entities can be used to improve the results. For instance, detection can be restricted to the function level easily. The syntactical information may also be used in further activity like the assessment of removal opportunities. Moreover, differences in the code representation, such as the order of function modifiers in Java programs, are normalized during parsing and will not distort the clone detection. Baxter's approach was part of the comparative study by Bellon and colleagues and delivered the highest precision of all approaches [23].

### Weaknesses

The downside of syntactic approaches is their complexity. They require a complete tokenization and parsing of the code. If pre-processor directives are used, which is often the case with C and C++ programs, the detection process must take care of these. Baxter reports on three possible methods to achieve this [19]: First, running the preprocessor on the code prior to clone detection, which will result in one of many possible code configurations. Second, inline or ignore includes. Third, add the directives to the language syntax so that they can be processed by the parser, which will only work, when the directives contain complete code blocks. That is, the clone detection is performed on one of many possible code variants, but not on the code representation the programmer actually writes and maintains. If any of these preconditions cannot be met, AST-based clone detection will provide no result at all, which makes it less robust than textual and token-based techniques. If a program contains syntactical errors it cannot be analyzed at all. Furthermore, holding and comparing the AST requires more memory and time compared with textual and token-based techniques [23]. Bellon's comparison of techniques reports a lower recall compared to token-based detection techniques [23].

### 3.1.4 Metric Comparison

The clone detection techniques discussed so far all rely on the structure and presentation of the code. Similarity, however, may also be expressed by other properties of program elements. Metric based approaches to clone detection split programs into smaller units, measure certain properties of these and compare the measurements with each other to find similar units. Units are typically source files, types, methods, or blocks. These approaches usually require an AST to identify the units and may use further program representations, such as data and control flow graphs, to collect metric values.

The metrics used are manifold. Mayrand and colleagues quantify 21 different aspects of functions, such as comments, calls to other functions, statements, declarations, and more [126]. Merlo and Patenaude add metrics on the type hierarchy to this list [129, 141]. Many other metric variations have been published [5, 11, 37, 38, 103].

In order to find clones, the metrics for the previously detected program units must be compared with each other. The simplest, way is to compare the metrics for all program units pair-wise [37, 126]. An approach that is more popular in the literature is to build vectors from the metrics of a unit and compare all vectors using clustering and distance measurement [5, 11, 103, 141]. Other techniques facilitate dynamic programming [103]. Similar approaches are also applied to find clones in web sites [29, 41].

#### Strengths

Metric based approaches can largely abstract from program syntax and layout and, therefore, are less prone to subtle differences of this kind. They may also find different kinds of clones that are not similar because of their structure, but because of their properties. The algorithms used for metric comparison are usually very efficient in terms of speed and memory consumption. The evaluation of Bellon and colleagues included Merlo's metric based detector, which provided one of the best precisions among the compared approaches for type-3 clones [23].

#### Weaknesses

More than syntactical approaches, metric-based techniques require a substantial amount of preparation. Most metrics are computed on intermediate program representations that need to be generated. That is, in order to analyze a program's source code it must be parsed into an AST and further steps, such as data and control flow analysis, must be applied. Metrics on cross-module dependencies will also require name resolution. These steps require time and will only work when the source code has been pre-processed (if necessary) and is free of syntactical and semantical errors.

Another weakness of metric-based approaches is that they only compare programs on the basis of a predefined unit such as functions or classes. Smaller clones, for instance a smaller part of a code block, may not be found if the remainder is not similar enough to the other code block.

Bellon and colleagues found Merlo's approach to provide a low recall [23]. The choice of metrics, however, has a strong effect on the results, as shown by Shawky and Ali who compared the effectiveness of different metrics [161].

### 3.1.5   Dependency Comparison

The approaches discussed so far utilize the program's representation, its structure or quantifiable measures. Another approach is to use *Program Dependence Graphs* (PDG) to detect clones. PDGs are similar to ASTs, but add edges that represent data and control flow dependencies between the nodes. Clones can be detected by searching isomorphic subgraphs in PDGs. Komondoor and Horwitz use program slicing to find isomorphic subgraphs in the PDGs of functions in C programs [101]. Krinke finds similar subgraphs in PDGs created for C programs by searching for similar paths in the graphs [110]. His approach builds up possible paths within the compared graphs simultaneously and uses a threshold to limit the length of possible matches.

**Strengths**

PDG-based techniques are capable of finding clones the aforementioned techniques will miss. The approaches are not sensitive to different statement ordering or gaps between the cloned statements because they analyze how statements interrelate but not how they occur in the code. This allows finding non-contiguous clones. In Bellon's experiment, Krinke's approach performed well in the detection of type-3 clones [23].

**Weaknesses**

Like metric based approaches, this kind of clone detection requires a substantial amount of preparation. Again, programs must be free of errors so that the intermediate representations can be generated. Furthermore language-specific implementations that extract the data and control dependencies must exist. Because of the NP-hard nature of the graph comparison problem the techniques can only approximate a solution. The algorithms require significant time to evaluate. Although finding a reasonable amount of type-3 clones, Krinke's clone detection approach was outperformed in terms of precision and recall by most other techniques in Bellon's experiment [23]. His technique, however, was disadvantaged because the tool comparison was based in continuous code fragments, whereas PDG-based approaches may detect clones that consist on non-consecutive lines of code. Higo improve PDG-based approaches by adding *execution dependencies* as an additional kind of dependency that represents the order in which the statements are executed to improve the capabilities of finding contiguous clones [71].

### 3.1.6   Other techniques

Besides the most common approaches that were discussed before, further techniques for clone detection were proposed.

Marcus and colleagues use the information retrieval technique of *latent semantic indexing* to find similar high-level concepts, such as data types, in programs [124]. Their technique uses identifiers and comments and abstracts from the program structure. Leitao and colleagues combine AST, metric, and dependency information to improve the results of clone detection [118]. Davis and Godfrey detect clones in the assembler code of programs [39]. Kim and colleagues use static analysis to compute abstract memory states for the procedures of a program and search for similarities in these states [96].

## 3.2  Evolution

Conventional approaches to clone detection, as discussed before, find the clones in one version of a program's source code. Many questions, including those about the effects clones have on the maintainability of software, can only be answered in the light of the history of the clones. The sheer presence of clones does not indicate a threat to maintainability. Problems may arise when clones change, especially when this happens inconsistently. Such cases can only be detected when clones are tracked across the versions of a program in some way. Based on tracking information, such as clone mappings and change deltas, changes to clones and common change patterns can be detected. This section will first discuss how clones can be detected efficiently using incremental algorithms. Then it will focus on how the evolution of individual clones can be extracted and which patterns can be derived from clone history. A detailed overview on techniques and patterns is given by Pate, Tairas and Kraft [140].

### 3.2.1  Incremental Detection

A perquisite to efficiently analyze the history of clones is a detection approach that scales up to the problem of detecting clones in many consecutive versions. Göde was the first to present an incremental clone detection algorithm, building up on Baker's suffix-tree based method [59, 60]. His approach utilizes the fact that usually only small portions of the source code change between versions. The first version is analyzed in a conventional way, but the clone detection for all following versions reuses suffix trees, token information, and clones from the previous one. For each new version Göde's technique analyzes the code for changes and then updates the data structures he kept. A *generalized suffix tree* [62] is used, because suffixes can be added and removed to update the structure after code updates. In a comparison with conventional clone detection the incremental approach is faster if not more than 30% to 40% of the code changes between two versions. In exemplary cases where just a single file was changed, the incremental detection required only 35% of the time compared to the original approach. Göde's incremental approach is based on the idea of updating the information that conventional token based detectors, such as Baker's, need. That is, all advantages of these techniques, including the detection of type-1, type-2, and type-3 clones, also apply to his incremental detection.

Other previously published clone detection techniques have also been extended to work incrementally. Nguyen and colleagues perform incremental AST-based clone detection. They adapted an approach that detects AST-subtrees as clones by clustering vectors of syntax-related metrics for similarity [136, 137]. Li and Thompson extend their conventional clone detection technique, which we discussed earlier. In their incremental variant they transform the problem of subtree clustering into an incremental distance-based clustering problem [119]. An incremental approach to PDG-based clone detection was presented by Higo and colleagues [72]. Cordy and Roy added an incremental mode to their text-based clone detector [36].

Other techniques have been originally designed to work incrementally. Hummel and Jürgens perform index-based clone detection [77]. They first detect tokens, which they join together to statements. Then the statements are grouped, fingerprinted, and duplications are searched comparing the fingerprints. The essential difference to other techniques is that a central clone index maintains all hashed sequences which are mapped to their occurrences in files. Incremental updates only require to create the fingerprints for the new or changed files, which are then added to the existing index and the now obsolete fingerprints to be removed. This approach, however, does not handle type-3 clones. Barbour, Khomh and Zou presented an approach that uses a central server to maintain the clone information [14]. Different conventional clone detectors are used and an incremental mode is built on top of them. After the clones for the first version have been detected conventionally the next versions are analyzed as follows. For each known clone class a representative fragment is chosen. Then conventional token or text-based detectors are applied to the changed files and the representatives to find new clones. Newly found clones are then merged into the central clone information storage. This approach does also not detect type-3 clones.

## 3.2.2   Tracking Clones

Incremental detection alone does not necessarily provide the relationships between clones across versions. Different approaches to recognize previously existing clones in subsequent versions have been proposed. The following describes the general approaches to track individual clones that may be used to build general models. For many empirical studies, analyses have been implemented that investigate only specific characteristics of clone evolution, but are not suitable to provide a general overview of how clones evolve.

Kim and colleagues coined the term of *clone genealogies*, following the idea of biological ancestry [98, 99]. To map clone classes across versions they first compute the textual similarity and locational overlap of the clone fragments detected in both versions. Textual similarity is determined using a conventional clone detector on the clone fragments of both versions. To map clone classes Kim and colleagues define a set of logical rules how clone classes may evolve across versions based on both the locational overlap and the textual similarity of their fragments. Their rule set also includes a definition for clone classes that were not changed since the previous version. The rules are applied to identify the mapping between clone classes and the changes applied to them in a single processing step. If all fragments in a clone class in version $v_{i-1}$, for example, appear in a clone class in the next $v_i$, all fragments have a text similarity over a given threshold and all fragments overlap with their counterparts in $v_{i-1}$, then a consistent change is detected from $v_{i-1}$ to $v_i$. That is, the detection of change patterns also defines the mapping between clone classes. This approach is largely based on pattern detection, thresholds, best matches, and the clones that were provided by the clone detector. One clone class in $v_{i-1}$ may be mapped to several clone classes in the next version, which creates a genealogy of clone classes that may split up or even join over time. The clone genealogy can be used to track clones forth and back through history and to inspect the type of their changes at the same time.

Instead of using similarity measures to track clones, Göde has presented an approach that actually tracks individual clone fragments across versions taking the code changes into account [55, 56, 60]. The technique is integrated into his incremental token-based clone detector, which reuses all data structures and updates them with every new version. Göde utilizes the fact that his incremental detection knows the changes to the token sequence from $v_{i-1}$ to $v_i$, to calculate the precise position of all clone fragments in $v_i$. After this mapping step, clones are detected in $v_i$. If the clone detector finds a fragment with the same position as a fragment that was updated from $v_{i-1}$ to $v_i$, these two fragments are identified as the same. Other than Kim, Göde does not map clone classes, but fragments. He represents the fragment ancestry and the clone classes together in one clone evolution graph. This graph can be inspected manually to analyze the history of fragments and their membership in clone classes, but also automatically to identify change patterns based on the clone membership in classes and the changes applied to the fragments in the classes. Göde's approach also allows tracking fragments that are not part of a clone class anymore. These *ghost fragments* may reappear in a clone class in some later version because an inconsistent change was corrected in a later version. Compared to the approach of Kim and colleagues, Göde's method is more precise as it actually tracks fragments based on code changes instead of approximating ancestry based on some similarity and overlap metric. A similar approach, that works text-based instead of token-based was presented by Thummalapenta and colleagues [165]. A *diff* algorithm is used to track changes to fragments.

Saha, Roy, and Schneider extract clone genealogies at the function level [157, 158]. They first apply robust parsing to identify the functions in $v_{i-1}$ and $v_i$. As next step they apply clone detection and map the detected clone fragments to the functions they are contained in. The authors then exploit the fact that they only need to compare the fragments that are contained in the same functions of consecutive versions. If more than one fragment is contained in a function the *longest common subsequence* algorithm is used to find the most likely ancestor by text similarity. As a last step change patterns are detected by comparing the fragments using *diff*. This approach requires a clone detector that detects clones on a function level.

Bakota built a clone tracker [9] on top of the AST-based clone detection from Koschke, Falke, and Frenzel [108]. To map clone fragments across versions Bakota defines a *similarity distance function* that is based on four different measures: first, the similarity of the fragment's lexical structure, second, the textual similarity of the file names, third, the name of the containing class or function, and forth, the position overlap of the fragments in the class or function. After the mapping has been established, patterns are detected.

Nguyen and colleagues also track clones in the context of AST-based clone detection [136, 137]. Their tracking technique is integrated into their clone detection approach, which we discussed previously in Section 3.1. They define incremental clone detection as a problem of incremental distance-based clustering.

Another technique to track individual clone fragments are *Clone Region Descriptors* (CRD) that were presented by Duala-Ekoko and Robillard [42, 43]. CRDs encode structural and syntactic characteristics of the a clone fragment, such as the filename, the name of the class, the signature of the method, the type of the cloned code block (for instance a `for` loop), and other details as conditionals or loop invariants. The idea behind CRDs is that these information rarely change so that they can be used to relocate previously known fragments in later versions of a program. In order to use CRDs clone fragments must align with syntactic blocks and syntactic analysis must be applied to the code.

### 3.2.3   Evolution Patterns

Incremental detection and clone tracking give insight into important properties of clone evolution, such as a clone's life time. How changes to clones affect software maintenance largely depends on how they change. Different patterns indicate different effects. An inconsistent change, for example, may indicate an incomplete code change that could cause a new bug. In contrast, a consistent change may indicate that the programmer was aware of the clone and able to manage the co-change of its fragments. Consistent changes, however, may indicate increased change effort because of the clone. Evolution patterns describe different kinds of changes to clones and how they can be detected combined with clone tracking techniques. Harder and Göde have discussed the challenges in modeling clone evolution [64].

Kim and her colleagues first defined a set of common change patterns to clone classes [99]. They described six different change patterns which can occur solely or together for the same clone class between two versions $v_{i-1}$ and $v_i$. The simplest case is that no change took place, which the authors named the *same* pattern. Fragments may also be *added* or *subtracted* from a clone class. Other patterns model changes to the existing fragments of a clone class. In a *consistent change* all fragments change in the same way, whereas in an *inconsistent change* at least one fragment changes differently than the others. The *shift* pattern models cases where fragments have moved. Figure 3.2 on the next page shows how these patterns may interrelate. multiple patterns can be assigned to a clone class from $v_{i-1}$ to $v_i$. For instance, one fragment may be deleted entirely, while all others change consistently. These patters, especially those on change consistency, have been widely adopted by the scientific community. While most authors refer to the terminology coined by Kim and colleagues, some of them modified the definition of the patterns. Göde, for example, regards the case where one fragment disappears while the others change consistently as an *inconsistent* change because the deleted fragment did not undergo the same changes as the other fragments [56].

Aversano, Cerulo, and Di Penta further refined the pattern of inconsistent change into *inconsistent evolution* and *late propagation* [6]. Inconsistent evolution means that the deviation of the fragments continues, whereas a late propagation is a pattern where the inconsistency is eliminated after some time. Late propagations terminate either by revoking the inconsistent change or by changing the other fragments so that consistency

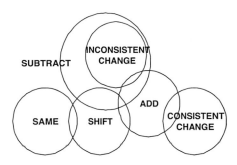

**Figure 3.2** – Venn diagram on how the patterns defined by Kim and colleagues interrelate [99].

is restored belatedly. The notion of late propagation has been used in many other studies, as we pointed out in Section 4.2, before. A peculiarity of late propagations is that they require multiple versions to occur, which makes them different to the change patterns from Kim and colleagues, which all span over just one version step.

A similar, but less comprehensive set of change patterns was described by Bakota, Ferenc, and Gyimóthy [10]. Their pattern set aims to reveal suspicious changes to clone classes that may indicate clone-related code smells. The pattern of *vanished clone instance* models the case where a previously known clone fragment is no longer detected as part of the class in the next version. The authors see this as a possible indication for the case that inconsistent change occurred and the clone detector does not find the fragment because its similarity dropped under the threshold used by the clone detector. The pattern *occurring clone instance* models the situation where a new fragment appears in a previously known clone class. The authors see this pattern as a possible indication that either a new clone fragment was created or that—in the terms of Aversano and colleagues—a late propagation occurred. The case that a fragment disappears in one clone class and appears in another between two versions is called *moving clone instance*. Occurrences of this rare pattern may also indicate inconsistent changes to clone classes. Finally, there is the pattern *migrating clone instance*, in which a fragment moves to another class from $v_{i-1}$ to $v_i$, but reappears in the original clone class in $v_j$, with $i < j$. This pattern is similar to Aversano's late propagation, but differs in the fact that the migrating fragment must be part of a clone class at all times, which a late propagation does not require.

## 3.3  Clone Detection for this Thesis

This thesis describes two empirical studies on clones that analyze clone evolution retrospectively in the source code of different programs. We will use clone detection, clone tracking, and evolution pattern detection. This section explains which of the aforementioned techniques are applied, why we chose them, and how their shortcomings are addressed.

### 3.3.1   Detection and Tracking Approach

Empirical studies on clone evolution must analyze long time periods for many reasons. Changes to clones may differ over time and over the life-cycle phases of a software system. Too few data may make the results too specific and not generalizable. Previous research found that clones tend to live years so that studies on their evolution should analyze time spans that are long enough to capture the whole evolution of long-lived clones. Hence, we aim to analyze the ideal time span which is the whole life time of a project. We analyze up to $10,930$ consecutive revisions and up to $11.6$ years of program history. That is, clone detector, tracker and pattern detector must scale up to these requirements.

We chose token-based clone detection, because it meets our high performance requirements and, at the same time, provides high recall along with a reasonable precision and is robust against syntax errors in the code or grammar changes which necessarily occur in project histories that exceed a decade. The possibility to analyze programs in the presence of pre-processor directives extends the number of possible subject systems, which are difficult to find for such extensive studies. Göde's incremental detection and pattern extraction is chosen for evolution analysis because both analyses are integrated into the incremental detection process and perform well.

### 3.3.2   Improving Precision

As discussed in Section 3.1.2, token-based clone detection provides a high recall, but has some limitations regarding precision. Since no syntactical information is used in the process structural boundaries in the code cannot be taken into account during clone detection. Less interesting parts of the code, such as import statements, cannot be excluded from the detection because their location in the token stream is unknown to the clone detector. We applied pre-processing to the code files and the token stream to mitigate the effect of these problems.

First, all code files that have been generated from a formal specification are removed prior to analysis. These files are mostly parsers that were generated from a language grammar. Such files naturally are highly repetitive because they are built from code patterns. The cloning in such files does not affect the maintainability of the code because it is not maintained by hand. If changes are required, the specification is updated and the code is regenerated. Redundancy in such files may even be desired to improve the runtime performance of the code. Mechanisms such as polymorphism mainly help the programmer to understand the code and to manage reuse, but cause longer execution times because of dynamic binding. Prior to clone detection we use text search to find generated files, which are then removed from the code in all versions. We search for terms, such as *generated, parser,* or *ANTLR* (a parser generator). We then inspect all search results manually before we decide whether to remove or keep them.

```
public void setFoo(int foo) {
  this.foo = foo;
}
```

**Figure 3.3** – A set-method in Java

The second improvement of precision is statement exclusion. Import and package statements often appear as clones. Even if the names of the package and the imports differ these statements will cause an abundance of type-2 clones. Although these sequences represent proper clones from a technical point of view, they are not interesting when the effect of clones on software maintainability is analyzed. Their redundancy cannot be avoided and most IDEs manage them automatically, today. Hence, we remove all of these statements by filtering the token stream before it is passed to the clone detector.

Array initializer statements are another case which we exclude from our analysis. When an array is initialized with a long sequence of values, for instance an encoding table in a word processor, it usually appears as cloned with other array initializers. In many systems these statements make up a large amount of clones that are not interesting to clone detection because the reported clones are usually occurrences of unrelated arrays that mostly contain static data. These statements are also excluded from the token stream before it is passed to the clone detector.

As a third improvement we use method separation. Due to a token-based clone detector's missing knowledge about syntactic structures, clones may embrace more than a single method or function in the source code. That is, clones may start in one method and continue into the next method. To eliminate these artifacts, we pre-process the token sequence of each file prior to clone detection. The boundaries of methods, functions, and procedures are detected with regular expressions. Unique sentinel tokens are inserted between these syntactic units. The clone detector recognizes these special tokens and will not report any clones that overlap them. This mechanism is similar to the file delimiters used in Baker's technique to avoid clones that span over more than one file.

As a side effect, method separation prevents the detection of get- and set-methods as clones. In many programming languages get- and set-methods must be defined for every publicly accessible member of a class to ensure information hiding. These methods usually follow a common pattern that makes them type-2 clones from a technical perspective. Nevertheless, they usually do not change. Often they are generated by the IDE. If method separation is applied and the minimum length is set to a value that exceeds the length of these methods, they will not be reported as clones. In our studies the lowest minimum length threshold for a clone is 50 tokens. A set-method in Java does not exceed 15 tokens as can be seen in Figure 3.3. A side-effect of this decision is that whole files that are cloned will not be reported as a continuous file clone, when they contain identical sequences of methods. The methods, however, will be reported as clones, if they are long enough.

It is important to note that method separation does not cause the clone detector to detect method clones only. It only prevents clones to overlap method boundaries. The reported clones may represent parts of methods, functions, or procedures.

### 3.3.3   Detection Thresholds

Token-based clone detection requires the definition of thresholds that control the similarity and the size of the clones of interest. Göde's clone detection tool `iclones`, which is used for all our studies, allows the detection of type-1, type-2, and type-3 clones [56]. At the time the studies were performed, pattern detection for type-3 clones was not defined. In each study we will explain which types of clones are detected.

The minimum length setting of `iclones` defines how many tokens a clone fragment needs to have to be considered relevant. Choosing a smaller value increases the recall because more clones are found. Choosing a larger value increases the precision because fewer shorter clones are detected that just happen to be similar due to common programming patterns. In our studies we decided to use three distinct values to compare the effect of the minimum length on the results. The values we chose are 50, 100, and 150 tokens. According to a study by Koschke and Bazrafshan one SLOC, a source line excluding blank lines and comments, consists of roughly 6 tokens in programming languages such as Java, C, C++, or C# [107].

To detect type-3 clones `iclones` merges smaller exact matches with gaps between them. The threshold for the allowed maximum gap between the exact matches depends on the length of the exact fragments that are merged. Two fragments are merged if the token length of gap between them does not exceed the token length of the shorter fragment. This procedure is performed for all merge candidates until one fragment cannot be merged because of the gap size.

## Conclusion

This concludes our discussion on existing clone detection techniques and our choices for the empirical studies. Before we describe these in Part III we will discuss the current body of knowledge on the relationship of code clones and software engineering in the following chapter. This will guide us to the research perspectives of our work.

# Chapter 4

# Causes and Effects of Clones

The reason why software clones attract so much attention is the common belief that they negatively affect the creation and maintenance of software systems. After the field of clone research focused on the technical challenge of detecting clones in the source code, scientific investigations about the role of clones in software engineering arouse interest. It is important to understand why and how clones come to existence. On the one hand, insight in the reasons may help to find ways how clones can be avoided. On the other hand, it may reveal cases where cloning is reasonable. More important is the question whether clones do actually effect software quality. Answers to this question are necessary to provide a solid justification for the efforts to find clones and to manage them. Nevertheless, empirical evidence may as well reveal that the effects are too small to justify costly countermeasures. Clone management, that is, the tools and processes designed to prevent and remove clones, to mitigate their effects as well as to support developers handling clones, can only be developed in the light of empirical knowledge on the effects of clones. Today, there is no clear answer to the question how clones affect software. Despite the lack of justification, the detection of clones is more often stated as primary interest of researchers than the analysis of clone-related effects and clone evolution, according to the answers to two surveys by Chatterji, Carver, and Kraft in 2015 [31]. This illustrates the importance of the questions this thesis is dedicated to as the answers will help to guide the efforts of the research community in the right direction.

This chapter summarizes the existing scientific work on how clones relate to software engineering. First, we discuss why clones come to existence. Then we will review the existing empirical evidence on the effects clones have on software engineering. In this part we will also derive the research questions for this thesis from the current state of the field. Finally, we describe the existing methods to manage clones.

# 4.1    Causes

Despite the common belief that clones should be considered harmful and, hence, avoided, they do exist in software systems. The reason that seems most natural is that programmers use copy and paste. But this is just a device that creates clones and not the reason why they are created.

Kim and colleagues conducted an ethnographic study in which they observed programmers during work and report on different copy and paste patterns that explain why and under which circumstances clones are created [97]. Kapser and Godfrey also report on copy and paste patterns including many cases where cloning may be reasonable or inevitable [94]. Zhang and colleagues interviewed industrial programmers about their intentions when creating and removing clones [182]. They suggest to categorize the reasons of cloning into technical, organizational and personal ones. In the following, we will summarize the reported reasons from the aforementioned studies and others using these three categories.

## 4.1.1    Technical Reasons

Programmers may choose to create clones for technical reasons. Programming languages and frameworks may make cloning inevitable. Copy and paste may also be used to avert technical problems.

### Missing Abstraction Mechanisms

Technical shortcomings of the programming language may cause programmers to create clones. One example is the implementation of the same algorithm for different types, when generic programming is not available (as in Java versions prior to 1.5)[97, 99]. Cloning the implementation and changing the types may be the only way to solve the problem. A similar case is the use of programming languages that do not support polymorphism [94]. Instead of reusing code through inheritance the programmer may be forced to copy it.

### Idioms

Programming languages, application domains and libraries often involve common code patterns that are idiomatic. These will appear as clones although they may not have been created by copy and paste. Idiomatic clones will often be created by accident. Kapser and Godfrey distinguish such idioms into two groups [94]: First, language or algorithm specific idioms, such as checking the return after allocating memory in C programs. Second, API and library specific protocols, such as the Java Swing API. The sequence of operations needed to create a button, adding listeners, and adding it to the GUI will usually be very similar.

Another example for idioms are common programming patterns. Kapser and Godfrey report that programmers copy very small snippets of code throughout the code frequently because they represent common language usage, such as collection iterations in Java [94].

Finally, design patterns can also cause cloning. The factory pattern, as Gamma described it [51], is an example. It implements classes with the purpose to create new instance of some kind of object. In many cases the implementations will be very short and similar so that they appear as clones.

### Program Correctness

Copying code can help to avoid defects in the code. One possible strategy is to clone code that proved correct in the past. If an identical or similar solution is required elsewhere, the correct code can be reused in another location. Cordy reports that programmers may do so to save test effort [34]. This observation, however, is not based on empirical data.

It has also been observed that cloning was used to prevent new bugs in existing code. Every change to code entails the risk that new bugs are introduced. So if additional behavior is needed, programmers may create a clone to implement the new behavior and leave the original untouched. Such activity has been observed in the driver implementations of the Linux operating system. When a new version of a hardware device becomes available, a copy of the driver is created for the new version. Changes are only applied to the copy, while the original remains untouched [94]. Zhang and colleagues report that 42.9% of the developers they interviewed create clones to avoid breaking existing features [182].

### Performance

Performance considerations may also be a reason for creating clones. In environments with high performance requirements, such as real-time computing, calling a method or evaluating polymorphy may be too time consuming. Hence, the code may be copied to all locations where its functionality is needed, to save that time [7]. This assumption by Baker has not been investigated empirically, though. Most modern compilers will identify inlining opportunities automatically so that this problem should be of low practical relevance, today.

### Automatic Code Generation

Some disciplines on computer science have reached a maturity which allows them to generate the source code for their applications from formal specifications. Parsers that are generated from grammars or GUI generators are such examples. Generated code tends to be very repetitive because the same code templates are instantiated many times. Such clones, however, are not created manually, neither will the code be maintained by hand in most cases. In all subject systems we analyze in this thesis we have found that no manual adjustments were made to the generated code files we identified as such. Consequently, we omitted this code from our analyses.

## 4.1.2   Organizational Reasons

Reasons for cloning may also be of organizational or social nature. The way how the software development process is organized and other external influencing factors can cause programmers to create code clones.

### Ownership, Rights, and Communication

When a programmer needs to change some existing behavior he may not be able to access the original implementation. This can be the case if it is part of a library that is maintained by someone else or the programmer does not have the necessary rights to change the original code. The programmer could also be unable or unwilling to discuss potential effects of changes to the original code with the responsible developer and, thus, prefer to create a copy that he can adjust to his needs [182].

In such cases cloning could be applied to overwrite the original implementation using inheritance and polymorphism or by creating a copy in a completely new location and calling this one instead of the original. Kapser and Godfrey observed that this strategy was used to implement workarounds for bugs where the defective code passage is not accessible to the programmer [94].

The involvement of more than one programmer in the maintenance of clones may also create the risk that changes are applied inconsistently by accident because not all programmers are aware of the existence of the clones [13, 58].

### Architectural Considerations

The architectural design of a software system may cause cloning. Architects are faced with the challenge to divide the functionality into modules and subsystems and to manage their dependencies. When the same functionality is required in more than one module or subsystem, but these are not allowed to depend on each other, cloning the functionality in all of them may be a compromise. Creating a new shared module with the functionality may not always be the preferable strategy, because it adds dependencies and bloats the architectural design.

Forking a new product from an existing one is another reason for creating clones. If the new product needs to be similar to the existing one, the development of a common platform may be advisable. Creating such a platform, however, comes with high initial costs and may only amortize after several products have been deviated. Therefore, the investment into a platform may be delayed and the first product variants may be created as copies of the original until it becomes clear whether a platform will pay off and which variations it must support [128].

### Time and Budget

When under pressure, copy and paste gives programmers a quick win. Roughly half of the programmers interviewed by Zhang and colleagues stated that time pressure is a reason why they occasionally prefer creating clones instead of planning and implementing a proper abstraction [182].

### 4.1.3  Personal Reasons

Software is created by people. Education, attitude, or personal habits may cause programmers to create clones. The interaction between individual programmers also plays a role [182].

**Lack of Professionalism**

There is a common sense among professionals that cloning is a bad practice. Among others, popular advice to avoid code duplication was given by Beck and Fowler [50] and Martin [125]. Empirical evidence for this assumption is still rare, however, this is also the case for any other so called code smell. Thus, the best advice for practitioners is probably to follow the guidance of these experienced engineers, until further evidence becomes available. Indeed, Zhang and colleagues observed in their study that the more skilled developers tend to have a stronger attitude against cloning compared with their less skilled colleagues [182].

Reasons why programmers use copy and paste to create clones are the unawareness of commonly known best practices, the incapability to solve their problem without cloning, or maybe even ignorance. Programmers may be incapable of avoiding clones because they do not know how to use abstraction mechanisms, such as method extraction, language preprocessors, generic programming, object-oriented decomposition, or polymorphism [182].

**Explorative Programming**

When complex implementations are to be developed the proper solution often cannot be foreseen at the beginning. In such cases programmers may start to explore the solution space with pragmatic programming. This may include the cloning of existing code, in order to adapt it to the new purpose. As their understanding evolves, opportunities for abstraction become apparent and are applied [97, 99]. Hence, clones may live in the code for a limited time until a refactoring becomes possible. Learning and discovery was named as a reason for cloning by 42.9% of the participants in the study of Zhang and colleagues [182].

Modern programming paradigms even encourage programmers to proceed this way. Test-driven development suggests to perform a most pragmatic implementation until the tests pass. Not until then, should the code be improved using refactoring, which may include clone removal [22].

Kapser and Godfrey also identified the copy and paste pattern of *experimental variation*, in which changes and new features are tested in a temporal copy of the original code. This allows experimentation without risking the correctness of the existing code. They also report that programmers may use the code of a similar solution to start a new piece of code that will evolve separately in the future. The copy can than be incrementally changed so that it develops to a new and distinct solution. The clone relationship will vanish over time [94].

Although these approaches should only create short-lived clones, when applied properly, there exists a risk that the clone removal may be omitted because of time-pressure or lack of attention. In such cases, clones will remain in the code for a longer time.

## 4.2  Effects

A main reason for the scientific interest in software clones are the presumed effects on maintainability. The beliefs on this relationship need support by empirical evidence. Hordijk and colleagues reviewed the state of this research in 2009 [73]. Figure 4.1 shows a causal model for the effects of clones that they built based on the findings of the existing studies at that time. The model is hypothetical because few studies existed and some provided contradictory results. It does, however, give a comprehensive overview of the effects assumed by researchers and, therefore, helps us to structure our discussion on the matter. The model shows different factors and how their presence influences other factors. One factor can either strengthen (+) or lessen (−) another one. For example, inconsistent changes make program errors through bugs more likely. Hence, the factor *Inconsistent Change* strengthens the factor *Errors*.

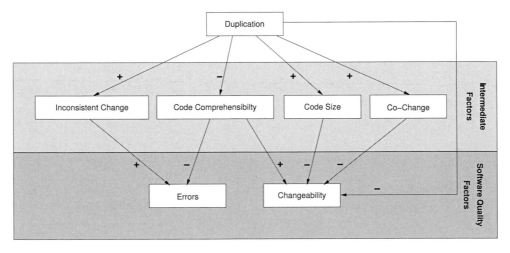

**Figure 4.1** – Cause-effect model on the consequences of cloning from Hordijk and colleagues [73].

In the following we will describe the perceptions behind the causal model of Hordijk and colleagues. It is important to note that these perceptions are hypothetical and not facts. After this theoretical part on the effects of clones, we will compare the assumptions with the current state of the research and derive open questions.

According to the model, clones indirectly affect the likelihood that errors occur and the changeability of the source code. Program errors are obviously a phenomenon that should be avoided. Changeability is an important property of software, because it must be changed to fix bugs, implement new features or to adapt to altering requirements.

Hordijk and colleagues identified four factors through which clones may affect the two aforementioned software maintainability attributes: inconsistent changes to clones, code comprehension, code size, and co-change. The occurrence of errors becomes more likely when clone fragments are changed inconsistently. Unintentionally inconsistent changes may cause inconsistent program behavior, which may cause bugs. It is also possible that bugs contained in clones are removed in only some fragments while others remain defective. Inconsistent changes are only defined on cloned code, therefore, code duplication makes inconsistent changes possible. Errors may be less likely to occur, when a high degree of code comprehension exists among the developers. Code comprehension may, however, be affected negatively by code clones. More code may be more difficult to understand, the same code has to be comprehended multiple times and the programmer must clarify why the duplication exist and whether there is a valid reason for it. That is, clones impede code comprehension which is needed to avoid bugs. Therefore, clones could abet errors.

The changeability of code may be positively affected by good code comprehension. It is probably easier to change something that can be understood well. Since Hordijk's model presumes clones have a negative effect on code comprehension, they may also affect changeability in a negative way. Changeability could be reduced by the size of the code. The idea is: the more code exists, the higher the effort to change it. Moreover, clones increase the code base as they are redundant passages of code. The necessity of co-changes that clones impose is also seen as a limiting factor to changeability. That is, changes are believed become more expensive when clones are present, because they probably need to be applied for each fragment. Finally, Hordijk and colleagues also presume a direct negative relationship between duplication and changeability. This comes from the fact that some researchers analyzed the direct relationship between clones and the change rate of the code. It is assumed that duplication causes more changes. The reason for this relationship is probably the fact that clones cause co-changes and, thus, increase the total amount of change.

Hordijk and colleague do not only suggest negative effects through clones on maintainability. Indeed there may be cases where clones are beneficial to maintenance and quality. One obvious case of positive influence is the speedup that copy and paste programming allows. Copying code may be faster than finding and implementing an abstraction. Reasons why cloning may be beneficial are also stated in Section 4.1. Some studies even imply that clones may change even less often than other code.

In the following we will describe the current state of research on the effects clones have on the maintainability of programs. An overview on such studies was also given by Pate and his colleagues [140]. Our discussion on the effects of clones in this section is organized into three major effect categories that follow Hordijk's model: First, the effect of clones on the changeability of programs, second, the effect on the correctness of programs and, third, the effect of clones on program comprehension. The latter category is not a direct effect in Hordijk's model, but it influences both changeability and correctness, so that we will discuss it in an own section.

The upcoming discussion of the related work in this area will also lead us to the three research perspectives we have introduced in Chapter 1. Concrete research questions for each perspective are defined in the respective chapters in Part III, where we describe our empirical studies.

## 4.2.1   Program Changeability

Changeability is the first of the two quality factors clones affect according to Hordijk and colleagues. It is degraded by the intermediate factors co-change and code size, but there are also direct factors through which clones impede changeability. The literature also names work effort and code instability as such factors. We discuss these influencing factors on changeability in the following.

### Co-Change

The existence of clones in the program code makes co-change necessary. First empirical evidence was provided by Kim and colleagues, who analyzed how code clones evolve in two open-source Java systems. They found that 32%–38% of all clone classes changed consistently at least once in their lifetime [98, 99]. This co-change could not be avoided completely because 64%–68% of the clone classes could not be removed for different reasons. While co-change is inevitable they also found that many clone classes are only short-lived. Depending on the analyzed system 48%–72% of the clone classes disappeared within eight check-ins to the source code repository.

Saha and colleagues conducted a similar study on the changes to clone genealogies on the release-level [156]. A total of 17 open-source systems, written in C, C++, C#, and Java were analyzed. The study extends the work of Kim and colleagues with more diverse subject systems. Where Kim and colleagues analyzed clones on the revision level Saha and colleagues chose the broader release level. Their findings support Kim's earlier study, but they also found that most genealogies that change, change consistently. They also found many long-lived clones.

Aversano and colleagues [6] found further empirical evidence for co-changes to clones. They analyzed changes to clones in a small and a mid-sized open-source system. Most changes to clones (45–74%) were carried out consistently to all fragments. That is, co-changes to clones do occur in software maintenance.

Krinke analyzed the consistency of changes to clones in five open-source systems [111]. For each change to a clone class between versions, as they were recorded in the source code repository, he evaluated whether the clone fragments have been changed consistently or inconsistently. He then quantified these changes for each system and found that roughly half of the changes to clones are inconsistent with minor differences between the analyzed systems. He also evaluated whether inconsistent changes are corrected in late propagation belatedly, which we will discuss in Section 4.2.2.

Göde and Koschke analyzed the evolution of clones in three systems written in Java, C and Ada [60]. They found that most clones live longer than one year. If, however, their lifetime is shorter than one year, it is mostly very short. They also observed that inconsistent changes to clones outnumber the consistent ones by a factor of almost five. Nevertheless, changes to clones appeared rarely—82% of the clones never changed. In another study on nine different subject systems Göde reported that the results regarding the lifetime of exact clones are strongly system-dependent [55]. Bazrafshan extended Göde's work by analyzing type-2 and type-3 clones and confirmed that the lifetime of clones varies between systems. He also found that near miss clones live even longer than exact ones. They also change more often, but it was not analyzed why. A possible reason may be that clones that were created to start off something new may be subject to reoccurring changes intentionally. Thummalapenta and colleagues also found that clones do co-change in two Java-systems and two written in C [165]. In some systems consistent evolution appeared even more often than inconsistent evolution. Wang and Godfrey analyzed how clones change in the history of the Linux SCSI drivers [172]. They categorized changes into the four categories *consistent change, inconsistent change, deletion of clones,* and *addition of new clones.* They found that inconsistent changes occurred more often than consistent ones. In most years of the analyzed period more clones where deleted than changed. For most of the analyzed years, however, the addition of new clones was the top category of changes to clones.

Göde and Harder analyzed whether co-changes of the same clone class do reoccur during its lifetime [58]. We defined the notion of change pairs for clones. Two consecutive co-changes to the same clone class form a change pair. Three small and mid-sized software systems in Ada, C, and Java where analyzed for such change pairs. We found that 83%–94% of all clone genealogies contain no co-changes or just a single one. That is, reoccurring changes to clones are rare. Most of the change pairs embodied two consecutive consistent changes (37%–41%), but consistent changes followed by an inconsistent one also appeared frequently (29%–33%). Inconsistent changes that were followed by another inconsistent change accounted for 18%–22% of all change pairs. The inconsistent changes where inspected manually and most of them were found to be intentionally inconsistent.

Geiger and colleagues attempted to establish a correlation between change couplings of source code files and the clone coverage in the files [52]. Although the correlation could not be confirmed statistically, they found a reasonable number of cases where the presumed relation exists. This conclusion was made by inspecting the data visualized in polymetric views. The absence of a statistical correlation between change couplings and clones does not mean that they are not related. Change couplings, however, could as well be caused by other influencing factors than clones.

### Instability

Krinke established the notion of *code instability* to measure the change volume source code is exposed to over a period of time [112]. If cloned code changed more often than non-cloned code, because of the necessary co-changes, then a higher instability of the cloned code must be observable. Krinke analyzed 200 weeks of the evolution of five open-source software systems and compared the instability of their cloned code with the instability of their non-cloned code. Instability was measured as the amount of changed lines divided by the number of total lines. This metric was calculated for cloned and non-cloned code separately and cumulated over all analyzed versions. Contrary to the common assumption that cloned code causes more change effort, Krinke found that the non-cloned code was less stable for all systems, altogether. A separate analysis of additions, deletions and changes to code lines showed, that clones are more stable with respect to additions, but less stable to deletions. For changes to code lines, the results differed among the systems.

Krinke's conclusions surprisingly contradict the common belief that clones cause higher maintenance effort. This unexpected new facet of clones may be an important building block to understand the nature of clones and, hence, requires further support by more research. Krinke's work opened a new perspective, but as a first study its focus was naturally narrowed on few systems with similar attributes and only one kind of clones. Whether his observations can be generalized to other conditions has yet to be investigated. That is, this initial study on the matter shed first light on clone stability and requires replication. Krinke examined clone instability only for open-source systems and restricted his observations to exact clones. The techniques used, did not utilize the best precision and recall, that can be achieved. Thus, it is necessary to further investigate the generalizability of his results using more fine grained analysis methods and taking also industrial software into account. We have done this [57, 67]. Chapter 6 describes this research.

Hotta and colleagues researched these questions simultaneously with us [74]. The research efforts on instability led to further work by Mondal and colleagues [131]. We will discuss this related work after we have described our own in Chapter 6.

While his original study focused on the likelihood and amount of change over time, Krinke also investigated the age of cloned and non-cloned code [113]. For each of three open source-software systems he selected one snapshot and compared the code age per line. The age was defined a the time since the line has been changed last. He found that in 81% of the files that contain clones, the cloned lines are older on average. In two of the three systems the analyzed cloned code was generally older, while in one of them the non-cloned part was older.

Monden and colleagues compared the number of changes to files that contain clones with files that do not contain clones [134]. They analyzed a 20 year old software system used in the public sector written in a programming language similar to COBOL. Contrary to Krinke they found that files without clones change less often than files that contain clones. The longer the cloned sequences in the files, the higher the number of file revisions. It was also observed that younger files contain a higher percentage of cloned code than older ones.

### Work

Lozano and colleagues defined the work required to maintain methods as a combination of the likelihood of changes to the method and the impact changes to the method have on the whole code base,. They define the impact as the amount of co-change caused in the remaining code [122]. They conducted an empirical study to investigate whether the work required to maintain a method increases when it contains clones. This relation could not be confirmed statistically. The results, however, show that in the four analyzed open-source Java-systems the required work differs. Their results show that in more than half of the cases the required work to change methods with clones is even lower. On the one hand the effort is lower in most cases. On the other hand in the fewer cases where the effort is higher, cases exist where it increases strongly.

Mondal and colleagues defined the metric *change dispersion* as an attempt to express the work required for a change [132]. Change dispersion measures the degree to which co-changes are scattered over the code. They assessed cloned and non-cloned code of twelve software systems with their metric. It was found that changes to cloned code have a higher dispersion for the systems written in Java and C. Only for the C#-Systems the dispersion of changes to non-cloned code was higher.

### Summary

It is evident that clones do cause co-change in the evolution of software systems. Although the results of the different studies vary in respect to the balance of consistent and inconsistent change, they document many cases where consistent co-evolution of cloned fragments took place. Different studies agree in the observation that the amount of co-change and the consistency depend on the system analyzed.

While the quantification of co-change is necessary to understand how clones affect the changeability of code it is not sufficient to answer the question whether clones have a negative effect. As we have discussed, different studies came to the conclusion that changes to clones occur rarely. The balance of consistent and inconsistent changes would be secondary if changes are so scarce that their overall effect is only small. When we consider clones as a risk to software quality, we should discuss it along the rules of risk management. It categorizes each risk by its impact in the case of an event but also by the probability of the occurrence of the event. While we cannot clearly assess the first, we have indication that the last is rather low. Another, yet not investigated, cause for the low change frequency could also be the fact that developers avoid changing clones because they fear the risk changing them.

One shortcoming of the investigations on co-change is that they do not compare the overall change effort with non-cloned code. The bare existence of clone-related co-changes does not necessarily mean that clones cause more change effort than other code. It may just mean that changes to them follow different patterns. When we assume that clones raise the costs of change in software, we should expect them to cause higher change effort than non-cloned code.

Krinke's idea of code stability fills this gap in the co-change observations. His unexpected results contradict common sense as they suggest that clones have a positive effect of changeability. If his findings, which do not contradict the results of the co-change analyses, can be supported, the common verdict about the increased maintenance costs through clones has to be reconsidered. Hence, the results on clone instability require support from broader investigations and deeper analysis than Krinke's first efforts could provide. Consequently, we make this the first research focus of this thesis.

> **Research Perspective A:** *How do clones affect the instability and, therefore, changeability of source code?*

Chapter 6 is dedicated to this question and follows Krinke's idea of code instability to investigate how clones affect the changeability of code. The controversial results of Krinke's study need confirmation, which is why we replicate his study using other and more fine-grained techniques. We also broaden the analysis to different software systems from different application domains, different programming languages and analyze different time periods in the life cycle of the systems. The related research we have discussed above indicates that the effects of clones often depend on the subject system. Consequently, we analyze whether the findings can be further generalized. Research Focus A on the preceding page will be further decomposed into research questions in Chapter 6.

## 4.2.2  Program Correctness

The second threat clones are believed to impose on software systems is that they cause bugs. This assumption has been investigated from different angles. The following discusses the work in this area ordered by the analytical approach.

### Analyzing Inconsistent Clones

A popular assumption is that inconsistent changes to existing clones cause bugs to occur. That is, if a programmer forgets to change all fragments of a clone class through an oversight, the fragments may behave differently when executed. This could mean that a new feature or change was applied incompletely or that a bug-fix was not propagated to all places where it is required. The following studies, therefore, investigated inconsistent clones, that is type-2 and type-3 clones, to assess how often such situations occur and whether the inconsistencies are indeed bugs.

Li and colleagues used their clone detector *CP-Miner* to search for clones with inconsistent identifier renaming, which they regard as candidates for cloning related bugs [120]. If source code is copied to another location and adapted to the new context identifiers may be renamed. If this is not done consistently, that is, each occurrence of an identifier $i$ has been renamed to the same new identifier $i'$, the programmer may have overlooked one occurrence. In total 995 such candidates have been identified automatically in four open-source C-Systems. The authors reported each of these back to the software developers who assessed the candidates. Although 91% turned out to be intentionally inconsistent, 87 cases where identified where the inconsistent renaming was indeed a bug. That is, variable renaming in cloned code fragments does cause bugs. In most cases, however, variable renaming is intentional.

In an analysis of five industrial and one academic software systems Juergens and colleagues reported on cases where inconsistent changes to clones caused actual bugs that were confirmed by the developers [90]. They identified *unintentionally* inconsistent clone classes through manual inspection. Of all inconsistent changes to clone classes 10%–37% where identified as actual bugs.

Wagner and colleagues analyzed type-3 clones in three industrial Java systems with a total size of roughly one million lines of code [170]. In the most current versions they found 235 gapped clones, which they correlated with documented program faults from the companies issue tracking system. They found that 17% of the gapped clones were related to documented bugs.

## Change Patterns that Indicate Bugs

While the previously discussed studies investigated the inconsistencies themselves, a much more popular approach is to analyze how the changes occur over time. Various studies have tracked clones and categorized their changes into patterns. The ratio between consistent and inconsistent changes gives a hint how often programmers manage to co-change clones properly. Most interesting, however, are cases where an inconsistency is turned into a consistent clone belatedly—these are called *late propagations*.

Kim and colleagues were the first to extract clone genealogies to identify different change patterns [99]. Although they define *inconsistent change* as a pattern, they did not quantify its occurrences in their empirical studies.

The notion of inconsistent changes was further refined and quantified by Aversano and colleagues [6]. They distinguish two types of inconsistent changes. First, those that are followed by a late propagation and, second, those that continue to evolve independently. In a case study on two small and mid-sized open-source systems they found that most changes to clones are consistent. Inconsistent changes occur but often fall into the category of independent evolution. Late propagations made up 13%–16% of all changes to clones. Indeed, they found that some of these late propagated changes were bug fixes. Thus, clones involve the risk that bugs remain in the system because of inconsistent changes. They conclude, however, that not all late propagations are problematic. Most of the cases they encountered were considered harmless.

In his aforementioned study on consistent and inconsistent changes Krinke also evaluated whether inconsistent changes are corrected later [111]. He compared how clone classes changed over different time spans from one to ten weeks. He found that the relation between consistent and inconsistent changes does not change notably when the time frame is widened. This finding suggests that most inconsistent changes are not followed by late propagations, that is, corrective changes that propagate the missing adaptations to all fragments. Krinke reports that such cases do exist as they have been found in manual inspections. But these exceptions are too few to be noticed in the large amount of inconsistent changes.

Göde further investigated the change consistency of clones with a more sophisticated methodology using an incremental clone detector that tracks individual clone fragments through their whole lifespan [55]. Like Krinke, he found that inconsistent changes are frequent, their ratio, however, varies strongly for different software systems. The rate of inconsistent changes to clones varied from 28% to 74% in the nine systems analyzed. Göde also pursued the question how often inconsistencies are corrected at a later point of time. His approach detects such late propagations of any duration. He found 27% to 74% of the inconsistent changes to be propagated subsequently.

Thummalapenta and colleagues confirmed the earlier finding that most clones—about 70%—change consistently in practice [165]. In their study on clone evolution in four open-source systems, only 16% of the clones where affected by a late propagation. They correlated bug-fixing changes with the changes to clones and found that these are more likely to occur in clones that undergo late propagations. Not every late propagation, however, is related to a defect. They conclude that programmers are able

to change clones consistently most of the time. Their attention should be directed to
the few cases where they fail to do so.

Göde and Koschke analyzed the history of three software systems and concluded
that bugs caused by inconsistent changes to clones are rare [61]. First, 87.8% of all clone
genealogies never changed. Second, only 14.8% of all changes to clones were identified
as unintentionally inconsistent, and third, only few were of a noteworthy severity.
The intention behind inconsistent changes was evaluated manually by inspecting all
occurrences of inconsistent changes in one of the three systems of which the authors
had in-depth knowledge.

Barbour and colleagues analyzed late propagations in two open-source Java
programs [15]. They found an unusually high number of late propagations compared
with other studies on the same matter. 4.700 such cases were found for one program
alone, which contradicts the findings of most other studies on the frequency of such
changes. The authors categorized the late propagations into eight categories based on
the sequence of the changes. For instance, a late propagation may take place in just
a single fragment that it changed back and forth. But it may also occur in different
ways. Barbour and colleagues extracted bug data from the log messages of the issue
tracking systems of the analyzed projects. They combined these data with their late
propagation categories to identify fault-prone late propagation types. The most fault-
prone category was found to be late propagations that occur because the diverting
change was reverted. The category of late propagations in which all fragments do always
change at the same time, but with different modifications, follows in second place. In
these two top categories up to 72% of the late propagations introduced a fault.

While most researchers have analyzed changes to clones in every revision of the code,
Bettenburg and colleagues focussed their analysis on inconsistent changes on the release
level [24]. They argue that this way, only finished and quality assured code versions are
analyzed and the chaotic change in-between, which likely contains try-and-error, is left
out. In their analysis of three open-source systems they found that only 1% to 4% of
all clone genealogies introduced software defects in released software. They conclude
that developers are capable of managing clones in most cases because many changes to
clones exist that do not cause bugs.

Xie and colleagues define different change patterns than most other authors. In a
study they analyzed how *mutation* and *migration* affect the likelihood of bugs [178].
Clone *mutation* takes place when the clone type of a genealogy changes, for example,
when identifiers are renamed in some fragments of a type-1 genealogy, so that it becomes
a type-2 genealogy. Clone *migration* describes the movement of clone fragments between
the files of a project. Analyzing three open-source Java systems Xie and colleagues
found that most clones change consistently. The most frequent migration pattern is
the change from type-1 to type-2. The authors correlated the different mutation and
migration patterns with bugs that were caused by the clones code. The data was
collected searching for issue-tracking keys in the logs of the source code repositories.
They conclude that clone genealogies that mutated from type-1 to type-2 have the
highest fault-proneness. How this, however, relates to the fault-proneness of non-cloned
code has not been investigated, so that it remains unclear whether clones are more
fault-prone than non cloned code. Regarding clone migration it was found that clone

genealogies, in which the distance of the fragments increases, are most prone to faults. Most genealogies are stable in terms of distance.

## Bug Prediction through clones

A different approach to investigate the effect clones have on program correctness is to turn the relation of clones and bugs around. If clones do cause bugs to a considerable extent, it should be possible to use clone information to predict bugs.

Selim and colleagues used statistical models to find out whether certain properties of clones can be used as predictors for defects in methods [160]. They compared the prediction quality of commonly used metrics in bug prediction research, such as lines of code, with clone related metrics such as number of copies. They also evaluated which clone characteristics make a good predictor and which may be redundant. Analyzing two open-source Java systems, they found that the prediction quality of clone related metrics depends on the analyzed system. While cloning metrics provided a better prediction for one program, the common metrics performed better for another. They also observed that methods tend to be more defect-prone the longer they exist.

Kamei and colleagues conducted a study on whether fault-prone modules can be predicted using metrics on software clones [91]. Based on different versions of the `eclipse` IDE they investigated whether clone metrics outperform conventional metrics, such as complexity measures, as bug predictors or whether they can improve the prediction results when combined with conventionally used predictors. Neither was found to be the case in general. For large components, however, the clone metrics performed slightly better.

## Correlation of clones with bugs

An obvious strategy to link clones with bugs is to correlate the cloned code with the defective code in some way.

In their aforementioned study on clones Monden and colleagues also compared the number of faults per line in files that contain clones with files that do not contain clones [134]. Surprisingly, files containing clones that are up to 199 lines long had a lower fault density than files that do not contain any clones. The highest fault density was measured for the files with clones larger than 200 lines.

Rahman and colleagues pursued the question how likely bug-fixing changes occur in cloned code compared with non-cloned code [145]. They extracted defect data from issue tracking systems and linked this information to code changes in the source code repository that reference a bug in their log message to find the bug-fixing changes. For these bug-fixing changes they analyzed whether they occurred in clones. Rahman and colleagues came to the following three conclusions. First, in absolute numbers, bugs mostly occur in non-cloned code. Only few appear in clones. Second, the clone rate in the bug-fixing changes is lower than in other changes. That is, cloned code seems to be less defect-prone than non-cloned code. Third, no strong evidence was found that the number of fragments in a clone class is correlated with the risk of bugs.

## Bugs caused by social aspects

A factor that has rarely been considered is the social one. As discussed in Section 4.1 personal issues are a reason for clones to come into existence. Therefore, social aspects, such as the authorship of clones, may be initiators for clone-related bugs.

Balint and colleagues defined a visualization that illustrates who changes clone fragments over time [13]. Their *clone evolution view* combines the point of time at which each line of the clone fragments was changed last with the individual programmer who applied that change. They used this view to identify recent inconsistent changes to clones and to evaluate whether different programmers were involved in these changes. The clones of three open-source software systems were analyzed using this method and different change patterns were identified by the authors. They conclude that, in practice, clones are created and maintained by both single programmers and multiple programmers. They report that inconsistent changes to clones seem more likely when more than one programmer is involved. These findings only provide a vague idea how the number of involved programmers affects inconsistent changes to clones, because the authors do not systematically provide empirical data in form of numbers to explain their conclusions. Nevertheless, the work of Balint and colleagues raises the question whether the number of involved developers can cause unwanted inconsistent changes and, therefore, bugs. This question has not been further investigated, since.

Cai and Kim further support the previously discussed assumption that the number of authors involved has an influence on how clones evolve [28]. They found that clones live longer the more developers participate in changing them. They conclude that clones maintained by multiple developers may be more difficult to remove because a longer life-time was observed for them.

## Conclusion

The studies on inconsistent clones and change patterns have shown that clones, in fact, do cause bugs that could not have appeared without clones. These situations may not make up for the majority of cases where clones change, nevertheless, the two studies by Li and colleagues as well as by Jürgens and colleagues reported on 194 confirmed bugs in eight software systems. This number alone justifies attention to clones. It has also to be considered that these bugs were all present in actual running software. As Boehm and Papaccio summarize, the costs for fixing a bug raise by 50–200 times when they are found in the field and not earlier [26].

Although clones cause a non-negligible number of bugs, they do not seem to be a primary cause for bugs in general, as some studies found clone-related bugs to be rare. If clones are compared with the non-cloned part of the code, there is no evidence for an overall increased disposition to bugs. Some studies, however, indicate there are certain kinds of clones that are more error prone than others.

Altogether, this raises the question whether it is possible to identify characteristics that make clones more likely to contain bugs. So far, most studies quantified clone-induced bugs, but did not seek for common causes. That is, we merely investigated the symptoms, but not the causes which could be counteracted. One possible factor that may complicate the maintenance of clones is the number of developers involved in creating and changing them. While a single developer may be able to keep track of the copies she or he made, copying someone else's code without letting her or him know, could result in unintended inconsistent changes to the clones in the future. So far, possible authorship effects like these have rarely been researched. The aforementioned study by Balint and colleagues indicates that multiple authors may make a difference [13].

The relationship between code clones and code authorship is the second research focus in this thesis. Chapter 7 is dedicated to the following research focus, which will be refined into more fine-grained research questions there.

**Research Perspective B:** *How do multiple developers affect the evolution of clones? Are different authors a key reason why clones are changed inconsistently and cause bugs?*

## 4.2.3   Program Comprehension

In contrast to changeability and correctness, program comprehension is an intermediate factor in the cause model of Hordijk and colleagues. But it is special in the way that it influences both correctness and changeability. Therefore, we discuss it separately from the two other factors.

According to the cause effect model proposed by Hordijk and colleagues, clones may affect program comprehension negatively. When the same piece of logic is repeated in different locations it may be more difficult for the programmer to understand the code as a whole. Copying also produces more code for the programmer to understand. She will have to keep the cloning relations in mind in order to keep the clone fragments in sync. These possible effects are speculative. Indeed the opposite may as well be the case as Balazinska and colleagues illustrated when they explored automatic refactoring for clones [12]. Simple copies with minor differences may be easier to understand than more complex unified solutions that require parameterization, more control flow paths, and maybe even more complex structure to provide the same semantics.

Empirical knowledge about the effect clones have on program comprehension is still missing. Although many efforts in the area of clone management are directed to assist developers with understanding clones—we will describe these in Chapter 5—the idea that clones affect program comprehension negatively is an assumption. Roehm and colleagues observed and interviewed professional software developers to learn how they comprehend software [149]. They found that programmers occasionally created clones to avoid program comprehension. That is, they copied foreign code that solved their problem so that they do not need to understand how it works and how modification would affect the original. This, however, only explains how clones are created because of comprehension problems, but not whether they impact comprehension themselves.

Latoza and colleagues interviewed professional software developers to learn about their work habits and the mental models they apply in their daily work [116]. The authors identified six different patterns of cloning from the answers. The participants agreed to 28%–42% that the clones of a specific category are problematic. Whether the problems arise because of comprehension problems is not answered.

### Conclusion

The effect clones have on program comprehension is mostly unclear. The existing publications provide insights as a side effect, as they did not make clones and program comprehension to the central question. Hordijk's cause-effect model makes clear that program comprehension may influence the effects clones have on software quality in multiple ways.

Questions of program comprehension are difficult to answer because the programmers must be involved to gather data. Most of the studies on the effect of clones have been performed retrospectively, using archived data. While this provides a basis for many research questions, it lacks major parts of the development process. Investigations on the effect clones have on the human performance are essential and may lead to different results. The need for human-based experiments is emphasized by Carver and colleagues [30]. The authors state that human-based behavior cannot be validated without the use of empirical studies that involve the developers. When for instance revisions and changes are extracted from a source code repository, the work that was necessary to create these changes is not available. Software development is often a process of trial-and-error and the final solution may not be clear to the programmer first. Problems regarding program comprehension will appear between the archived program revisions. Consequently, the effect of clones cannot be understood with retrospective analysis of archived project artifacts alone. The programmer at work, performing real tasks, must be observed and the effects of clones must be measured at the same time to learn about this facet of software development. This is the third research focus of this thesis.

> **Research Perspective C:** *How do clones affect performance of programmers in real software engineering tasks?*

In Chapter 8 we describe the first controlled experiment on clones that pioneers this new perspective on the effects of clones. Detailed research questions are derived there.

## Conclusion

This concludes our discussion on why clones come to existence and what is known about their effects on software quality aspects; namely on changeability, correctness, and comprehensibility. As we have discussed, negative effects of clones are evident. Nevertheless, they need to be further compared with the properties of non-cloned code. We also need to find out whether certain properties of clones, such as authorship, cause clones to be problematic while others remain unsuspicious. And we also need to investigate the relation of clones and software quality from a more active perspective, which is measuring the developer's performance while at work.

Our three research perspectives address these general questions and will be the basis for our studies in Part III. Our overview on software clones and the related research in the field would not be complete, if we left out clone management. Before we can plunge into the empirical part of this thesis, we need to visit this last topic of clone research. It is important to our thesis, as our research is directed to provide a justification for clone detection and management activity. Moreover we investigate in which cases— considering all the individuality of clones, subject systems, application domains, and influencing factors—clone management can help to improve software quality efficiently. Consequently, Chapter 5 briefly describes the related research on clone management.

# Chapter 5

# Managing Clones

Clones do have certain negative effects on the maintainability and correctness of programs, as we have discussed in Section 4.2. Although it is yet unclear to which extent clones cause problems, *clone management* aims to counteract clone related problems. Laguë and colleagues as well as Giesecke divide the possible measures into the categories of *preventive*, *compensative*, and *corrective* clone management [53, 115]. Preventive measures aim to avoid the creation of clones. If clones do exist in a program they may be either dealt with using compensative measures, such as guidance with consistent changes, or using corrective measures that remove the clone so that it does not need to be managed any longer. Hou, Jablonski, and Jacob speak of *proactive* clone management which is similar to compensative management but emphasizes active tracking of cloning instead of counteracting after clones came into existence [75, 76]. Zibran and colleagues postpone clone management to the release time, which they call *post-mortem* clone management[184].

Besides these types of clone management activity it may also be deliberately chosen not to counteract a clone at all. The discussion on effects in Section 4.2 has shown that clones do not necessarily have negative effects. Some empirical evidence even supports the thesis that clones may be rather stable and hassle-free code. Since all management activity comes at a cost, the benefits of managing clones should be pondered [86]. Today, no cost-benefit model exists that can verify the economic efficiency of clone management measures.

Recently Roy, Zibran, and Koschke gave a comprehensive overview on the state of the field of clone management and raised future research questions [154]. The following will give an overview of clone management ordered by the three categories of Laguë and Giesecke.

## 5.1 Preventive

Laguë, Proulx, and Merlo describe *preventive control* to avoid the creation of new clones [115]. They suggest that clone detection should be integrated into the development process and triggered whenever new code is committed into the projects source code repository. If clones are found the system architect should decide whether the clone is acceptable.

Wang and colleagues use the machine-leaning technique of Bayesian networks to predict the harmfulness of a clone [173]. In the moment the programmer copies a piece of code a risk evaluation is performed. The authors use different metrics on the history of the code (such as lifetime and change frequency), the copy destination (such as similarity of the file names, similarity of the source and the target method), and the code itself (such as length and number of invocations). To train the Bayesian network existing clones were categorized into harmful and harmless using the unconventional assessment that a clone class that never changes or only changes inconsistently is harmless, while a clone that changes consistently at least once is harmful. The authors evaluated their tool and measured precision values above 90%. Nevertheless, the definition of harmfulness needs to be discussed. Zhang and colleagues extended this approach with an event mechanism that inspects commits to the source code management and notifies different stakeholders about clone-related changes [181].

## 5.2   Compensative

Besides *preventive control* Laguë, Proulx and Merlo also describe *problem mining* as a compensative measure [115]. When a developer commits changes to existing code, it is automatically checked whether cloned code was changed. If this is the case, the programmer is presented with the clones and may decide to take back his commit and change the cloned fragments as well.

Nguyen and colleagues implemented a clone-aware source code management system named `Cleman` [136, 138]. Clone detection is performed on check-ins of code and the results are persisted within the SCM system. When a programmer updates her working copy of the code, the persisted clone data is also retrieved and updated when new changes are committed. On each commit, the consistency of changes to clones is checked. Detected inconsistencies reported to the user. If the user decides to apply the changes to all other fragments, `Cleman` will perform this modification automatically.

Hou, Jablonski, and Jacob use the programmer's IDE to continuously track clones from their creation on [75]. Their *Eclipse* plug-in `CnP` records all copy and paste actions to identify new clones. Once clones are detected their positions are constantly updated when the code changes. The plug-in will also highlight clones in the source code and allows the programmer to navigated to the other fragments of a clone. It also highlights renamed identifiers and literals and checks whether these have been renamed consistently between the fragments. Their approach, however, will only work if the programmers exclusively use the plug-in to edit the code. A similar method has been presented by de Wit and colleagues [40].

Duala-Ekoko and Robillard also integrate their clone management tool into `Eclipse` [43]. They use their previously discussed tracking method of *Clone Region Descriptors* to track the positions of clones while the code changes. The clone detection is performed with a AST-based detector. Once clones have been detected their plug-in `CloneTracker` warns the user about changes to existing clones and presents the other fragments that may require changes. They also provide a list of all known clone classes and the possibility to navigate to their fragments in the code. Similar to the solution of Hou and colleagues, `CloneTracker` requires the developer to use the tool exclusively to ensure correct clone tracking.

Toomim, Begel, and Graham present *linked editing* as a technique that eases changes to clones methods [166]. Cloned methods can be selected for a linked editing mode. All changes to one fragment will automatically be applied to all linked fragments as well. The linked fragments may also contain differences which will be highlighted in a different color. For a better overview of the differences the tool allows programmers to hide the common parts of the code so that they can focus on the differences in the linked fragments. In a user study with 13 university students the authors found that common maintenance tasks on cloned code were fulfilled faster, when linked editing was used.

Zhang and colleagues apply a query-based filtering approach to analyze clones on higher abstraction levels [183]. First, they search for reoccurring configurations of simple clones—clones as the approaches mentioned in Chapter 3 will find—within methods or files and group these into higher-level clone classes. Examples for such classes are repeating clone configurations in the same method, different methods, or files. To help the user analyze these data, different visualizations are proposed. Sortable tables give a generic overview of all simple clones. A more sophisticated search allows the user to define queries in a query language that allows filtering by many different clone class attributes, such as files containing fragments, length, number of fragments, etc. They also propose a new visualization, in which the files of a system are represented as side by side bars in which the occurrences of clones are highlighted. A color scheme indicated which clones belong to the same class. This side by side view helps to identify files with similar clone configurations.

Adar and Kim use a similar filtering and visualization approach to display the evolution of clones [2]. They use the graph exploration system GUESS that uses a graph-based query mechanism that is controlled via a python API. They use the clone genealogies defined by Kim and colleagues, which are graphs, and define different visualizations that can be manipulated using the query language.

Another visualization tool suite has been presented by Harder and Göde [66]. Our tool *Cyclone* visualizes clone genealogies in three synchronized perspectives. The evolution view interactively presents clone genealogies, highlights changes to clone classes and allows filtering. The code view shows the cloned code and allows the user to navigate through clone classes and fragments. The tree-map view elevates cloning information to the file and directory level. A colored tree map indicates the clone rate within files and directories. It also shows interactively which files or directories contain clones in other files or directories. The tool is based on the generic clone management data format *Rich Clone Format* (RCF), which provides programming APIs for versioned clone data analysis. The tool *RCFViewer* serves as a generic viewer for RCF data.

Steidl and Göde use decision trees to predict bugs in inconsistent clones [162]. The authors assume that many inconsistencies will not cause bugs, but some will. Hence, a bug prediction would help to identify the inconsistencies that need attention, which makes this an compensative approach to clone management. They use characteristics of the clones themselves, such as length, and characteristics specific to gaps in type-3 clones, for example the presence of null checks or loop breaks, to estimate the likelihood that the inconsistency will cause a bug. The decision trees are build using the human assessment of bugs in clones.

Chatterji and colleagues conducted an empirical study to evaluate whether clone reports, as they are provided by clone detectors, help programmers to manage clones [33]. They found that programmers tend to use text-based clone reports incorrectly when they were not trained beforehand. Their results also indicate that these reports do not help programmers to locate errors because of inconsistencies, but helps them to find other faulty locations after they identified one.

## 5.3   Corrective

Fanta and Rajlich describe strategies to remove clones in existing code with automated code refactorings supported by standard development tools [47]. They suggest that clones should be removed using extract method refactorings. They conclude that these operations should be performed by experienced programmers only. Komondoor and Horwitz present an automated approach to remove clones in difficult cases where the fragments contain gaps or statements are in different order [102]. They use PDGs to detect clones, to compute extraction solutions and to ensure semantic identity of the original code and the solution. Balazinska and colleagues apply a similar approach based on ASTs [11, 12]. Jarzabek and Li presented a technique based on generative programming to deal with clones that are difficult to refactor [81].

Basit and colleagues analyzed to which extend generics can be used to remove clones [18]. In a case study they found that only 40% of the clones could be removed this way because many clones differ in other aspects than just type parameters. Schulze and colleagues suggest to use aspect oriented programming (AOP) as an alternative to refactoring to remove clones that implement cross-cutting concerns in the code [159].

## Conclusion

This concludes our digression on clone management and also the part on software clones. In Part III, we will shift the focus on the empirical research we have conducted to investigate our three research perspectives we defined in Chapter 4.

# Part III

# Empirical Studies on the Effects of Clones

# Chapter 6

# Clone Stability

Software systems need to change during their lifetime. Existing bugs must be corrected and the system's functionality must be adjusted to the changing requirements. Every change to the program code causes costs. This makes changeability a key quality of software systems. Software engineers use principles, such as clean code development [125] or modularization [139], to ease future changes.

It seems plausible that redundant code fragments, caused by copy-and-paste, lower the changeability of the source code. Whenever cloned code needs to be changed, chances are that the changes must be applied redundantly to all clone fragments. This would multiply the required effort by the number of existing copies. Our first research perspective is directed to this possible effect of clones.

> **Research Perspective A:** *How do clones affect the instability and, therefore, changeability of source code?*

If cloned code proves to change more than non-cloned code, this would provide evidence for the assumed negative effect on maintainability. Thus, we empirically analyze how the *stability* of cloned and non-cloned code differ, to find out whether clones are less stable, indeed. That is, we measure and compare the relative amount of change in cloned and non-cloned code.

As we have discussed in Section 4.2, the question on clone instability was first formulated by Jens Krinke [112]. In his case study he found that cloned code is more stable in general—that is, it gets changed less with respect to its size. Nevertheless, cloned code was found to be less stable than non-cloned code when considering only deletions. Based on these results, he concluded that *"it cannot be generally assumed that the maintenance of cloned code is more expensive than the maintenance of non-cloned code"*. This finding is unexpected as it contradicts the wide-spread assumption that clones increase maintenance effort. It suggests that cloned code is more stable and therefore may require even less maintenance effort than non-cloned code.

In this chapter we present our research on the stability of clones by replicating and extending Krinke's original research. In Section 6.1 we refine our research focus into concrete research questions for our work. Section 6.2 presents Krinke's study on the matter in detail and how ours differs. Section 6.3 outlines our study procedure and Section 6.4 presents the results. We list possible threats to the validity of our study in Section 6.5 and discuss our results in Section 6.6. Finally, Section 6.7 discusses research on the same matter by others that was performed at the same time as ours or later. Section 6.8 concludes.

The contents of this chapter have been previously published and presented at the *15th European Conference on Software Maintenance and Reengineering* [57]. An extended version also appeared as invited paper in Wiley's *Journal of Software: Evolution and Process* [67]. This version presents additional data, provides an extended discussion of the results, and also summarizes further research on the matter performed by others.

## 6.1  Research Questions

Krinke's results are surprising as they contradict the common assumption that clones increase the effort required to maintain source code through additional changes that have to be applied to the code. Although Krinke's work is sound and conclusive, many factors can have an influence on the measurement. Replicating studies to verify and generalize their findings is a good practice in general, but especially when the initial results are controversial.

One possible threat to validity of the original study are the measurement techniques used to gather the data. Krinke decided to detect clones and changes to code based on source code lines and to analyze weekly snapshots of the subject systems. We believe that his results may at least partially be explained by these decisions. When source lines are analyzed, small changes that only partially affect one character will be counted as if the whole line changed. That is, small changes could be overrated. Because the analyzed code snapshots were taken on a weekly basis, overlapping changes that happened within one week cannot be measured separately. One reason that clones cause higher maintenance costs could be repeated changes to clones. Such repeated changes to clones could have been overlooked by the original study. A more fine-grained measurement, using a token-based clone detector and change analysis approach, could reveal changes that Krinke was not able to measure. For the systems he analyzed, all revisions of the source code management system are available for analysis. These provide a more detailed view on the events. This leads us to our first research question.

> **Question A1:** *Can we confirm the findings of the original study using more fine-grained measurement techniques?*

To this end, we choose to analyze some of the systems also used in the original study on the level of tokens and on a per-revision basis.

The stability of clones may depend on the software systems that were analyzed. Krinke has analyzed five different open-source systems written in different, but yet structurally similar languages—Java, C, and C++. This raises the question whether clones in different languages differ in their stability. To explore the generalizability of his results, we extend the analysis by analyzing systems from academia and industry that are written in Ada and COBOL, respectively.

**Question A2:** *Do the findings of the original study also hold for academic and industrial systems and for different programming languages?*

Clone detection parameters, such as the minimum size and similarity, have a significant effect on the detected clones. The stability of clones could depend on these factors as well. The original study considered only clones that are at least 11 lines long and exact copies of each other. We extend the original study by varying the minimum length that clones are required to have. We investigate how clones of different size and similarity affect the results.

**Question A3:** *How do the clone size and similarity influence the relation between the stability of cloned and non-cloned code?*

Krinke's results suggest that the stability of clones is significantly lower regarding deletions. While Question A1 is directed to replicate this finding, we also investigate whether this also holds for other systems. On the one hand, we analyze the reason for this phenomenon statistically and, on the other hand, we manually inspect particularly large deletions.

**Question A4:** *What makes deletions differ from the other change types?*

Software systems undergo different development phases—for instance new development versus maintenance—in which the effects of their clones may differ. The stability of clones may vary when different periods of a project's history are inspected when changes to clones are not equally distributed. Hence, we analyze the stability of clones for different time windows.

**Question A5:** *Does the stability of cloned code vary in different time periods?*

## 6.2   The Original Study Compared to Ours

Our goal is to repeat Krinke's original study on clone stability, validate his findings and get a better understanding of the reasons. In contrast to his study, we use a much more fine-grained measurement, take more influencing factors into account, and analyze systems that differ in their domain, language and development environment.

We perform a partial replication of the original study because we do not reuse the exact techniques and methods Krinke applied in the original study. We deliberately made this decision to answer the same research question as the original study using more fine-grained techniques. Research Question A1 is directed to the partial replication, while the new Questions A2 and A3 explore the generalizability of the original findings. With Question A4 we aim to explain the particularity of deletions to clones Krinke observed. He did not investigate possible reasons. Question A5 adds a new dimension to the discussion of clone stability. This makes our work a comprehensive report containing the results of the previous studies and new results, providing deeper insight into how probable and voluminous changes to clones are compared to non-cloned code. Our discussion on later findings by others in Section 6.7 will make this report complete. The differences of our study compared to the original study are described in this section.

We use a *token-based* program representation to detect clones and analyze changes to them. This allows a more detailed analysis compared to text-based clone detection using line granularity, which was used in the original study. We exclude code *generated* by `antlr` which Krinke did not exclude, but which he found contributes a large percentage of the clones. As this generated code is not maintained by hand, clones do not require change propagation.

We include every *revision* of our subject systems into our analysis whereas the original study used weekly snapshots. This allows us to detect changes that are hidden when using weekly snapshots.

We measure code stability not only for exact clones (*type-1* clones) as the original study did, but for clones with differences in variable names and literals (*type 2*) and clones with differences in their token sequence (*type 3*)—which play an important role in software maintenance—as well. Apart from the type of clones, the *minimum clone length* has a significant influence on the number of detected clones. Consequently, it may also have an effect on the stability measures. We, therefore, use different lengths to evaluate their effect on the stability.

We also widen our observations to systems with different properties. Krinke analyzed only open-source systems written in C-style languages—namely C, C++, and Java. With `ArgoUML` and `SQuirreL` we analyze two of the systems that were also used in Krinke's study. Since the fine-grained stability analysis is time and resource consuming we chose only two of Krinke's systems. This allows us to make room for the analysis of additional systems. We add three new systems from academia and industry written in Ada and COBOL to evaluate whether clones in these systems have the same properties regarding stability. The different requirements and goals of open-source, academic and industrial development may lead to different processes, development styles and team structures. These may have an effect on the clones in these systems. Finally, we measure

|  | Original study | Our study |
|---|---|---|
| Systems | ArgoUML, SQuirreL, Emacs, FileZilla, jdt.core | ArgoUML, SQuirreL, clones, Cobol-A, Cobol-B |
| Systems domains | 5 open source | 2 open source, 1 academia, 2 industrial |
| Interval | weekly | each subversion revision |
| Languages | C, C++, Java | Java, Ada, COBOL |
| Granularity | lines | tokens |
| Preprocessing | pretty printer | exclusion of files generated by antlr, package-statements, import-statements, with-statements, and array initializations. Separation of methods. |
| Clone types | *type-1* | *type-1*, *type-2*, and *type-3* |
| Minimum clone length | 11 lines | 50, 100, and 150 tokens |

**Table 6.1** – Comparison of the original and our study setup.

the stability for different time periods, to evaluate whether it varies over time. A comparison of Krinke's study setup and our study setup is given in 6.1.

## 6.3 Study Setup

This section describes the setup of our study including the subject systems and the methods we have used to collect relevant data. Where possible, we approximated the settings used in Krinke's study to maximize the comparability of both studies.

### 6.3.1 Clone Detection

Our approach to detect clones can be briefly summarized as Göde's incremental clone detection [56], which works token based. To circumvent common shortcomings of token based approaches, we augment the detection process with the exclusion of generated code, the exclusion of array initializers and imports, and the separation of methods in the token stream. These properties of our clone detection approach are discussed in detail in Section 3.3.

The parameters for the degree of similarity and the size of the clones have a strong influence on the results. In the following we will explain how we chose these for this study. Very strict parameters result in only few clones, whereas more tolerant parameters result in a much larger number of clones. Consequently, the clone detection parameters must be varied to learn about their effect on clone stability.

The strong effect of configuration settings for clone detectors is supported by a study from Wang and colleagues [171]. They used a search based approach to find clone detector settings that show a good performance when used against the Bellon benchmark [23]. Their evaluation included Göde's incremental approach that we use in our study. They found that the default setting often do not provide the best results. Consequently, we vary the settings for clone detection. We configured our clone detector in the following way.

**Degree of Similarity**

This parameter to clone detection defines which types of clones are detected and included in our analysis. We consider two possible settings for this parameter. The first setting detects only type-1 clones. The second setting detects clones of type 1, 2, and 3. We deliberately analyzed the systems using both settings to evaluate their effect on the results.

**Minimum Clone Length**

This value determines how many tokens a clone needs to have to be considered relevant. Choosing a smaller value increases the recall because more clones are found. Choosing a larger value increases the precision because fewer shorter clones are detected that just happen to be similar due to common programming patterns. We decided to use three distinct values to compare the effect of the minimum length on the results. The values we chose are 50, 100, and 150 tokens. The original study used 11 *lines* as minimum clone length. In the subject systems we use in our study one SLOC—source line excluding blank lines and comments—of code consists of 2 to 4 tokens on average. However, in the original study blank lines and comments were removed. The pretty printer `ArtisticStyle` was also applied to the source code. It applies code transformations, such as pulling the braces on the same line as the method signature. These measures produce a representation of the source code that is more compact. We expect that our setting with 100 tokens comes closest to Krinke's setup. By adding the 50 and 150 tokens to our setup, we aim to extend the study with two samples that contain larger and smaller clones, respectively.

## 6.3.2  Subject Systems

In total, we used five subject systems. The first two systems have been analyzed in the original study—namely the UML modeling tool `ArgoUML`[1] and the database administration program `SQuirreL`.[2] Both are open-source software. In addition, we analyzed the source code of our own scientific clone detection tool `clones` written in Ada. The remaining two subject systems were provided by one of the top-ten companies in Germany's insurance and home-savings business. Both systems are written in COBOL and have been in use for more than ten years. System `Cobol-A` is dedicated to life insurance whereas `Cobol-B` provides functionality for commission calculation, which is a common concern to different services.

---

[1]Website: http://argouml.tigris.org/
[2]Website: http://squirrel-sql.sourceforge.net/

| System | Language | Start Date | End Date | Years | Size [KLOC] | CR [%] |
|---|---|---|---|---|---|---|
| ArgoUML | Java | 2002-08-08 | 2006-06-01 | 3.8 | 144 – 308 | 4 – 20 |
| SQuirreL | Java | 2002-12-01 | 2006-09-24 | 3.8 | 78 – 218 | 1 – 17 |
| clones | Ada | 2005-01-01 | 2009-12-31 | 5 | 5 – 35 | 2 – 15 |
| Cobol-A | COBOL | 2007-10-31 | 2010-09-24 | 2.1 | 337 – 413 | 12 – 28 |
| Cobol-B | COBOL | 2008-05-17 | 2011-03-17 | 2.8 | 424 – 582 | 9 – 21 |

**Table 6.2** – Subject system properties

The time periods we analyzed for each system and further details are summarized in Table 6.2. For ArgoUML and SQuirreL we chose exactly the same time periods Krinke used in his study. For the other systems, the choice of versions was guided by organizational constraints. For clones we chose a period of five years. For the two industrial systems all revisions beginning from the date where the company started to use subversion were chosen. For Cobol-A the time period had to be shortened at the end because of hardware limitations during our on-site analysis at the company.

We extracted the source code for the open-source systems and the program clones from their subversion repositories and included all revisions in-between the bounds specified in Table 6.2 that changed at least one relevant source code file. That is, we considered changes with the most detailed granularity possible. Otherwise, repeated changes to the same code may be hidden if they occur between two snapshots. For Cobol-A and Cobol-B, all versions that were deployed in the production environment within the specified bounds—all of them containing relevant changes—were analyzed.

### Size

The size of all subject systems increased during our study period. Basically, we observed two different patterns. The first pattern applies to ArgoUML, SQuirreL, and clones. All three systems exhibit a notable and more or less steady increase in their size. That is, there has been a considerable amount of code and functionality added to these systems during the study period. The evolution these systems' size is shown in Figure 6.1 on the next page. Krinke observed a drop in ArgoUML's size that is not visible in our data. This drop was caused by the removal of several files that contained generated parser code. Is is not present in our data because we excluded generated code from our our analysis.

The second pattern applies to Cobol-A and Cobol-B. These systems increased in size as well, but the increase is less steep. Figure 6.2 on page 71 shows how the number of lines and tokens changed during the evolution of these systems.

### Clone Ratio

Apart from the size of the systems, we measured the clone ratio, which is defined as the percentage of tokens that are part of at least one clone fragment. The clone ratio allows us to get an impression of the overall extent of cloning within a system. The clone ratio

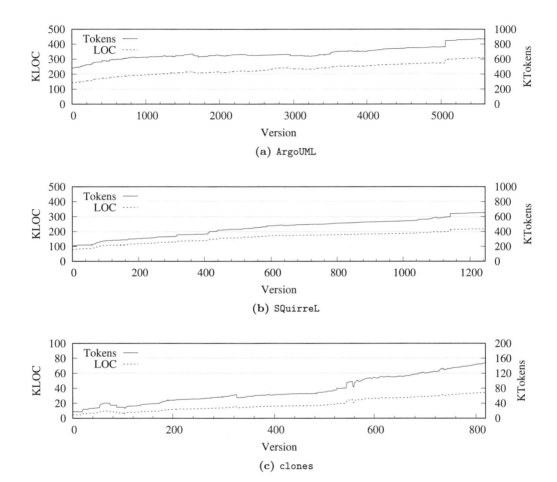

(a) ArgoUML

(b) SQuirreL

(c) clones

**Figure 6.1** – Size evolution of growing subject systems.

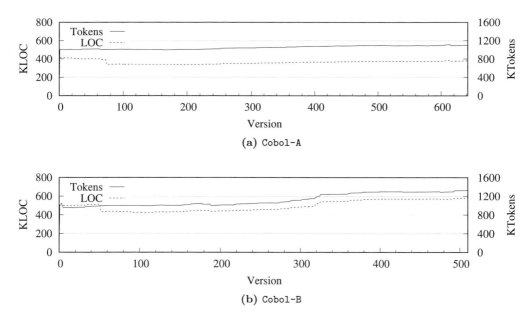

**Figure 6.2** – Size evolution of slowly growing subject systems

depends on the specific clone detection parameters used. The last column of Table 6.2 on page 69 contains the variation of the clone ratio (CR) for each system considering all settings of clone detection parameters described in Section 6.3.1.

Again, we identified two different patterns. For two systems—namely ArgoUML and clones—the clone ratio decreases during our study period. For the remaining systems, the clone ratio remained relatively stable during our analysis. The clone ratio for each subject system is shown in Figure 6.3 on the following page. Again, Krinke observed a notable drop of the clone rate in ArgoUML that is not present in our data. The reason is again the removal of some highly cloned code files that were automatically generated from a grammar. The phenomenon is not present in our data because the respective files were excluded from the analysis.

### Subversion Usage

Table 6.3 summarizes some numbers about the subversion usage of each project, which gives some insight into how the projects are developed and at which level of granularity the change data was available. The table shows how many different users made commits within the analyzed period and how many of the commits were contributed by the four most active users. CI is the commit interval, which is the time that elapsed between commits as average (avg) and median (mdn) value. Average and median differ strongly because commits often occur as series of consecutive actions followed by longer periods of inactivity (day vs. night time). The number of committers for the two open-source systems reflects the number of users who applied the changes to the subversion

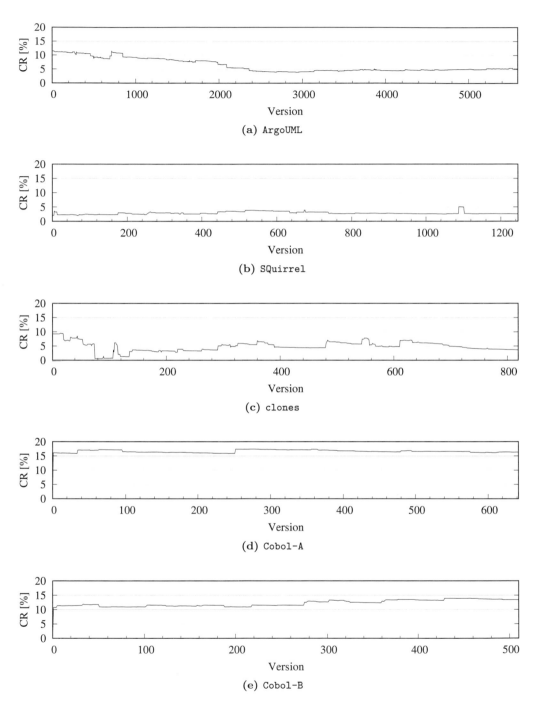

**Figure 6.3** – Clone ratio for type-1 clones with 100 tokens minimum length

| System | Commiters | Revisons | Versions | Top-4 | CI avg (h) | CI mdn (h) |
|--------|-----------|----------|----------|-------|-----------|-----------|
| ArgoUML | 20 | 2195–10656 | 5590 | 67.2% | 5.98 | 1.08 |
| SQuirreL | 7 | 800–2556 | 1247 | 97.8% | 20.91 | 2.15 |
| clones | 15 | 15271–28897 | 820 | 78.0% | 53.30 | 7.53 |
| Cobol-A | ≈ 1 | 4–6978 | 642 | - | 38.79 | 19.70 |
| Cobol-B | ≈ 1 | 686–8348 | 511 | - | 48.65 | 23.87 |

**Table 6.3** – Subject system `subversion` metadata

repository. In open-source development it is common that changes are suggested by unprivileged users and then applied by users who have write access to the code. That is, the number of actual contributors is larger than the number of committers denoted in Table 6.3, but each change to the code was at least approved by one of the actual committers. The usage data for the COBOL systems is limited, because the available `subversion` meta data did not contain actual user names.

In the systems `ArgoUML` and `SQuirreL` commits usually contain changes that leave the source code in a compilable and working state. Nevertheless, the work on one feature, bug fix or refactoring may be distributed over several commit actions. In our manual inspection we found many of such change series. `ArgoUML` has a policy that request commits to always leave the code in a working state. In `clones` the developers aim to keep the code in a working state. In some cases this may require a sequence of consecutive commits over a short period of time. `SQuirreL`'s developers are warned via the mailing list when the code base may be broken for some revisions. Nevertheless, these are guidelines and there is no guarantee that they are adhered every time. For the two COBOL systems we only analyzed the revisions that were deployed to the production environment. Hence, the commits are at a coarser granularity.

Branching was not used for parallel development in any of the projects. Changes are usually applied to the main branch and, therefore, for all five systems we analyzed only this branch. The open-source projects use branches to backport bug fixes to older releases. We did not analyze these.

## Development Process

The way software is developed may have an effect on the cloning phenomena within the code. Nevertheless, we do not aim to evaluate the effect of single differences among the systems on clone stability. There are too many of them to isolate single variables and measure their effect on clone stability. Instead, with our explorative case study we intend to evaluate whether the findings of the original study can be reproduced with systems having different characteristics.

All five systems have in common that they are developed in an incremental fashion. According to their publicly available information, `ArgoUML` follows a rather strict road map with regularly scheduled releases. `SQuirreL` also has incremental releases, but does not follow any schedule. New releases are published when the small development team feels that it is time for a release. `clones` as well as the two COBOL systems do not have public releases. Their development is driven by research or respectively business needs. Features are added as needed and—for the COBOL systems—deployed on a daily basis.

The team structure and the collaboration of developers differ among the systems. `ArgoUML` has a large base of contributors who can suggest solutions for open problems. But only a small group is granted write-access to the repository. These developers perform commits on behalf of the other users. In contrast, `SQuirreL` is developed primarily by a single person. This person, however, changed within the analyzed period. There are other developers who make only few changes. `clones` is developed by a small group of equally active researchers. Most changes are limited to the researchers' own code. The two COBOL systems `Cobol-A` and `Cobol-B` have the same development style. Each program has a single programmer who is responsible for the development. Developers usually keep this role for the whole life-time of the program. Interactions between the developers of different programs are rare. Both COBOL systems conceptually exist for more than ten years, but are subject to massive code churn. Most of the files we analyzed were not older than 1.5 years.

### Clone Management

During our study period, the industrial systems have not been subject to any clone control measures. For `clones` and the two open-source systems, individual small clones have been removed sporadically. Still, no systematic clone control measures were taken for these subject systems as well.

## 6.3.3   Data Collection

For each of our subject systems, we analyzed a sequence of versions $V$ and the changes that affect the source code between these versions. Using clone detection, we can tell for each token in a version $v \in V$ whether it belongs to a clone or not. Let $C(v)$ be the total number of tokens[3] that are cloned in version $v$. Likewise, $N(v)$ denotes the number of tokens that are not cloned. The total number of tokens that exist in $v$ equals $C(v) + N(v)$.

For every version, we measure the number of tokens that are deleted, added, or changed in cloned and non-cloned code, respectively. The difference information is obtained using the Longest Common Subsequence algorithm [135] which we have adapted to token sequences. Figure 6.4 illustrates the three different types of changes to a token sequence.

$DC(v)$ is the number of tokens that have been deleted from cloned code between versions $v-1$ and $v$. Analogously, $DN(v)$ is the number of tokens that are deleted from non-cloned code. Looking at Figure 6.4, tokens 1 and 2 are deleted. If these are part of a clone in version $v-1$, $DC(v)$ is incremented by two. If they are not part of a clone, $DN(v)$ is incremented by two. If one token is part of a clone and the other is not, both values are incremented by one.

---

[3]In Krinke's study, $C(v)$ is a set of source lines and not a plain number. The only information used, however, is the cardinality of the set. Consequently, we define $C(v)$ and the following variables as numbers straight away.

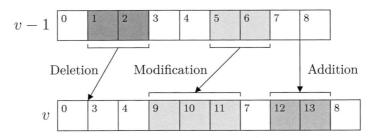

**Figure 6.4** – Changes to a token sequence

Let $AC(v)$ be the number of tokens that are added to cloned code and $AN(v)$ be the number of tokens added to non-cloned code between versions $v - 1$ and $v$. Every addition of a contiguous token sequence does either increase $AC(v)$ or $AN(v)$ depending on where the addition occurred. We say the addition occurred in cloned code when the tokens left and right of the newly added tokens were part of a clone in $v - 1$. Regarding Figure 6.4, the additions of two tokens occurs in cloned code and leads to an increase of $AC(v)$ when tokens 7 and 8 in version $v - 1$ are part of a clone. If one of them is not, the addition occurs in non-cloned code and $AN(v)$ is increased accordingly.

Finally, $MC(v)$ denotes the number of tokens that are changed in cloned code while $MN(v)$ is the number of tokens that are changed in non-cloned code. Modifications occur when the location of a deleted sequence of tokens in version $v - 1$ overlaps with the location of an added sequence of tokens in version $v$. Unlike deletions that affect a sequence of $x$ tokens in version $v - 1$ and additions that affect a sequence of $y$ tokens in version $v$, modifications affect both a sequence of $x$ tokens in version $v - 1$ as well as a sequence of $y$ tokens in version $v$. In Figure 6.4, for example, a sequence of two tokens is affected in $v - 1$ and changed into a sequence of three new tokens in $v$. To determine how many tokens affect cloned code and how many tokens affect non-cloned code we proceed as with a deletion. However, we need to account for modifications where just a few tokens are changed into a much longer token sequence. Consequently, we take the maximum of $x$ and $y$ to determine how many tokens are affected by the modification. If $x \geq y$ then $MC(v)$ and $MN(v)$ are updated according to the number of tokens in $v - 1$ that are cloned or are not cloned respectively. If $x < y$, we multiply the increments for $MC(v)$ and $MN(v)$ with $\frac{y}{x}$.

For all the above type-3 clones we regard all kinds of the above changes to the gaps as changes to non-cloned code.

The sum of all changed cloned tokens in version $v$ is denoted by $*C(v)$, the sum of all changed non-cloned tokens in version $v$ is denoted by $*N(v)$. They are defined as:

$$*C(v) = AC(v) + DC(v) + MC(v)$$

$$*N(v) = AN(v) + DN(v) + MN(v)$$

The values $C(v)$, $N(v)$, $DC(v)$, $DN(v)$, $AC(v)$, $AN(v)$, $MC(v)$, and $MN(v)$ are calculated for each version $v \in V$ during incremental clone detection. Note that $DC(v)$,

$DN(v)$, $AC(v)$, $AN(v)$, $MC(v)$, and $MN(v)$ are 0 for the very first version as it does not have a predecessor and, consequently, there are no changes.

Our instability measurements for a version $v$ consider only files that exist in both versions $v - 1$ and $v$. That is, we do not add the tokens of newly added files to $AC(v)$ and $AN(v)$, nor do we add the tokens of deleted files to $DC(v)$ and $DN(v)$. Including file additions and deletions would not be adequate because we use changes to individual tokens to measure instability. This provides an accurate measure of change for most cases, because every token that gets touched by a developer gets counted. In case of file additions and deletions, this cannot be applied because these are atomic actions that add or remove all tokens in the file at once—the effort for this change does not relate to the amount of tokens, it is constant. Hence, we do not consider additions and deletions of files. Nevertheless, adding or deleting a file can lead to costly co-changes in related files. Such changes are covered by our measurements. Our approach also tracks file movements and renames. When a copy of a file is created, the copy will be regarded as a newly added file. According to its definitions, the original study analyzed a fixed set of files over all versions. That is, his measurement of $AC(v)$, $AN(v)$, $DC(v)$, $DN(v)$ $MC(v)$, and $MV(v)$ did not consider additions and deletions of files as well.

## 6.3.4 Measurement

To answer our research questions, we need a measure for the stability of source code. We follow Krinke's approach and use the *instability* which is the ratio between the number of changed tokens and the number of all tokens of a given category. Instability will be denoted with the symbol $\iota$. The instabilities of cloned and non-cloned code to deletions, for example, are:

$$\iota_{DC} = \frac{\sum\limits_{v \in V} DC(v)}{\sum\limits_{v \in V} C(v)} \quad \text{and} \quad \iota_{DN} = \frac{\sum\limits_{v \in V} DN(v)}{\sum\limits_{v \in V} N(v)}$$

Both $\iota_{DC}$ and $\iota_{NC}$ compute the instability over a set of consecutive versions $V$ of the source code. That is, the metric values represent the instability over a given time period, which can be varied to obtain the stability in different periods by adjusting $V$. Likewise we define the instabilities with respect to additions as:

$$\iota_{AC} = \frac{\sum\limits_{v \in V} AC(v)}{\sum\limits_{v \in V} C(v)} \quad \text{and} \quad \iota_{AN} = \frac{\sum\limits_{v \in V} AN(v)}{\sum\limits_{v \in V} N(v)}$$

Consequently, the modification instabilities of source code are defined as:

$$\iota_{MC} = \frac{\sum\limits_{v \in V} MC(v)}{\sum\limits_{v \in V} C(v)} \quad \text{and} \quad \iota_{MN} = \frac{\sum\limits_{v \in V} MN(v)}{\sum\limits_{v \in V} N(v)}$$

These metrics resemble the measurements of the original study. Our metrics differ in their definition being based on tokens and also slightly in their names (for example

$\iota_{AC}$ vs. AC% and $\iota_{MN}$ vs. CN%). The following metrics extend the measurements of the original study.

We also determine the general instability of the cloned and non-cloned code over all of the three operation types:

$$\iota_{*C} = \frac{\sum\limits_{v \in V} *C(v)}{\sum\limits_{v \in V} C(v)} \quad \text{and} \quad \iota_{*N} = \frac{\sum\limits_{v \in V} *N(v)}{\sum\limits_{v \in V} N(v)}$$

These eight $\iota$-metrics allow us to compute the instability of cloned and non-cloned code separately. If we want to compare the overall instability of cloned and non-cloned code within a time period, we can simply compare $\iota_{*C}$ with $\iota_{*N}$ for the same set of consecutive versions $V$. The higher of the two metric values represents higher instability.

All eight metrics represent ratios. For example, $\iota_{*C}$ denotes the ratio of existing cloned tokens that were changed. Hence, the metrics for the same change type can be compared directly, because they are not affected by the absolute amount of cloned and non-cloned code in the system. Nevertheless, the $\iota$ values for cloned and non-cloned code must be compared with care. Assume $\iota_{*N} = 0.2$ and $\iota_{*C} = 0.1$, then the non-cloned code would be less stable regarding deletions, because of the higher $\iota$ value. While this gives us the tendency it still does not suffice to express the magnitude of the difference between both values. In our example $\iota_{*N}$ exceeds $\iota_{*C}$ by a value of just 0.1, but at the same time the instability of $\iota_{*N}$ is twice as high as $\iota_{*C}$'s. Let us now assume $\iota_{*N} = 0.9$ and $\iota_{*C} = 0.8$. Again, the non-cloned code is less stable and, again, the metric values differ by 0.1. Nevertheless, the relative difference of both is much smaller. That is, in the first example, non-cloned code is notably less stable, while in the second, it is just slightly less stable. Consequently, we define four additional metrics for the *relative* difference of the code's instability.

$$\iota_{D\Delta} = \frac{\iota_{DN} - \iota_{DC}}{\iota_{DN} + \iota_{DC}} \qquad\qquad \iota_{M\Delta} = \frac{\iota_{MN} - \iota_{MC}}{\iota_{MN} + \iota_{MC}}$$

$$\iota_{A\Delta} = \frac{\iota_{AN} - \iota_{AC}}{\iota_{AN} + \iota_{AC}} \qquad\qquad \iota_{*\Delta} = \frac{\iota_{*N} - \iota_{*C}}{\iota_{*N} + \iota_{*C}}$$

Positive values of $\iota_{*\Delta}$ indicate that cloned code is more stable than non-cloned code. Accordingly, a negative value means that non-cloned code is more stable. We divide the difference of the two instability values by their sum to normalize the metric. This makes $\iota_{*\Delta}$ relative to the absolute amount of the two instabilities. A difference of 0.1 is more significant if $\iota_{*N}$ and $\iota_{*C}$ are low: $\iota_{*N} = 0.2 \land \iota_{*C} = 0.1 \Rightarrow \iota_{*\Delta} = 0.333$. It is less significant if both $\iota_{*N}$ and $\iota_{*C}$ are high: $\iota_{*N} = 0.9 \land \iota_{*C} = 0.8 \Rightarrow \iota_{*\Delta} = 0.059$. The four metrics provide values between 1, that is, only cloned code changed, while non-cloned code did not, and $-1$, that is, only non-cloned changed and cloned code did not. A value of 0 means that cloned and non-cloned code changed to the same relative amount. The $\iota_\Delta$ metrics are undefined for time periods without change, where $\iota_{*N} + \iota_{*C} = 0$. Because we skip versions without changes to the system's token stream, this case cannot occur in our case studies.

The $\iota_\Delta$ metrics follow the concept of the *attributable risk* or *risk difference* from epidemiology [100]. For example, $\iota_{*\Delta}$ computes the absolute difference between the two probabilities $\iota_{*N}$ and $\iota_{*C}$. That is, $\iota_{*N} - \iota_{*C}$ is the increased risk of change that can be attributed to being not-cloned. The division by the sum of both probabilities turns the difference into a percentage and, as we explained before, takes the size of the underlying probabilities into account. Another possible metric would have been the *odds ratio* [100]. An odds ratio variant of $\iota_{*\Delta}$ would be defined as follows.

$$OR_* = \frac{\sum\limits_{v \in V} *C(v) \times (N(v) - *N(v))}{\sum\limits_{v \in V} *N(v) \times (C(v) - *C(v))}$$

A problem of $OR_*$ would be that it is undefined for $*N(v) = 0$ (no non-cloned tokens change) or $(C(v) - *C(v)) = 0$ (all cloned tokens change). The $\iota_{*\Delta}$ metric will always be defined as long as two criteria are met: First, $C(v) > 0$ and $N(v) > 0$ (cloned and non-cloned tokens exist) and, second, at least on token changed for all analyzed periods. The restrictions for $\iota_{*\Delta}$ are unproblematic because cases where these are not met are not interesting to our analysis. The restrictions of $OR_*$ would not allow us to measure the instability for versions in which non-cloned code does not change, which is not acceptable.[4] Because $OR_*$'s results scale from 0 to infinity, it must be normalized to a scale from $-1$ to 1 using a association measure like Yule's $Q$ [180], which computes as follows.

$$Q(OR_*) = \frac{OR_* - 1}{OR_* + 1}$$

Besides these technical differences, both $Q(OR_*)$ and $\iota_{*\Delta}$ provide almost identical results. We computed both for all our results and measured differences at the level of the third decimal. The largest difference we measured accounts to 0.001186.

To answer Questions A1 and A2, we calculate $\iota_{AC}$, $\iota_{AN}$, $\iota_{DC}$, $\iota_{DN}$, $\iota_{MC}$, and $\iota_{MN}$ for both subject systems and compare the values to the results of the original study. To ensure comparability, we parametrized our clone detector to use a minimum clone length of 100 tokens and detect type-1 clones only.

We approach Question A3 by repeating the above procedure with different settings for our clone detector. In particular, we vary the minimum clone length using the values 50, 100, and 150 tokens. In addition, we compare our results for only type-1 clones to the results obtained from considering type-1, type-2, and type-3 clones. The results allow us to analyze how these parameters affect the stability of cloned and non-cloned code.

Question A4 is answered by analyzing modifications of tokens in more detail—their size and frequency in particular. In addition, we manually inspect deletions that removed a large number of tokens to explore their rationale.

---

[4]Indeed, we did not encounter situations where the non-cloned code did not change. This, however, could not be foreseen before our analysis and may also not hold for systems that will be analyzed in the future.

For Question A5, we use a sliding window of one month and three months, respectively, to measure $\iota_{*\Delta}$ and analyze how it varies between different phases of our subject systems.

# 6.4 Results

## 6.4.1 Validation of the original studies' results

In this section we answer Question A1 by comparing the stability of cloned code to the stability of non-cloned code for ArgoUML and SQuirreL, both of which have been analyzed in the original study. We applied a minimum clone length of 100 tokens and configured our clone detector to detect only identical clones. This resembles Krinke's setup who used 11 lines as minimum and detected only exact clones. We have measured the stability of cloned and non-cloned code with respect to deletions, additions, and modifications. Figure 6.5 on the next page shows our results compared to the results of the original study which we took from [112].

The first thing to be noticed is that our instability values are much lower than those from the original study. This is due to the use of a different interval between versions and our measurement being based on tokens instead of lines. Our short version intervals result in a significantly smaller ratio between the number of changed tokens and the number of all tokens encountered during our analysis. Hence, we cannot compare the absolute but only the relative values of the instability measure. We present Krinke's and our results on different scales so that it is easier to examine the relative proportions of the instability values.

Regarding ArgoUML, the instability of cloned code with respect to additions, $\iota_{AC}$, is notably lower than the instability of non-cloned code $\iota_{AN}$. Regarding deletions, the instability of cloned code is slightly higher compared to non-cloned code. Looking at modifications, $\iota_{MC}$ is notably lower than $\iota_{MN}$. Consequently, the stability of cloned code is higher than the stability of non-cloned code when considering additions and modifications. For deletions, however, the deviation of the instabilities is very small. Non-cloned code seems to be slightly more stable. The same relation has been found by Krinke. Although the ratio between the instability of cloned and non-cloned code for each type of change are slightly different compared to Krinke's results, we can confirm his findings in general.

The instability values for SQuirreL are all higher compared to ArgoUML indicating more changes. Nevertheless, the relations $\iota_{AC} < \iota_{AN}$, $\iota_{DC} > \iota_{DN}$, and $\iota_{MC} < \iota_{MN}$ also hold for SQuirreL. Again, this confirms Krinke's findings. In summary, we can confirm his findings that cloned code is more stable in general but less stable with respect to deletions compared to non-cloned code.

The instability measurements we present are all mean values. It has to be noted that the distribution of the values, these arithmetic means are computed from, differ thoroughly. This is due to the fact that the cloned code is less often affected by changes. But, if it is affected by a change this does cause higher instability as it would in non-cloned code. We further discuss this in Section 6.5.

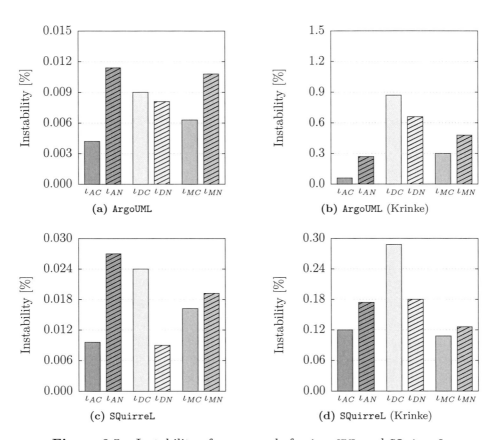

**Figure 6.5** – Instability of source code for `ArgoUML` and `SQuirreL`

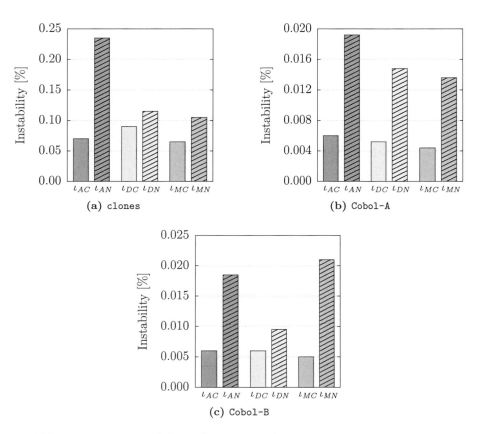

**Figure 6.6** – Instability of source code in clones, Cobol-A, and Cobol-B

## 6.4.2   Generalizability

Although the original study analyzes five different systems written in different programming languages (C, C++, Java), all of them are open-source systems and the programming languages used are structurally similar. To test the generalizability of his findings and answer Question A2, we extend the analysis by measuring the instability values for three more systems from academia and industry written in Ada and COBOL. The results are given in Figure 6.6 on the preceding page.

Analogous to the other systems, we can observe that for `clones`, the instability of non-cloned code is higher than the instability of cloned code regarding additions and modifications. Unlike the other systems, however, the instability of non-cloned code is also higher regarding deletions—that is, cloned code is more stable with respect to every type of change. This also holds for the industrial systems `Cobol-A` and `Cobol-B` written in COBOL. A peculiarity of `clones` is, that cloned as well as non-cloned code is by far less stable compared to the other systems. In other words, there are more changes to the code. The instability values are larger by a factor of ten approximately.

We also observed that the distance between the instabilities of cloned and non-cloned code is bigger for the COBOL systems. That is, the clones in these systems are much more stable compared to non-cloned code as in the other systems. The difference is caused by the high instability of non-cloned COBOL code, while the instability values for the clones do not differ significantly among the systems (except for `clones`).

In summary, the higher stability of clones found in the original study can also be found in systems using different languages, development styles and serving different application domains. However, the lower stability of cloned code regarding deletions is not generalizable to these systems. In the following section, we analyze the effect of the clone detection parameters, because these have a notable influence on the detected clones and, hence, the stability measures.

## 6.4.3   The Relationship of Detection Parameters and Stability

In this section we answer Question A3 by varying the requirements to be regarded as a clone. We achieve this by changing the parameter settings of our clone detector for the minimum length of clones and the minimum similarity. As minimum length we choose 50, 100 and 150 tokens. The setting of 150 tokens will only provide clones that are at least 150 tokens long. The 50 tokens setting will provide clones that are at least 50 tokens long, but also all longer clones. This includes all clones found with the 100 and 150 tokens settings. That is, the smaller values for this setting cause the clone detector to provide more results. For clone similarity we choose the following two settings: First, only type-1 clones. Second, type-1, type-2, and type-3 clones. Again, the latter setting will provide more clones as it is less restrictive.

The three length settings and two similarity settings multiply to the six possible parameter combinations:

- Type 1 / 50 tokens

- Type 1 / 100 tokens

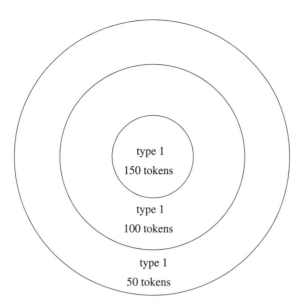

**Figure 6.7** – Overlapping of the results provided by the different clone detector settings for type-1 clones as Venn diagram.

- Type 1 / 150 tokens

- Types 1–3 / 50 tokens

- Types 1–3 / 100 tokens

- Types 1–3 / 150 tokens

As we have discussed in Section 6.3.1, the setting *type 1 / 100 tokens* comes closest to the settings of the original study. For each subject system we collect instability data for all six clone definitions. The settings that detect smaller clones also provide the larger clones. The Venn diagram in Figure 6.7 shows how the three settings for type-1 clones overlap. When type-1 clones with a minimum length of 50 tokens are detected, clones with more than 100 or more than 150 tokens length will also be included in the result because the parameter defined the minimal size a clone may have. The setting for type-1 clones with at least 150 tokens will not provide clones that are shorter than 150 tokens. The same holds for the settings that will detect type-1, type-2 and type-3 clones. These will always contain the type-1 clones as well.

We used the chi-square test of independence [142] to assess the statistical significance for the difference we measured between the stabilities of cloned and non-cloned code. We use this non-parametric test because our samples differ in size—there is less cloned code than non-cloned code. We applied the test to the results for each of our six parameter settings. All tests provided a p-value of 0.0001 or less. This is the case for both the results for all change types combined and the individual results for each change type. That is, the differences we report in the following are statistically significant.

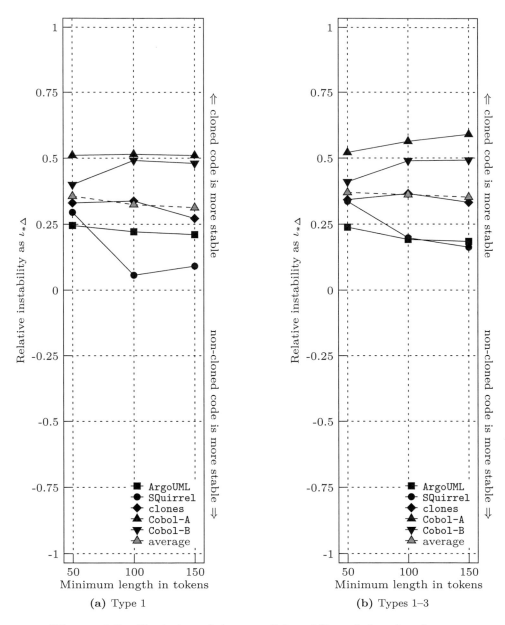

**(a)** Type 1  **(b)** Types 1–3

**Figure 6.8** – Deviation of the overall instability of cloned and non-cloned code for clones of different minimum length

Figure 6.8 on the facing page shows the difference of the instabilities between cloned and non-cloned code for each system and parameter setting. These two charts compare the overall instability $\iota_{*\Delta}$. How the instability differs for the three change types *additions*, *deletions*, and *modifications* will be discussed later.

The most obvious finding is that, regardless of the detection parameters chosen, cloned code is more stable than non-cloned code in total. This is indicated by the constantly positive $\iota_{*\Delta}$ for all systems. It is also clear that the instability of cloned and non-cloned code varies for different detection parameters for all systems. Cobol-A in the type-1 settings is an exception where the differences for clones of different length are minimal. In general, the variation of $\iota_{*\Delta}$ is rather small for most systems. It also does not follow a common pattern as $\iota_{*\Delta}$ increases with the minimum clone length for some systems while it decreases for others. All systems, however, have in common that the variation of the detection parameters does not cause negative $\iota_{*\Delta}$, which would mean that non-cloned code is more stable.

Notable effects of the detection parameters can be observed for SQuirreL and Cobol-B in the step from type-1/50 to type-1/100. In SQuirreL larger clones with a minimum size of 100 and 150 tokens are less stable than the smaller ones. In Cobol-B the opposite is the case.

When the results of type-1 clones in Figure 6.8a on the preceding page are compared to those for type-1, type-2, and type-3 clones in Figure 6.8b, similar results can be observed for the systems. The effect of the variation in clone similarity also differs per system. Less similarity causes higher clone stability in SQuirreL and Cobol-A. The effect on the other systems is only small. Two cases exist where the minimum clone length has different effects when the two similarity settings are compared. The first is Cobol-A in which exact clones of different length do not differ in their stability, while the stability of near-miss and gapped clones increases with the minimum length. The second is SQuirreL, in which clones with a minimum length of 100 tokens have the lowest stability, whereas near-miss and gapped clones have the lowest stability when they are at least 150 tokens long. Again, we can conclude that differences exist, but are not decisive in a way that they turn the balance of code stability in favor of non-cloned code.

The average of all values indicates that $\iota_{*\Delta}$ decreases slightly for longer clones. Given the lack of common patterns among the systems, this tendency should be considered with care.

So far we considered only summarized $\iota_{*\Delta}$ values. To go further into detail we inspect the difference between the instability of cloned and non-clone code for additions, deletions, and modifications separately.

## ArgoUML

Figure 6.9 on the following page shows the parameter effect split according to the three types of operations for ArgoUML. For this system we can observe that varying the minimum clone length affects the three types of operations differently. Switching from 50 tokens to 100 tokens decreases the difference in the code instabilities for modifications and deletions, whereas it increases the deviation of additions. The instability of cloned

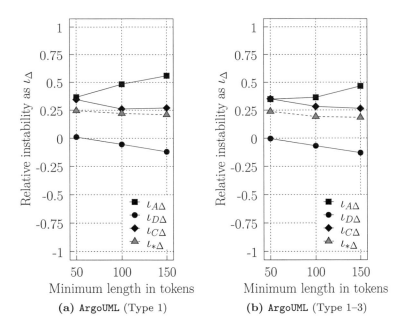

**Figure 6.9** – Deviation of the instability of cloned and non-cloned code for `ArgoUML`

code with respect to deletions, $\iota_{D\Delta}$, becomes negative. This indicates that cloned code is actually less stable than non-cloned code regarding clones of at least 100 tokens length and considering only deletions in `ArgoUML`. For 150 tokens minimum length, $\iota_{A\Delta}$ further increases, $\iota_{D\Delta}$ further decreases, and $\iota_{M\Delta}$ increases slightly. In general, the deviation between the stability of cloned and non-cloned code in `ArgoUML` is notably different for the three types of operations.

The domination of deletions that was observed in the original study also holds for different settings. In `ArgoUML` longer clones tend to be more instable than shorter ones.

**SQuirreL**

The results for `SQuirreL` are similar to those for `ArgoUML`. The difference in the stability of cloned and non-cloned code is more distinct. Clones are even more stable regarding additions, but also even less stable regarding deletions. In terms of deletions non-cloned code is more stable for any of our six detector parameter settings. Like in `ArgoUML` longer clones are less stable in this regard than shorter ones.

A common pattern for all three operation types is that the $\iota_\Delta$ values decrease when the minimum length of clones is increased from 50 to 100. That is, the smaller clones are less stable. This trend does not continue when the minimum length is increased to 150 tokens.

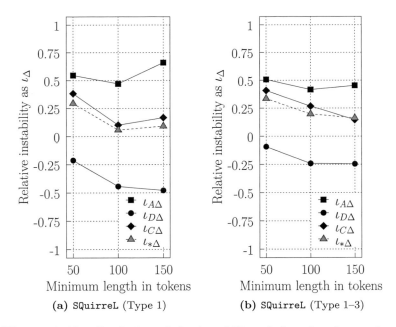

**Figure 6.10** – Deviation of the instability of cloned and non-cloned code for SQuirreL

Varying the similarity setting also has different effect on the $\iota_\Delta$ values. Near-miss and gapped clones are still less stable than the non-cloned code, but the difference is smaller. The other differences do not follow systematic patterns.

### Clones

In `clones` the variation of the detection parameters has only small effects when the 50 and 100 tokens settings are compared. Nevertheless, clones of at least 150 tokens length differ. The most outstanding differences are the high stability of long exact clones regarding deletions and the low stability of long clones to changes. Indeed, `clones` is the only system in which clones are less stable regarding only changes. This, however, can only be observed for the longest exact clones.

Besides the aforementioned exceptions the values are similar to those of `ArgoUML` and `SQuirreL`: Clones seem to be most stable in terms of additions, followed by changes and deletions. The values differ when the detection parameters are changed, but no common pattern can be observed.

### Cobol-A

`Cobol-A` shows the most uniform picture. The stability varies between the settings and change types, but the variation is minimal as are the differences between the patterns. When the similarity settings are compared it can be observed that the stability of clones

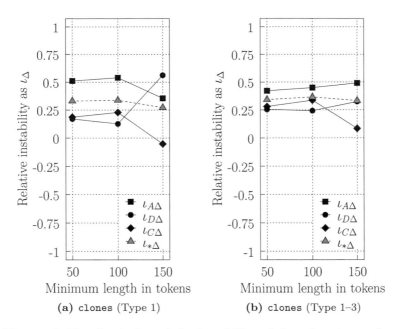

**Figure 6.11** – Deviation of the instability of cloned and non-cloned code for `clones`

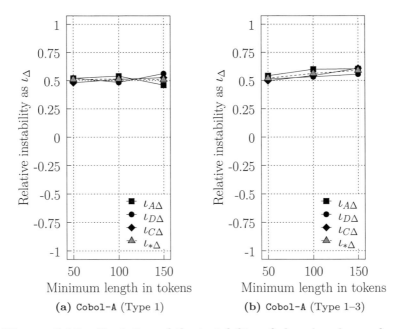

**Figure 6.12** – Deviation of the instability of cloned and non-cloned code for `Cobol-A`

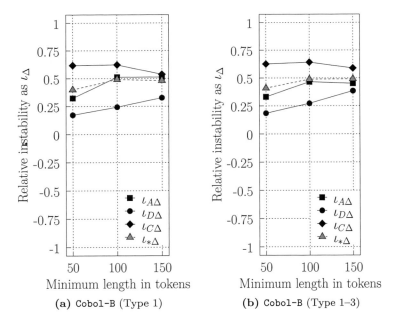

**Figure 6.13** – Deviation of the instability of cloned and non-cloned code for `Cobol-B`

increases slightly with their minimum length for all three types. For exact clones the clone length has less effect. Nevertheless, these differences are marginal.

### Cobol-B

In `Cobol-B` the deviation between $\iota_{A\Delta}$, $\iota_{D\Delta}$, and $\iota_{C\Delta}$ is larger compared with `Cobol-A`. The tendency that longer clones are more stable can be observed here too with one exception for changes. The minimum similarity setting has minimal effect on the values.

### Summary

In summary, we observed that the choice of parameters has an effect on the stability values. `ArgoUML`, `SQuirreL`, and `clones` have in common that in most cases clones tend to be most stable regarding additions, followed by changes. The domination of deletions in `ArgoUML`, `SQuirreL` can be observed for most detection parameter settings, but does not appear in `clones`. In the two Cobol systems longer clones seem to be more stable in most cases.

On the one hand the answer to Question A3 is that different detection parameters do have an effect on the stability of clones. On the other hand, these differences are mostly small and do not follow common patters over the systems. Most importantly, these differences do not invert the relative stability between cloned code and non-cloned code.

Our observations do not conclude in a clear advice whether clones detected with specific parameters require more attention because they cause higher change effort. The overall observation that clones are more stable than non-cloned code seems to be independent from the parameter settings or the system. Only in ArgoUML and SQuirreL clones where less stable than non-cloned code regarding deletions. There are subtle differences between systems, parameter settings, and change types, but they do not follow common patterns besides the fact that cloned code mostly is more stable than non-cloned code.

### 6.4.4   Deletion Characteristics

Our aforementioned results show that, in the open-source systems, clones are less stable regarding deletions. For the academic and industrial systems this is not the case. In the original study, Krinke eliminated the versions with high $DC(v)$ and got results similar to ours for clones, Cobol-A, and Cobol-B. This leads to the question how the difference in the stability with respect to deletions is caused (Question A4 on page 65).

The instability of clones regarding deletions may be caused by a high frequency of deletions, a large average size of deletions, or a combination of both. We will analyze these two possible causes.

#### Frequency

To determine the frequency of changes that delete tokens we need to find out how many versions out of all contain deletions to clones. For each of the $AC$, $AN$, $DC$, $DN$, $MC$, $MN$ values we define the subset of versions that contain changes of the respective type in the respective portion of the code as:

$$V_{DC} = \{v | v \in V, DC(v) > 0\} \quad \text{and} \quad V_{DN} = \{v | v \in V, DN(v) > 0\}$$

$$V_{AC} = \{v | v \in V, AC(v) > 0\} \quad \text{and} \quad V_{AN} = \{v | v \in V, AN(v) > 0\}$$

$$V_{MC} = \{v | v \in V, MC(v) > 0\} \quad \text{and} \quad V_{MN} = \{v | v \in V, MN(v) > 0\}$$

$$V_{*C} = \{v | v \in V, *C(v) > 0\} \quad \text{and} \quad V_{*N} = \{v | v \in V, *N(v) > 0\}$$

We also define the frequency of versions with changes of a specific type to clones as follows.

$$DC_{freq\%} = \frac{V_{DC}}{|V|} \times 100$$

$$AC_{freq\%} = \frac{V_{AC}}{|V|} \times 100$$

$$MC_{freq\%} = \frac{V_{MC}}{|V|} \times 100$$

Table 6.4 on the facing page shows the values for the *type 1 / 100* setting. Surprisingly, changes that delete tokens from clones are least frequent in ArgoUML

|              | ArgoUML | SQuirreL | clones | Cobol-A | Cobol-B |
|--------------|---------|----------|--------|---------|---------|
| $AC_{freq\%}$ | 4.38%   | 3.54%    | 2.68%  | 10.26%  | 9.59%   |
| $DC_{freq\%}$ | 3.85%   | 2.25%    | 3.17%  | 10.11%  | 9.59%   |
| $MC_{freq\%}$ | 5.64%   | 2.81%    | 3.78%  | 9.33%   | 8.81%   |

**Table 6.4** – Frequency of change types (*type 1 / 100*)

and SQuirreL. Additions and modifications appear more frequently. Consequently, the instability to deletions cannot be caused by a high frequency of such changes. The phenomenon must be caused by the size of the deletions.

**Size**

To get a better impression, we calculate the average size of each operation for cloned and non-cloned code, which we define as:

$$\overline{DC} = \frac{\sum\limits_{v \in V_{DC}} DC(v)}{|V_{DC}|} \quad \text{and} \quad \overline{DN} = \frac{\sum\limits_{v \in V_{DN}} DN(v)}{|V_{DN}|}$$

$$\overline{AC} = \frac{\sum\limits_{v \in V_{AC}} AC(v)}{|V_{AC}|} \quad \text{and} \quad \overline{AN} = \frac{\sum\limits_{v \in V_{AN}} AN(v)}{|V_{AN}|}$$

$$\overline{MC} = \frac{\sum\limits_{v \in V_{MC}} MC(v)}{|V_{MC}|} \quad \text{and} \quad \overline{MN} = \frac{\sum\limits_{v \in V_{MN}} MN(v)}{|V_{MN}|}$$

Figure 6.14 on the next page shows the results. In most cases, changes to non-cloned code are much larger in size than changes to cloned code. This is plausible because clones are relatively small code fragments compared to the vast amount of non-cloned code. ArgoUML and SQuirreL differ in their average deletion sizes. Deletions to clones in ArgoUML are almost as large as deletions to the remaining code. In SQuirreL they are even larger on average. This means the domination of deletions in these systems is caused by the deletions' size.

To learn more about the characteristics of the deletions we manually inspected the top-10 versions in which the most cloned tokens have been deleted for all systems. That is, we inspected the ten versions having the highest absolute $DC(v)$. A closer look into these versions of ArgoUML and SQuirreL explains why the clones in these systems are more instable to deletions.

**Top-10 $DC(v)$ Versions in ArgoUML**

The sum of the $DC(v)$ values for the top ten versions of ArgoUML contributes 37% of all token deletions from cloned code throughout our analysis. Revision 3092 has the

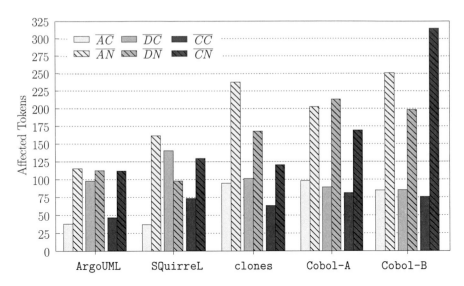

**Figure 6.14** – Average size of operations

highest $DC(v)$ value of all versions with 3065 tokens being deleted from cloned code. Our investigation of the commit revealed that a Pull-Up-Method refactoring has been applied that elevates the handling of button clicks from specialized GUI elements to the common super class. The accompanying commit message indicates that the refactoring was specifically targeted at removing duplication and improving maintainability.

In total, we have classified 4 out of 10 commits as refactoring. We encountered 2 Pull-Up-Method refactorings, 1 Extract Method refactoring, and 1 Rename refactoring. The remaining commits are 1 bug removal, 3 removals of code that was not needed anymore, and 2 cases of general restructuring. Regarding all 10 commits, 4 affected a single contiguous source code section only, while the others involved multiple locations. Our results from analyzing the changes and accompanying commit messages indicate that only 3 commits were specifically targeted at removing duplication, while the others seem to affect clones only as a side effect. Nevertheless, all but one commit (the bug removal) are related to restructuring and clean-up activity.

### Top-10 $DC(v)$ Versions in SQuirreL

Regarding SQuirreL, the ten commits with the highest $DC(v)$ values contribute 87% of all tokens that were deleted from cloned code. Revision 1978 has the highest value with 1032 tokens being deleted from cloned code. The commit extracted multiple copies of different methods into a common utility class and is, consequently, an instance of the Extract Method refactoring. Regarding all ten commits, only 2 of them have been classified as refactoring. Seven commits removed code that provided specialized functionality which was, however, not needed anymore. The remaining commit was a general restructuring of GUI initialization code.

Half of the commits involved only a single contiguous source code location, whereas the other commits affected multiple locations. From our analysis of the changes and commit messages, we conclude that only two commits were targeted as specifically reducing duplication in the system. Analogous to ArgoUML, cloned code seems to be often deleted without a clear intent to reduce duplication, although most commits are related to restructuring and clean-up activity.

These findings for the open-source systems cannot be generalized for clones, Cobol-A, and Cobol-B for which we also inspected the top-10 $DC(v)$ versions manually. These do not contain comparable cleanup-activity, but rather added new functionality and deleted some cloned code incidentally. There was not a single case where the rationale of the change was clearly related to the fact that clones were present.

To summarize, the higher instability of clones to deletions in ArgoUML and SQuirreL is caused by code cleanup in the form of few but exceptionally large deletions. The majority of these changes were not performed because clones were present. The other systems were subject to restructuring and code cleanup too, but they do not contain changes that can be compared to the ones we described for the open-source systems. The deletion of cloned code seems to be a side effect of general restructuring.

## 6.4.5 Distribution Over Time

The instability measures we discussed so far were all computed over the entire history we had available for each system. They summarize the instabilities over a time period of two to five years. This way of measurement does not allow any conclusions on the temporal distribution of the changes. The $\iota_{*\Delta}$ value we measured over the whole period may essentially be swayed by a few changes that happened in a short period. Different time periods, thus, may have notably different $\iota_{*\Delta}$ values. For instance, clones may be less stable most of the time, but few exceptionally large changes to non-cloned code may make them more stable on average. Different phases in the life cycle of a software system may be a cause for such differences in the stability of clones. To evaluate this effect and to answer Question A5 on page 65, we repeat our instability measurements on shorter time periods and compare the results.

We use a sliding window technique to analyze subphases of the whole time period available. As size of the time window we choose one and three months. For each project we approximate how many versions fall into these periods on average. The resulting number of versions is used as window size. We approximated the number of changes per month to define the window size instead of using accurate time windows for two reasons. First, because the instability measure is not defined for time periods without any activity and second because instability measures could be influenced by the different number of commits in each window, which would have complicated the interpretation of the results. Because our subject systems have different development activity, the number of versions per window differs for the systems and is shown in Table 6.5 on the next page.

We let the window slide over the available history version by version, measuring $\iota_{*\Delta}$ each time. Figures 6.15 to 6.19 show the results for all systems. In the plots, each point stands for the $\iota_{*\Delta}$ value of one window. Each curve represents the results for a

| System | Versions | 1-month window | | 3-month window | |
|--------|----------|----------|-----|----------|-----|
|        |          | Versions | %   | Versions | %   |
| ArgoUML | 5590 | 121 | 2.2 | 364 | 13.0 |
| SQuirreL | 1247 | 25 | 2.0 | 75 | 12.0 |
| clones | 820 | 12 | 1.5 | 37 | 9.1 |
| Cobol-A | 642 | 19 | 2.9 | 57 | 17.8 |
| Cobol-B | 511 | 15 | 2.9 | 45 | 17.6 |

**Table 6.5** – Window Sizes

different minimum clone length. For clarity and to save space in this chapter we present the values for only type-1 clones, because the results for all clone types differ only marginally. Nevertheless, the data for all clone types is enclosed in Appendix A for the sake of completeness and transparency. There we also repeat all charts presented here in larger scale.

The smaller the window, the stronger is the effect of single changes to the $\iota_{*\Delta}$ value. It comes naturally that a higher fluctuation of the curve can be observed in the plots for the smaller window size. The curves for longer windows are smoothed, because single changes have less effect on $\iota_{*\Delta}$, which is an average value. We chose one month as the smallest window to avoid too strong fluctuation of $\iota_{*\Delta}$ that would make it impossible to interpret the results. One month should contain a sufficient amount of change and should be long enough to finish the work on most development and maintenance tasks.

In the following, we describe the results in detail and discuss situations where the stability values changed notably in the 1-month setting. For the COBOL systems we report only the numbers. We cannot provide deeper insight into the changes because of data confidentiality.

**ArgoUML**

Figures 6.15a and 6.15b show how $\iota_{*\Delta}$ varies in different windows for ArgoUML. Basically, we can observe that cloned code is more stable for the most part. Although the $\iota_{*\Delta}$ varies it mostly stays between 1—which means no clones are changed at all—and approximately 0—which means that there is no difference in the stabilities of cloned and non-cloned code. Nevertheless, there are some cases where $\iota_{*\Delta}$ drops below 0, which means that clones have been less stable for the respective windows.

The curves of both window sizes have their strongest drop to negative $\iota_{*\Delta}$ around window 500. The main cause for this transition are three huge interrelated operations on clones. The first one is a consistent change to cloned listener code that is implemented for different GUI components. It is duplicated several times. The rationale of the change was the addition of new interactive elements to the listener. Just a few revisions later the developers appear to react on this costly change and perform an extract method refactoring on the clone they had changed consistently before. In their commit message they state "to improve maintenance" as the reason for the refactoring. The third change

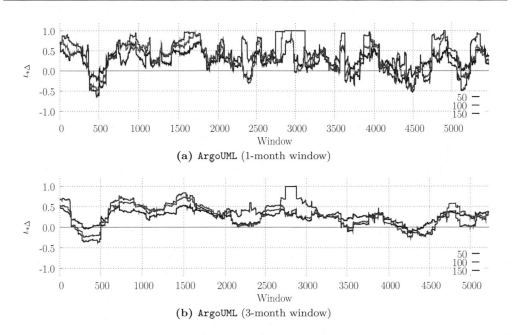

**(a)** `ArgoUML` (1-month window)

**(b)** `ArgoUML` (3-month window)

**Figure 6.15** – The $\iota_{*\Delta}$ values for type-1 clones using different time windows in `ArgoUML`

is another extract method refactoring. GUI code that loads icons and is duplicated several times is removed and replaced by a unified solution.

Another situation where clones were less stable in the 1-month setting begins at window 3638. The $\iota_{*\Delta}$ value drops from 0.94 to $-0.23$ because of an inconsistent change to a clone pair. Two parsers share the same 97-line long initialization sequence of a translation table. This is removed in one of the to parsers, but not in the other. A comment before the sequence, saying "TODO: I think this is so old we don't need it any more" indicates that the code became obsolete longer ago. A second situation that contributes to this drop is connected to changes to some logic for routing edges in a graph. The developers adapt some code they copied from another graph framework and start to restructure it according to their needs. In this process they copy 58 lines of routing code to another class and remove this copy only some revisions later. The stability value turns positive again after some windows because of an exceptionally large change to only non-cloned tokens—the cloned code became more stable in comparison because of changes in the non-cloned code.

The next phase where clones were less stable lasts from window 4415 to 4569 and is caused by three changes. The first of ·these has the highest impact. It happened when the developers added support for the assignment of multiple stereotypes to UML entities. The GUI, which is used to define these stereotypes, is cloned for nodes and edges. Both instances were changed consistently to support the new feature, deleting 203 and modifying 193 tokens in total. The second contributing change is caused by a temporary workaround. A new table model proved to be buggy. Hence, the developers reintroduced the previous implementation for this model as a nested class, but left the new and buggy one in the repository. Both models share many clones. Five revisions later they removed the old model again which causes a large deletion of cloned code. In the third change contributing to this drop, the code generation for C# is changed inconsistently to the code generation for Java.

A last drop to negative $\iota_{*\Delta}$ is located between the windows 5069 and 5239. One of its reasons is a change that was reverted in the very next revision. A combo-box model was copied from one to another class. The developers revert this change with their next commit without giving a reason. The second change that lowers the clone stability moves 74 lines of code from one class to another. For a single revision this code is present in the original and the destination class. The removal of the code from the original class is counted as a deletion to cloned code by our metric, but it should not be considered as a threat to maintenance.

For `ArgoUML` we can conclude that there are some time periods in which clones have been less stable according to our metric. These changeovers in stability are mainly caused by few changes. Among the revisions that contribute to these situations we identified four consistent changes to clones. We also identified five changes that removed clones in some way. All the drops to negative $\iota_{*\Delta}$ include at least one such change, which are relatively large in size compared to the consistent changes. That is, although we did observe consistent changes to clones—which may indicate increased maintenance costs—the phases where clones are less stable are strongly affected by deletions of clones.

## SQuirreL

In `SQuirreL` $\iota_{*\Delta}$ fluctuates much stronger than in `ArgoUML`. The curves are less distorted because there are less versions in each window compared to `ArgoUML`. In the 1-month setting, 66% of all windows contain no changes to clones at all—these are the windows where $\iota_{*\Delta}$ equals 1. But those windows that contain changes to clones tend to have very low $\iota_{*\Delta}$ values—the cloned code is much more instable than then non-cloned code. In Figure 6.16a on the facing page, these transitions appear as a recurring pattern. Most of these drops are caused by only one or two revisions with a high number of changes to clones. When such a revision is part of the window for the first time, $\iota_{*\Delta}$ drops and stays low as long as the revision is part of the window. In the first window that does not contain the revision anymore, $\iota_{*\Delta}$ increases steeply again.

For instance, in window 75 of the 1-month setting, $\iota_{*\Delta}$ drops from 1 to $-0.26$. This is the first window that includes a version in which 211 cloned tokens implementing a method that quotes strings are removed from one class. Before the change, the method appears in a dialog class as well as a utility class. It is removed only from the dialog and remains in the other class. Inspecting the clone's history gives more insight into what happened. The utility class was created 25 revisions earlier. This is also where the string-quoting function was copied. Apparently, the developers prepared for the case that the functionality is needed by different classes, but they did not remove it from the dialog, which they do belatedly in this change. The commit message says "Cleanup for 1.2 release". The $\iota_{*\Delta}$ jumps up again in window 100 because the version is no longer

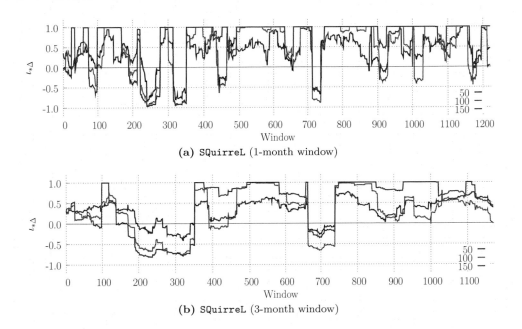

**(a)** SQuirreL (1-month window)

**(b)** SQuirreL (3-month window)

**Figure 6.16** – The $\iota_{*\Delta}$ values for type-1 clones using different time windows in SQuirreL

part of the sliding window. This downswing also appears in the 3-month window setting. Here, it is part for the downswing at window 25, but falls into the same window together with other changes to clones.

Between the windows 191 and 279 clones are also less stable for some time. Two changes are the major reason for this. The first is a consistent change to a long switch statement that appears twice in the same class. It is used to render values of different data types. For internationalization purposes 70 tokens were modified. This clone was created some revisions earlier because the same data rendering was needed in different table views. The second contributing change is closely related to the removal of the sting-quoting function that caused the first drop. This time it is the corresponding *un*quote function that is removed from the dialog, but not the utility class.

The drop between the windows 224 and 279 is caused by three changes that again relate to the long switch statement that renders different data types. After it was cloned and changed consistently once, the developers now start to modify one of the copies. The handling for the different data types is reimplemented in another method. Each time when the new methods support more data types, their old handling in the switch statement is removed. The other copy of the switch statement, however, is not changed at all. This seems to be a *replicate and specialize* pattern as Kapser and Godfrey describe it [94]. In this pattern developers copy code that solves a similar problem to the one they are solving and then modify the copy according to the different requirements.

Another case is located from window 317 to 353. One of the two changes making clones less stable in these windows is a consistent change where 10 lines of string manipulation are replaced by a one-line solution. This code appears as clones in six different classes. Each class serves as a wrapper to a SQL data type. The other contributing change again is an instance of the aforementioned *replicate and specialize* pattern. The *WhereClausePanel* is cloned to start the *EditableWhereClausePanel*. Shortly after the clone was created the new class was almost completely changed to start the development of the new panel. After this massive change both classes do not share any clones anymore.

A further occurrence can be found at windows 716 to 750. This is caused by a single commit. Two classes that contained the same method for inserting data into a database table are subject to "Massive refactoring and clean up" as the commit message states. Both files, which shared a clone of only 39 lines, are almost completely changed. After this, both instances of the clone are gone. From there on both classes have no cloning relationship anymore.

Like in ArgoUML clones are less stable for some time periods in SQuirreL. In total we identified nine changes as the main reason for the drops. Only two of them changed clones consistently. Four are instances of the *replicate and specialize* pattern, two removed code that moved to a new location belatedly, and in one case a clone disappeared because of massive restructuring. That is, clones that existed temporarily until one copy was specialized or were cleaned up are the main reason for the short periods in which clones were less stable and not costly consistent changes to clones.

## Clones

The results for clones are presented in Figures 6.17a and 6.17b. Like the open-source systems, clones has time periods where the cloned-code is less stable in terms of our $\iota_{*\Delta}$ measure. We manually inspected the six deepest dips in the 1-month curve.

The first one spans from window 62 to 74. It is caused by the removal of functionality that implemented some special behavior of the Baker algorithm. For each programming language the clone detector supported a clone of this functionality was present. The functionality became obsolete so that all clone fragments were removed.

The second dip around window 100 is mainly caused by three interrelated changes that form the beginning of a refactoring. A larger module containing code for post-processing steps after the clone detection was split into multiple new modules. The code was removed from its original module some time after it had been copied to the new one. While it was cloned, changes were applied to the new module but not to the older one which was removed after some time.

The next two dips at versions 325 and 370 are both related to the same test cases. Some code to set up the test environment is cloned in both test cases. In the first case the interface of the tested module changed so that the cloned code in both test cases had to be adapted. The second case changed only one of the two test cases, because it now needed another setup. The other test case did not have to co-change.

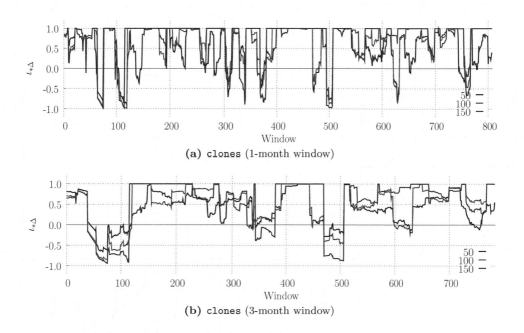

**(a)** `clones` (1-month window)

**(b)** `clones` (3-month window)

**Figure 6.17** – The $\iota_{*\Delta}$ values for type-1 clones using different time windows in `clones`

The fifth dip around window 500 must be regarded as an error in measurement. Several new functions were added *before* a clone and counted as change to the cloned code which is false and due to the underlying LCS algorithm.

The sixth dip around window 760 is another instance of the *replicate and specialize* pattern. Code that filters tokens as a pre-processing step appeared as clones in a module that filters on the basis of user-defined matching rules and in another module that inserts delimiter tokens between methods as a pre-processing step. This code had to be specialized for the method separation but not for the filtering.

Like in the other systems the turnovers to negative $\iota_{*\Delta}$ are caused by single changes and last for only short periods. The reasons for these changes are diverse. Nevertheless, only two of them were caused by cloned code that had to change consistently. The others were caused by cloned fragments that supposedly evolved independently or limitations of the measurement technique.

### Cobol-A and Cobol-B

Figures 6.18a and 6.18b show how $\iota_{*\Delta}$ varies in different windows for `Cobol-A`. Even though there is a notable variation of $\iota_{*\Delta}$ over time, it rarely turns negative. In the 1-month setting we can observe only two periods where clones were less stable than non-cloned code. Compared to the `ArgoUML`, `SQuirreL`, and `clones` these drops are

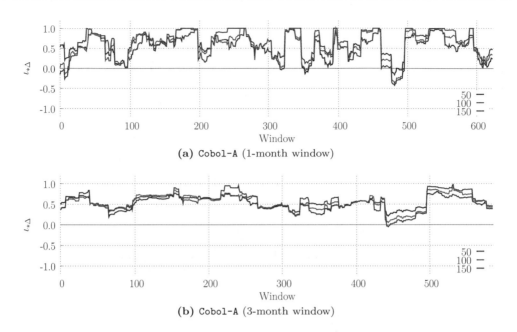

**(a)** `Cobol-A` (1-month window)

**(b)** `Cobol-A` (3-month window)

**Figure 6.18** – The $\iota_{*\Delta}$ values for type-1 clones using different time windows in `Cobol-A`

rather short and less distinctive. This matches our previous finding that the clones in the COBOL systems are more stable than in the other systems we analyzed.

The results for `Cobol-B` that are presented in Figures 6.19a and 6.19b are similar to `Cobol-A`. The value of $\iota_{*\Delta}$ rarely drops below 0, that is, cloned code is more stable most of the time. The drops below 0, however, are slightly stronger than for `Cobol-A`.

Unfortunately, we cannot provide more detail on the reasons of the changeovers in stability due to confidentiality.

## Conclusion

In general we can conclude that the chosen time period has a notable effect on the results. There are phases where the cloned code is indeed less stable than the non-cloned code, regarding to our metric. Nevertheless, these situations mainly depend on only few versions that make changes to clones and can be observed in the open-source systems and `clones` only. These situations are mostly caused by clones that were meant to evolve independently, the late removal of code that moved to another location, refactorings, or cleanup. We observed only few cases where consistent changes contributed to these situations. These changes were mostly small compared to the others mentioned before. Cases where consistent changes where *repeatedly* applied to cloned code, which would indicate a lasting maintenance problem, contributed to only one drop of the stability value. In some cases we observed how developers proactively removed clones.

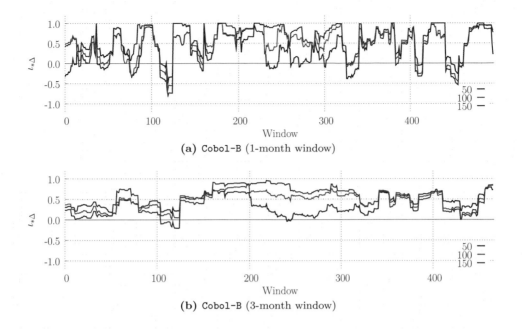

**(a)** `Cobol-B` (1-month window)

**(b)** `Cobol-B` (3-month window)

**Figure 6.19** – The $\iota_{*\Delta}$ values for type-1 clones using different time windows in `Cobol-B`

## 6.5   Threats to Validity

There are certain threats to the validity of our study, which we describe in this section, ordered by threats to internal, construct, and external validity.

### 6.5.1   Internal validity

The evaluation of clone stability has so far been done only in exploratory case studies like this one. This makes it impossible to control the many possible influences on the stability. Theoretically, there may be confounding factors common to all our subject systems, but unknown to us, that cause the stability of clones we observed.

Our sampling criterion whether a token is cloned or not may be connected to possibly confounding factors. The fact of being cloned puts a token into a relationship to the other tokens in the same clone fragment. That is, our samples consist of *code fragments*. Cloned and non-cloned fragments differ in their average size—non-cloned fragments are larger on average. The same change may have a larger effect on the instability if it hits cloned code, compared to the effect it would have on non-cloned code. The probability of a clone being changed may also be affected by the necessity of consistent —and therefore redundant— changes to clones. While the latter influence on the change probability is of interest to our study, the former may be a confounding factor. This possible confounding factor is also present in the original study and the follow-up studies we will discuss later.

Future research should be directed to the questions whether the size difference of the analyzed code regions has an effect on the results.

## 6.5.2   Construct Validity

### Clone Detection

Like most studies on code clones, the parameters used for clone detection—defining what is regarded as a clone—have a major effect on the results as they influence precision and recall. We have used a token-based clone detection approach which offers a good trade-off between precision and recall. Furthermore, the distinction between relevant and irrelevant clones depends on the use case. To cover many potential use cases and mitigate this threat, we have used—and analyzed the effect of—different parameter settings. A related threat is that state-of-the-art clone detectors are constructed to search for similarity in the code. They were not designed based on actual maintenance tasks, which means that they may find results that are not relevant to a specific task. Consequently, our results must be interpreted according to what our detector finds, not what software maintainers might be interested in. Furthermore, different clone detectors will produce different results because they use different definitions of similarity. We use a token-based approach because of its comparatively high precision and recall in regards of human oracles [23] and because it scales to the task of analyzing clones at the commit level.

### Difference Calculation

Another threat emerges from our calculation of difference information. Like the original study, we have employed a standard differencing algorithm that cannot detect movement of code and may produce artifacts resulting from ambiguous situations. Nevertheless, our manual inspection of samples and the top-ten commits regarding deletion of cloned code showed that these situations are rare. Still, using another differencing algorithm may affect the results.

The categorization of additions of tokens to clones may be inaccurate if the addition appears at the border of a clone. Inserting tokens at the exact border of a cloned sequence of tokens will be detected as an addition to the non-cloned code. When any addition occurs adjoin to a cloned token of a 100 token clone, than the probability that it occurs at the clone's border is $\frac{2}{101}$. That is, there are 99 possible insertion points between the tokens of the clone and two at its borders. This effect could increase the measured stability of clones.

### Belated Movement

Code that is moved to another location also has an effect on the results, if the relocation is not encapsulated in one commit. If the code is first copied and appears as clone for some revisions, then the completion of the operation—which is the removal of the original—will be measured as a deletion of cloned code. Nevertheless, in our manual inspections we encountered only few such situations.

**Choice of Interval**

We inspected every relevant revision from the source code repositories of our subject systems. The changes included in a single revision might, however, have been prepared over a longer period before they have been committed together. Consequently, our view on the data does not exactly resemble the actual programmer's work. Nevertheless, our replication shows that although we have used a different interval between versions compared to the original study, we came to similar results. Research Perspective C will be directed to the question what happens between the commits. We describe this in Chapter 8.

**Self-Contained Changes**

The development policies may have an effect on the granularity of the data. If commits to the repository are not self-contained, our method may, for instance, measure changes of temporal clones that only existed because the code was committed in the middle of a refactoring. Indeed, we identified such cases. Nevertheless, these lead to a decrease of the stability of cloned code. This means clones may be even more stable than measured.

A similar threat is that our metric differentiates between cloned and non-cloned code, but it can not interpret the rationale of cloning. We identified cases where code was cloned first to evolve independently afterwards. The customization of the cloned code will be counted as instability of the cloned part. The intention of measuring clone stability is that instable clones may indicate maintenance problems. But this is not the case in the aforementioned scenario, which should not be considered as a maintenance threat. Such cases may distort the results but they would cause a higher instability of the cloned code. Again, our conclusion that cloned code is more stable in general is not falsified by that. Clones could be even more stable than measured in our case study.

## 6.5.3 External Validity

We analyzed five subject systems and cannot rule out that the results differ for other systems. The systems `clones`, `Cobol-A` and `Cobol-B` were chosen because they differ by their academic respectively industrial development contexts and their programming languages. This choice was made to mitigate the threat that previous studies may have measured phenomena that are characteristic only to open-source systems. Our results show that despite some slight differences, the main conclusions also hold for the additional systems. Nevertheless, the number of non-open-source systems is still small and our results can most likely not be generalized to all systems of that kind.

Our results indicate some differences in clone stability among the systems—for instance the higher stability of the clones in the COBOL systems and the differences regarding deletions. It is not possible to identify the factors which cause these differences, because too many come into question—such as team structure, programmer experience, development processes, policies, public attention. Therefore, we discuss potential reasons in Section 6.6, which, however, remain speculative.

For all systems we were able to analyze how the stability changes during their iterative development. Although the analyzed periods for all systems covered several release cycles with all their phases, the data do not give insight into the very beginning of the development of the systems. While our study focuses on the effect of clones during maintenance, analyzing only the early phases may give different results.

## 6.6   Discussion

In this chapter, we approximate the maintenance costs of cloned and non-cloned code by their relative amount of changes. The less stable code is—that is, the more it is changed—the higher are the costs to maintain it. Generally, we assume that there is a relation between the stability of code and the costs to maintain it. While there are many good reasons for why this assumption holds, there may be situations where the relation between stability and maintenance costs does not exist.

If, on the one hand, clones undergo many changes, we can be relatively sure that they increase the maintenance costs. If, on the other hand, clones are stable and do not change much, we cannot conclude that they do not increase maintenance costs. It might just be too expensive or too risky to modify a cloned code fragment and its copies. Developers may modify other non-cloned code fragments instead as a workaround. Cordy noted that developers may refrain from changing code due to the risk of introducing new defects [34]. Although the clones are stable and did not change, they may indirectly increase the maintenance costs by requiring more or less costly workarounds.

Apart from source code changes, clones may also increase the maintenance costs in other ways, for example, they may negatively affect program comprehension or increase the effort needed for testing. Given that source code changes are not the only way in which clones can increase maintenance costs, we cannot conclude that stable clones do not increase the maintenance costs. In this study, we have used stability as one of many possible measurements for maintenance costs.

Our data show that the main conclusion—that cloned code is more stable overall—holds for different software systems with different characteristics. The most apparent difference is the instability regarding deletions clones have in the open-source systems, but not in the others. This may be caused by the way these systems are developed. Open-source projects are exposed to permanent public review and the developers can decide how the project advances—this at least holds for the systems we analyzed. The closed systems like clones, Cobol-A, and Cobol-B are developed by small teams which means that only a small group of people can comment on the development and help to make design decisions. The project schedule is not chosen freely, it is rather dictated by the business or research needs. This may lead to a more rushed and pragmatic development and leave less space for refactoring. Indeed, our results show that the instability clones have regarding deletions in the open-source systems is caused by restructuring and cleanup that did not happen to the same extent in the other systems. Our observation on the refactoring and clean-up activity in the open-source systems may be an indicator that clones are more likely affected by these than other changes like the addition of new functionality or bug fixing.

Another substantial difference between the open-source and the closed systems is the programming paradigm. Both ArgoUML and SQuirreL are object-oriented systems, while `clones`, `Cobol-A`, and `Cobol-B` are written in imperative languages. Object-oriented programming languages offer more sophisticated abstraction mechanisms and were designed to foster reuse. Indeed, the Java systems have a lower clone ratio than the COBOL systems—they have fewer clones. But, at the same time, the clones of the Java systems are the least stable in our study—they change more. This, again, could be related to the clean-up and refactoring activity we observed in these systems. Such changes could be easier to perform in object-oriented programs than in imperative ones.

The analysis of the fluctuation of clone stability over time shows that clones may be less stable for some time periods. This is mainly caused by changes that should not be regarded as maintenance problems. Especially the instances of the *replicate and specialize* pattern, where a clone is created to start the development of a different solution, may actually save maintenance costs by speeding up the development and avoid the effort of creating the code from scratch. Hence, the existence of these periods where clones are less stable should be considered with care. Most of them are not related to the assumption that clones change more because changes to one copy must be propagated to the others often.

A possible interpretation of the higher instability of clones regarding deletions in the open-source systems is that the creation of clones and changes to them do rarely occur at once for all fragments that exist in the clone's lifetime. These changes to clones may be hidden in the overall noise of changes to non-cloned code. Deletions of clones, however, may be more likely to appear at once, causing a high change volume in a single change. For instance, the fragments of a clone class may be added one-by-one over some time, rarely or never changed consistently, and removed at once when they start to be an annoyance to the developers. Such patterns could be an explanation why we tend to see instability because of deletions but not because of other changes.

One particularity about the COBOL systems is that their cloned code is much more stable than their non-cloned code. Among all systems in our study, their clones are most stable compared to the non-cloned code. Developers told us that they refrain from changing code that is known to work and prefer to create copies for the development of new features, which likely is a reason for this result. This method leads to many clones and both systems indeed happen to have the highest clone ratios among all we analyzed. Nevertheless, these clones appear not to require many consistent changes afterwards. This could be caused by the high code churn we already mentioned for the COBOL systems. They contain a lot of code that is needed only for limited time (for instance code for seasonal campaigns). Such code is deleted frequently and its rather short life-time lowers the probability of consistent changes.

The data for the `clones` system also exposed some peculiarities. Compared to the other systems its code is by far less stable in absolute numbers for cloned and non-cloned code. One reason seems to be its significant growth during the analyzed period. Indeed, it is significantly less stable regarding additions. But the instabilities of the other change types are also higher by orders of magnitude. We believe one reason is the experimental nature of the program, which is frequently adjusted to different studies and used to evaluate new methods to improve the results. Its functionality cannot be regarded as stable as those of the other systems. Being developed by experts in the field of clone detection may also have an effect. Surprisingly, neither is the clone ratio significantly lower than in the other systems, nor is the relative stability of the clones much higher—`clones` is close to the average of all systems in this regard. It seems that having sophisticated knowledge about cloning does not result in a notable difference in the extent of cloning and how much clones change.

Our five subject systems differ in too many attributes to make clear statements on which factor causes which difference in the instability values. Our results show that for all these systems with all their differences, code being cloned does not mean that it changes more in general.

Based on the results of our study, we suggest—analogous to Kim and colleagues [99]—to not aggressively refactor clones in every case. Although the previous part of our discussion indicates that even stable clones can increase the maintenance costs, one should carefully evaluate in which way a particular clone increases maintenance costs before choosing a counter measure. The variation of parameters in our study showed that clone stability depends also on the characteristics (for example, type and length) of clones. Therefore, we suggest to take these characteristics into account when deciding how to deal with individual clones.

## 6.7   Further Studies on Clone Stability

During and after our work on clone stability others have defined further metrics and applied these in case studies. In this section we will report on these metrics and studies to summarize the body of knowledge on clone stability. Where possible we will report the other metrics using the terminology we defined earlier in this chapter. Some metrics are based on lines instead of tokens. To ease comparisons we modify the original metrics to work on tokens.

### 6.7.1   Modification Frequency

Hotta and colleagues analyzed the *frequency* of changes to cloned and non-cloned code [74]. That is, they measured only the probability of change, not the amount.

**Metric**

The *modification frequency MF* represents the likelihood that code is affected by a modification. It can be measured for cloned code as $MF_d$ (d as in *duplicated code*) and for non-cloned code as $MF_n$ separately. A comparison of both values allows to compare the probabilities.

The $MF$ metrics are computed based on the set of revisions that contain changes to code files $R$. This set corresponds to our set of versions $V$. All modifications to the code are extracted from the source code repository. Each set consecutive lines that are changed between two revisions constitute one modification. If, for example, one file is changed in three different locations and the three locations form a set of consecutive lines, then three modifications are counted.

The absolute counts of modifications to cloned and non-cloned code are defined as $MC_d$ and $MC_n$. For each modification the authors analyze whether it overlaps cloned or non-cloned code. If the modification is completely enclosed in cloned lines, $MC_d$ is incremented by one. If the modification is completely enclosed in non-cloned lines, $MC_n$ is incremented by one. If the modification overlaps both cloned and non-cloned code, both $MC_d$ and $MC_n$ are incremented by one. The modification frequencies of cloned and non-cloned code are then defined as:

$$MF_d = \frac{\sum\limits_{r \in R} MC_d(r)}{|R|}$$

$$MF_n = \frac{\sum\limits_{r \in R} MC_n(r)}{|R|}$$

These metrics express the likelihood that cloned or non-cloned code is affected by a modification. Usually, there is more non-cloned code than cloned code so that the metric must be normalized to account for this difference. $LOC(r)$ is the number of lines in revision $r$ and $LOC_d$ and $LOC_n$ are the respective metrics for cloned and non-cloned lines.

$$normalized \ MF_d = \frac{\sum\limits_{r \in R} MC_d(r)}{|R|} \times \frac{\sum\limits_{r \in R} LOC(r)}{\sum\limits_{r \in R} LOC_d(r)}$$

$$normalized \ MF_n = \frac{\sum\limits_{r \in R} MC_n(r)}{|R|} \times \frac{\sum\limits_{r \in R} LOC(r)}{\sum\limits_{r \in R} LOC_n(r)}$$

The modification frequency emphasizes the likelihood that some code gets hit by a modification and disregards the amount of code that gets modified. Therefore, the metric analyzes a different aspect of stability, which is not covered by the $\iota$ metrics.

## Case Study

In their case study the authors apply their metrics to the history of 15 open-source systems. SQuirreL is the only subject system that was analyzed by us, too. Four different clone detectors were used to assess whether different clone detection mechanisms affect the modification frequency. One of these four detectors—CCFinder—uses a technique that is similar to the detector we applied in our study—iclones.

Hotta and colleagues come to the overall conclusion that, according to their metric, cloned code tends to change less frequently compared with non-cloned code. Although the difference was not statistically significant, the results indicate that cloned code is not less stable than non-cloned code according to the modification frequency.

The modification frequencies for SQuirreL were computed as roughly[5] $MF_d = 12.5$ and $MF_n = 18.0$. That is, the cloned code in SQuirreL changes less frequently than

---

[5]The authors did not provide numerical data. The values have been derived from the charts in their publication [74].

the non-cloned code. We have shown for the same system that the relative amount of code that changes is less for cloned code.

Similar to our analysis of different time windows, the authors also analyzed how *MF* varies in different time periods. Time periods where clones change more frequently exist, but are singularities in most systems. In SQuirreL clones change less frequently in all time windows.

## 6.7.2   Proportional Stability Metrics

Mondal and colleagues presented a set of metrics in their empirical study on clone stability [133]. Unlike $\iota$, which is essentially one metric, they define three of which the first represents the change frequency, the second the amount of change, and the third summarizes both.

### Metrics

The *unstable proportion UP* is the proportion of the commit operations that affect cloned and non-cloned code. It tells how many out of all commits affected cloned and non-cloned code, respectively. In the following we adjusted the original metric definitions to our symbols and to work on tokens instead of lines.

To compute *UP* we first need to identify all versions that change cloned code $V_{*C}$ and all versions that change non-cloned code $V_{*N}$. Mondal chose these sets of versions not to be disjoint. That is, versions that change both cloned and non-cloned code will be included in both $V_{*C}$ and $V_{*N}$. The proportion of commits that affect cloned and non-cloned cloned code are defined as:

$$UP_C = 100 \times \frac{|V_{*C}|}{|V|}$$

$$UP_N = 100 \times \frac{|V_{*N}|}{|V|}$$

Because $V_{*C}$ and $V_{*N}$ may or may not be disjoint, the values of $UP_C$ and $UP_N$ may or may not be the inverse of each other (that is, they may or may not sum up to 1).

The definition of *UP* is identical to our frequency metrics we used in our investigations on the characteristics of deletions in Section 6.4.4. There we defined $AC_{freq\%}$, $DC_{freq\%}$, and $MC_{freq\%}$. Nevertheless, we only defined these metrics on the level of the different operations types. We used these metrics to compare the frequency of these operation types only in cloned code.

Both $UP_C$ and $UP_N$ are sensitive to the different size of the cloned and non-cloned code. There is usually more non-cloned code than cloned code. Therefore, if the commits are equally distributed over the code, $UP_C$ will be smaller than $UP_N$ although the likelihood that code is affected by a commit does not differ between cloned and non-cloned code. Mondal and colleagues address this with the additional metric *UPHL*. According to the publication [133] it determines the likelihood of being modified per 100 tokens of a code region and is defined as follows:

$$UPHL_C = 100 \times \frac{UP_C \times |V|}{\sum\limits_{v \in V} C(v))}$$

$$UPHL_N = 100 \times \frac{UP_N \times |V|}{\sum\limits_{v \in V} N(v)}$$

The metric is easier to understand when we replace $UP_C$ and $UP_N$ with their definitions and simplify the fractions.

$$UPHL_C = 100 \times \frac{|V_{*C}|}{\sum\limits_{v \in V} C(v))}$$

$$UPHL_N = 100 \times \frac{|V_{*N}|}{\sum\limits_{v \in V} N(v)}$$

*PCRM* represents *how much* of the cloned or non-cloned code changes. Like the $\iota$ metric it computes the ratio between the number of changed tokens and the number of all existing tokens. It, however, differs in one important aspect: Other than the $\iota$ metric, it regards only versions with changes to cloned or non-cloned code, respectively. Therefore it is defined as follows:

$$PCRM_C = \frac{100 \times \sum\limits_{v \in V_C} *C(v)}{\sum\limits_{v \in V_C} C(v)}$$

$$PCRM_N = \frac{100 \times \sum\limits_{v \in V_N} *N(v)}{\sum\limits_{v \in V_N} N(v)}$$

Krinke's metrics deliberately take *every* change into account when the stability of cloned an non-cloned code are computed. That is, changes where no cloned code is changed are also part of the calculation of the instability of the cloned code. This is not the case for the *PCRM* metrics for cloned code $PCRM_C$ and non-cloned code $PCRM_N$, which consider only changes that affect cloned code or non-cloned code, respectively.

Both *UP* and *PCRM* are combined in the *Overall instability of code region* or *OICR*.

$$OICR_C = UP_C \times PCRM_C$$

$$OICR_N = UP_N \times PCRM_N$$

As we will see in the following discussion, *OICR* provides the same results as the $\iota$ metric. That is, *UP* and *PRCM* effectively are components of $\iota$.

## Comparison to our Metrics

$UP$, $PCRM$, and $OICR$ are similar to our $\iota$ metrics. In the following we will explain where they differ and where they are identical. Table 6.6 on the next page illustrates in six examples how the metric values are affected when the changes to the code are distributed differently over the versions. In all six examples each version has 200 cloned tokens and 800 non-cloned tokens. In each example 20 cloned tokens are changed and 80 non-cloned tokens are changed. Only distribution of the changes over the versions $v \in V$ differs between the examples. For simplicity the total amount of existing cloned and non-cloned tokens does not change from version to version.

> **Example 1**   All changes take place in just one version.
>
> **Example 2**   All changes are equally distributed over two versions.
>
> **Example 3**   Two versions; the changes to the cloned code only appear in the second version. The changes to the non-cloned code are equally distributed.
>
> **Example 4**   All changes are equally distributed over twenty versions.
>
> **Example 5**   Twenty versions; the cloned code is not changed in $v_1$ to $v_{10}$. The 20 changes to cloned tokens are equally distributed over $v_{11}$ to $v_{20}$. The changes to non-cloned code are equally distributed over all versions.
>
> **Example 6**   Twenty versions; the non-cloned code is not changed in $v_1$ to $v_{10}$. The 80 changes to cloned tokens are equally distributed over $v_{11}$ to $v_{20}$. The changes to cloned code are equally distributed over all versions.

For the $\iota$ metrics the difference of $\iota_{*C}$ and $\iota_{*N}$, namely $\iota_{*\Delta}$, equals 0 for all examples. That is, $\iota_{*\Delta}$ is not affected by the distribution of changes over versions. The metrics $\iota_{*C}$ and $\iota_{*N}$ respond to a change in the number of versions. The more versions, the lower the values. The $\iota$ metrics, however, were designed to compare the instabilities and not to interpret the absolute values. In summary, $\iota_{*\Delta}$ can be used to determine how the *amounts* of token changes are distributed over cloned and non-cloned code during the evolution of a system. They do not tell *how often* the code was changed to apply the changes.

$PCRM$ behaves differently than $\iota$. In the examples where cloned code does not change in every version (3 and 5) $PCRM_C$ computes a higher instability than $\iota_{*C}$. $PCRM_C$ answers the question *how much* of the cloned code changes *if cloned code changes*. That is, $PCRM_C$ penalizes the instability of cloned code when the same changes to the tokens are applied in few versions instead of being distributed over many smaller changes.

The difference between $PCRM$, $OICR$, and $\iota$ becomes clearer when it is explained using a simple example: Imagine two car engines. One has four ignition plugs the other eight. We ask the question which engine has the higher rate of ignition plug failures. Lets assume that during the past four quarters the smaller engine had two failures, while the larger had four. The $\iota$ metrics will answer this question with $\iota_\Delta = 0$. That

| Ex | $v$ | $C(v)$ | $*C(v)$ | $N(v)$ | $*N(v)$ | $\iota_{*C}$ | $\iota_{*N}$ | $UP_c$ | $UP_n$ | $PCRM_c$ | $PCRM_n$ | $OICR_c$ | $OICR_n$ |
|----|-----|--------|---------|--------|---------|-------------|-------------|--------|--------|----------|----------|----------|----------|
| 1 | $v_1$ | 200 | 20 | 800 | 80 | $\frac{20}{200}=0.1$ | $\frac{80}{800}=0.1$ | $\frac{1}{1}=1$ | $\frac{1}{1}=1$ | $\frac{20}{200}=0.1$ | $\frac{80}{800}=0.1$ | $1\times0.1=0.1$ | $1\times0.1=0.1$ |
| 2 | $v_1$ | 200 | 10 | 800 | 40 | $\frac{20}{400}=0.05$ | $\frac{80}{1600}=0.05$ | $\frac{2}{2}=1$ | $\frac{2}{2}=1$ | $\frac{20}{400}=0.05$ | $\frac{80}{1600}=0.05$ | $1\times0.05=0.05$ | $1\times0.05=0.05$ |
|  | $v_2$ | 200 | 10 | 800 | 40 | | | | | | | | |
| 3 | $v_1$ | 200 | 0 | 800 | 40 | $\frac{20}{400}=0.05$ | $\frac{80}{1600}=0.05$ | $\frac{1}{2}=0.5$ | $\frac{2}{2}=1$ | $\frac{20}{200}=0.1$ | $\frac{80}{1600}=0.05$ | $0.5\times0.1=0.05$ | $1\times0.05=0.05$ |
|  | $v_2$ | 200 | 20 | 800 | 40 | | | | | | | | |
| 4 | $v_1$ | 200 | 1 | 800 | 4 | $\frac{20}{4000}=0.005$ | $\frac{80}{16000}=0.005$ | $\frac{10}{10}=1$ | $\frac{10}{10}=1$ | $\frac{20}{4000}=0.005$ | $\frac{80}{16000}=0.005$ | $1\times0.005=0.005$ | $1\times0.005=0.005$ |
|  | $\cdots$ | $\cdots$ | $\cdots$ | $\cdots$ | $\cdots$ | | | | | | | | |
|  | $v_{20}$ | 200 | 1 | 800 | 4 | | | | | | | | |
| 5 | $v_1$ | 200 | 0 | 800 | 4 | $\frac{20}{4000}=0.005$ | $\frac{80}{16000}=0.005$ | $\frac{10}{20}=0.5$ | $\frac{20}{20}=1$ | $\frac{20}{2000}=0.01$ | $\frac{80}{16000}=0.005$ | $0.5\times0.01=0.005$ | $1\times0.005=0.005$ |
|  | $\cdots$ | $\cdots$ | $\cdots$ | $\cdots$ | $\cdots$ | | | | | | | | |
|  | $v_{10}$ | 200 | 0 | 800 | 4 | | | | | | | | |
|  | $v_{11}$ | 200 | 2 | 800 | 4 | | | | | | | | |
|  | $\cdots$ | $\cdots$ | $\cdots$ | $\cdots$ | $\cdots$ | | | | | | | | |
|  | $v_{20}$ | 200 | 2 | 800 | 4 | | | | | | | | |
| 6 | $v_1$ | 200 | 1 | 800 | 0 | $\frac{20}{4000}=0.005$ | $\frac{80}{16000}=0.005$ | $\frac{20}{20}=1$ | $\frac{10}{20}=0.5$ | $\frac{20}{4000}=0.005$ | $\frac{80}{8000}=0.01$ | $1\times0.005=0.005$ | $0.5\times0.01=0.005$ |
|  | $\cdots$ | $\cdots$ | $\cdots$ | $\cdots$ | $\cdots$ | | | | | | | | |
|  | $v_{10}$ | 200 | 1 | 800 | 0 | | | | | | | | |
|  | $v_{11}$ | 200 | 1 | 800 | 8 | | | | | | | | |
|  | $\cdots$ | $\cdots$ | $\cdots$ | $\cdots$ | $\cdots$ | | | | | | | | |
|  | $v_{20}$ | 200 | 1 | 800 | 8 | | | | | | | | |

**Table 6.6** – Comparison of Stability Metrics by Example

is, although the absolute number of failures differ, the failure rate is identical for both engines. For both engines 50% of the plugs failed within the year. It does not matter in when the failures occurred during the year. Let us further assume that we have the plug failure data on a quarterly basis. The two plug failures of the smaller engine occurred together in the last quarter, whereas the four failures of the larger engine occurred one per quarter. In contrast to the $\iota$ metrics, $PCRM$ tells the average fail rate for the quarters where plug failures occurred. $PCRM$ for the smaller engine computes to $\frac{2}{4}$, whereas $PCRM$ for the larger engine computes to $\frac{1}{8}$. That is, $PCRM$ is higher for the smaller engine because the plugs failed at once. $UP$ represents in how many quarters failures occurred per engine. It is $\frac{1}{4}$ for the smaller engine and $\frac{4}{4}$ for the larger. $OICR$ corrects the imbalance of $PCRM$ by multiplying it with $UP$. The consequence is that $OICR_\Delta$ and $\iota_\Delta$ are identical ($\frac{1}{4} \times \frac{2}{4} = \frac{4}{4} \times \frac{1}{8}$).

Our engine example illustrates that $UP$ and $PCRM$ are a proper decomposition of the $\iota$ metric. Nevertheless, it remains unclear how these two metrics add value to the discussion on clone stability. $PCRM$ increases when plugs fail at the same time—or the changes to the code appear together in the same commit. It is reasonable to believe that fewer interactions reduce costs because each interaction comes at a cost. Each plug failure requires the car owner to visit the dealership, each change to the source code may require the development process to be run through, including efforts for such things as software tests, releasing, and deployment. Hotta and colleagues argue that a high number of small changes could be worse for the maintenance cost than few large changes [74].

Mondal and colleagues present $PCRM$ as similar to the $\iota$ metrics [133]. They argue that the $\iota$ metrics for cloned code are also computed on versions in which the clones do not change and that $PCRM$ compensates this. As we have shown before, the $\iota$ metrics give proper indication on how the amount of changed tokens is distributed over the two code regions. Indeed, $PCRM$ answers a different question than the $\iota$ metrics and $OICR$ is the metric that is identical to the $\iota$ metrics.

## Case Studies

Twelve subject systems were analyzed using the aforementioned metrics. In contrast to all previous studies it was found that cloned code is less stable for the majority of the systems. According to $OICR$ clones are less stable in seven of twelve systems. In terms of $PCRM$ the values for $PCRM_C$ exceeded those of $PCRM_N$ for ten of the twelve systems. Nevertheless, our previous discussion on $PCRM$ shows that this does not allow the conclusion that one region of the code is less stable. Hotta's $MF$ metric was also used and for most systems the modification frequency of cloned code was found to be higher compared with non-cloned code.

The $MF$ and $OICR$ (aka. $\iota$) metrics lead to different conclusions than in the previous studies. The most likely reason is the selection of subject systems. The choice of Mondal and colleagues does not intersect with the subject systems of the other case studies. While all other researchers selected subject systems in which the clones are more stable than the non-cloned code, Mondal and colleagues predominantly analyzed systems where the opposite is the case.

Their case study analyzes less data than the others. On average Hotta's subject systems are 105,986 lines of code long and 4,526 versions were analyzed. Our subject systems average at 311,200 lines of code and 1,762 versions. Mondal's systems reach 42,239 lines of code an 575 versions. `QMail Admin`—the system where clones are least stable according to *OICR*—consists of only 4,000 lines of code. Of another system where cloned code is less stable according to *OICR*, only 32 revisions were analyzed. The smaller system size and the fewer versions could be the reason that different results were obtained.

The discrepancy in the results indicates that clones could be less stable in small software systems and more stable in enterprise scale systems.

## 6.8   Conclusion

In this chapter we have analyzed the stability of cloned and non-cloned code with respect to different types of changes. Regarding Question A1 on page 64, we can confirm the general findings of the original study with our more fine-grained measurement technique. Nevertheless, these findings could not be entirely generalized to other systems. We also found clones in closed-source systems to be more stable than non-cloned code, but the instability regarding deletions was not observed in these systems (Question A2 on page 65).

Our answer to Question A3 on page 65 is that clone detection parameters do influence the results but do not change the relation between the stability of cloned and non-cloned code. The effect of parameter variations differs among the systems we analyzed. Still, we can conclude that clones with different characteristics have different stability value and, thus, a different effect on the maintenance costs.

Regarding Question A4 on page 65, we have identified the above-average size of deletions in the clones of open-source systems as a primary cause for the high instability of their clones regarding deletions. These exceptionally large deletions are mostly part of larger clean-up and refactoring activity and tend to affect cloned code as a side-effect. In the closed-source systems, deletions are not larger than other change types on average and do not dominate the stability measures.

Finally, we evaluated how changes to clones are distributed over time to answer Question A5 on page 65. We found that if the time window is chosen small enough, clones are indeed less stable than non-cloned code, especially in some phases of the open-source systems. The changeover of the stability values is mainly caused by changes that should not be regarded as maintenance problems. Despite one case, we did not find repeating changes that had to be propagated across clones to be the root cause for phases where clones are less stable.

We have also reported on the findings of other studies that appeared during or after our work. Hotta's investigations on the modification frequency further supports the tendency that clones are more stable from the perspective of modification frequency. Mondal and colleagues have shown that clones may be less stable in smaller software systems.

In general, we were—analogous to Krinke—not able to validate the assumption that cloned code increases the maintenance effort because it is more frequently changed. As cloned code appears to be even more stable than non-cloned code, it could even be a factor that reduces the maintenance effort. Nevertheless, stability is only one of many factors that contribute to the effect clones have on maintainability. Our conclusions support recent research results indicating that it is not reasonable to forcefully remove clones in general. Measures regarding clones need to be carefully weighed up against the clones' possible consequences for maintainability.

# Chapter 7

# Clone Authorship

Software systems are developed in teams. The collaboration of multiple programmers helps to tackle large projects, accelerates the development, makes it possible to bring experts of different fields together, and reduces the risk that knowledge is lost when the sole developer parts. Many software projects would be impossible if they had to be undertaken by just one developer. At the same time, teamwork entails challenges and risks. Developers need to share information and to coordinate their work. Social structures, communication barriers, concurrent work on the same thing, or insufficient processes could cause misunderstandings or gaps in knowledge. Tools and techniques such as issue tracking systems, knowledge bases, source code management systems, or agile software development are used to mitigate these threats.

It is worthwhile to investigate whether code clones are also affected by the number of developers who create and maintain them. As we discussed in Section 4.2 and also concluded in Chapter 6, general tendencies that clones increase maintenance costs, the likelihood of changes, or the occurrence of bugs could not be confirmed. Nevertheless, previous research has proven that some clones do. As to now, no method to separate the 'good' from the 'bad' is known. The following research perspective, which we derived in Section 4.2 is directed towards this relationship.

**Research Perspective B:** *How do multiple developers affect the evolution of clones? Are different authors a key reason why clones are changed inconsistently and cause bugs?*

While a single developer may be able to keep track of the copies she or he made, copying someone else's code without letting her or him know, could result in unintended inconsistent changes to the clones in the future. So far, possible authorship effects like these have rarely been researched.

Balint and colleagues support the alleged relationship of clones and code authorship [13] as they found inconsistent changes by different authors to be a reoccurring pattern. Nevertheless, the frequency of such changes and whether the inconsistency was indeed unintended has not been evaluated, yet. Cai and Kim found that the number of developers has a strong positive correlation to the life-time of clones [28]. That is, clones, to which multiple developers contribute, remain in the system longer. It remains, however, unknown whether a long lifetime is positive (for instance code maturity) or negative (for instance difficult to remove).

Further indication that multiple developers may cause problems with clones is given by an observational field study on program comprehension by Roehm and colleagues [149]. They observed that developers tend to copy code from others instead of changing or extending it. Either because they do not fully understand the implementation or because they cannot foresee all consequences of changing the existing code fragment. When clones are created because of such uncertainty and communication is avoided, the question whether they lead to further problems arises. In a self-experiment we found it difficult to decide whether an inconsistent clone poses a problem, when the original and the copy where created by different developers [65]. It was particularly difficult to gather all required information from different people. A detailed discussion of the related work on clones and developers [13, 28, 97] was already given in Chapter 4.

In this chapter, we analyze the relationship between exact code clones and code authorship in a case study on five subject systems. Our aim is to shed light on the aforementioned assumptions. We investigate whether clone related problems are caused because the fragments of a clone class are created an maintained by different developers. The main contribution is the first empirical data on the effect multiple developers have on clones. We also provide first insights into the rationale of single-author and multi-author cloning. The results provide a basis for the decision whether the number of developers may be used to prioritize clone management activity. In order to detect code authorship, we also present a new method based on the meta data of `subversion` and the source code. Authorship is analyzed on the level of tokens, which is more precise than other methods that have been proposed previously. The contents of this chapter have been previously published and presented at the *29th International Conference on Software Maintenance* [63].

The remainder of this chapter is organized as follows. In Section 7.1 we define research questions based on Research Focus B. Techniques to detect the authorship of source code will be discussed in Section 7.2. There we report on existing approaches and define our own authorship detection technique. Section 7.3 describes the setup of our case study, which is followed by the presentation of the results in Section 7.4. In Section 7.5 we discuss possible implications of our results. Possible threats to validity are covered in Section 7.6. Section 7.7 concludes this chapter.

## 7.1 Research Questions

To investigate Research Focus B, we define the following research questions.

**Question B1:** *How often do multiple developers create and maintain clones?*

Before the effects of multiple developers can be evaluated, we need to examine how often clones are indeed authored by more than one developer. We define a mechanism to detect the authorship of cloned code fragments and quantify how often multiple developers are involved in the creation and maintenance of clones.

**Question B2:** *Do clones change more often when multiple developers are involved?*

We analyze whether clones that have multiple authors are more likely to change. An increased change frequency can imply higher maintenance effort. Each change entails the risk of an unintended inconsistency.

**Question B3:** *Are inconsistent changes more likely if multiple developers are involved?*

We also analyze the change consistency. That is, whether the changes to a clone are applied consistently to all copies. Inconsistent changes can cause faulty program behavior. If a cloned bug is fixed inconsistently, the system remains in a defective state.

The aforementioned questions will be pursued statistically. While statistics will shed first light on the general relationship, manual inspection of the clones and the changes made to them is essential to understand the rationale behind the cloning. Possible problems, such as unintended inconsistencies and bugs, can only be safely assessed with manual inspections.

**Question B4:** *Do multi-author clones cause unintended inconsistencies or bugs? Does the rationale behind single-author and multi-author cloning differ?*

## 7.2  Authorship Detection

To answer our research questions we need to identify the authors of the clones. Since clones are fragments of source code, we need a technique to detect the author of some code fragment. Different techniques have been presented by others and applied to research different questions. In the following we will give a brief overview of the existing techniques and discuss their applicability for our research questions. As none of the existing techniques can be applied, we also present our own approach.

### 7.2.1  Authorship vs. Ownership

Before we discuss how authorship can be detected, we need to clarify the difference between code authorship and ownership. The question who contributed a piece of code is frequently discussed under the term of *code ownership*. Being the owner of a thing implies possession, control, and responsibility at a certain point of time. These properties cannot be extracted from source code and its evolution alone. For instance, some code may not change over some time, but the responsibility for it may be transferred to another developer (for instance when the previous owner leaves the project). Meta data of source code management systems (SCM), which are used by all approaches, only tell who added, modified, or deleted code. Hence, we speak of *code authorship*, since authoring does only imply the creational aspect. This term is more precise for what approaches based on retrospective analysis of project archives can provide. We also use the term author to avoid confusion and misinterpretation of the results. From a technical perspective our approach uses the committer of a revision in the source code management system.

## 7.2.2   Existing Techniques

The existing approaches can roughly be partitioned into two categories. The first category quantifies the contributions of different developers on the file level, whereas the second works on the level of code lines.

Cai and Kim's work uses a file based approach, but does not provide detail how the data are gathered [28]. Weyuker and colleagues investigated whether the number of developers who contributed to a file can be used to enhance bug prediction models [176]. They found that this metric does not play a decisive role in this context. In a follow-up study by Bird and colleagues the notion of authorship was refined with contribution networks. These are also based on file-level data [25]. Their results indicate that bugs are more likely to occur when developers change code they are not experienced with. An approach by Gîrba and colleagues extracts the number of changed lines from CVS log messages to calculate the code ownership on the file level. They introduce a time-line visualization that shows code authorship and how it changes over time [54]. These metrics are easy to compute from the meta data of a SCM, but are not precise enough for a study on clones. Clones are local passages of source code which cannot be effectively analyzed on the file level, because many clones will be much smaller than the files containing them. Consequently, techniques that work on the file level are not applicable to answer our research questions.

Balint and colleagues use a line-based approach [13]. They utilize the CVS command *blame* that provides the version in which each line was modified last and the user who applied this change. Rahman and Devanbu use the same functionality of `git` to investigate who contributed to buggy fragments of code and conclude that the lack of experience in a particular file is a factor that may induce bugs [146]. Although such authorship detection methods provide data on a much more fine-grained level than file-based techniques, they are still not accurate enough for our study. Even if just one character is modified, the whole line will be regarded as changed, which may lead to an overestimation of changes. Furthermore, code formatting—often carried out automatically and in the large—could distort the authorship detection. More imprecision is caused by the fact that the tools used to obtain the author only provide who made the most recent change to a line. The previous history remains hidden.

Krinke and colleagues proposed a related method to detect which fragment of a clone pair is the original an which one is the copy [114]. For each code line of a clone fragment they extract the version in which the line was changed last. This information is gathered from the source code management system. Then they classify the clone pairs into different patterns based on the age of the lines. The general idea of their approach is that if the lines of one fragment are older than all the lines of another, the first fragment is considered to be the original.

## 7.2.3   Token-based Authorship Detection

The existing approaches for authorship detection are too inaccurate for our purpose. Consequently, we define a new approach that overcomes the shortcomings of the existing ones. We build up on our strategy from Chapter 6 that uses a detection mechanism on the token level. The general idea is to incrementally track the author of each token in the source code over all versions recorded in the code repository. Detecting authors on this level has the advantage that layout changes do not affect the measurements, because tokens abstract from whitespace and line-positions. By obtaining the authorship information from all available versions, we further ensure that no information is lost. The authors of code fragments and clones are aggregated from the detected token-authors. Changes to the code are extracted from a `subversion` repository. We aimed to analyze long-lived systems that provide complete records of their history. `Subversion` has been widely used for more than a decade and many projects used it during their whole life-time. In the following our approach is explained in detail.

### Token Authorship

The author of a token is the user who originally added it to the code. Whenever a developer adds a token it will be assigned to him. In contrast to our stability study our technique for authorship detection only handles additions and deletions. Modifications are not regarded as a special case because this distinction is not required for our algorithm to work. If existing tokens are modified, we decompose this action into a deletion and an addition of tokens. The newly added tokens will be assigned to the person who made the change. The change analysis differentiates between two kinds of changes: First, changes inside a file, that is, changes to the file's token stream and, second, changes on the file-system level, such as copying, moving, or deleting files. Changes to the token stream change the author information as described before, whereas changes on the file-system level are handled differently. When a file is moved from one location to another, the authorship of the tokens inside will not change. When a file is copied, the person making the copy will become the author of all tokens in the file. This distinction is made because we regard the copying of files as the creation of new clones, whereas moving files should not affect authorship. A file may undergo both types of changes (token and file-system level) in the same `subversion` commit. In such cases we split the change into two operations: First, a token level operation and, second, a file-system level operation. As an example, if person $p$ creates file $f$ and person $p'$ moves that file to another location $f'$, all tokens in $f'$ will still be authored by $p$. When $p'$

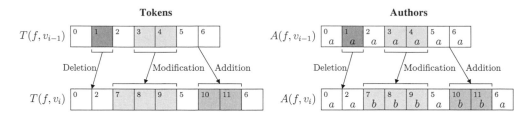

**Figure 7.1** – Changes to a token sequence and the according author information. Code that was authored by author $a$ is changed by author $b$ from version $v_{i-1}$ to $v_i$.

moves and changes $f$ in the same version, only the newly added tokens in $f'$ will be assigned to $p'$, while all other tokens in $f'$ will be assigned to $p$.

Formally, we analyze all relevant versions $v \in V$ from a project's subversion repository. As in Chapter 6, a version is relevant if it contains at least one change to a file of the analyzed programming language. In this chapter we further define a version as a tuple $v = (F, C, a)$, consisting of a set of existing files $F$, a set of changes to files $C$ as they appear in subversion's version log, and an author $a$ who is the committer of $v$ according to the subversion log (which we also will refer to as $a = author(v)$). For each file $f \in F$ we can extract its list of tokens in a specific version as $T(f, v)$. For each token $t \in T(f, v)$ we determine its author $a$. This gives us a list of authors for all the tokens in the file as $A(f, v)$. That is, we define a bijective mapping between $T(f, v)$ and $A(f, v)$ that also preserves the order of the elements. Hence, the author of the $n$-th token $t_n \in T(f, v)$ is the $n$-th author $a_n \in A(f, v)$ in version $v$. The calculated list $A(f, v)$ is stored along with the version $v$ so that it can be used for further analysis.

To obtain the token authors, we process all versions $v \in V$ in the order in which they were added to the repository. For each $v$ we process all changes $c \in C$ using the following rules:

**Additions**   If $c$ is an addition of a new file that was not present in $v_{i-1}$, we create a new author list $A(f, v_i)$ with the same size as the token list $T(f, v_i)$ and assign the version's author as the author of all tokens in the file $f$. Formally, $\forall_{a \in A(f, v_i)} : a = author(v_i)$.

**Modifications**   If $c$ is a modification of a file $f$ that existed in $v_{i-1}$, we compute the differences between $T(f, v_{i-1})$ and $T(f, v_i)$ using the Longest Common Subsequence algorithm (LCS) on the tokens. This gives us a list of change deltas $D$ between the two token lists. Each delta $d \in D$ is a tuple $d = (s, l, t)$, where $s$ is the start index of the change, $l$ is the length of the change in tokens, and $t$ is the type of the change, which is either an addition or a deletion of tokens. The deltas are ordered as they appear in $f$ from its beginning to its end. To apply the changes to $f$'s author information we first copy the previous author sequence to the current version by assigning $A(f, v_i) = A(f, v_{i-1})$. Then we iterate over each $d \in D$ in reverse order and apply each $d$ to $A(f, v_i)$ using the following rules: If $d$ is a deletion, we remove $l$ authors from $A(f, v_i)$ starting from $s$.

Figure 7.1 on the preceding page shows how author $b$ removes token 1 from the token stream and how the author information for token 1 is also removed from the author list. If $d$ is an addition, we insert $author(v_i)$ at position $s$ into $A(f, v_i)$ for $l$ times. This updates the author information for $f$ in $v_i$. Afterwards $A(f, v_i)$ is isomorphic to $T(f, v_i)$. In Figure 7.1 on the facing page author $a'$ adds tokens 10 and 11 between the existing tokens 5 and 6 and $a'$ is added as the author of these new tokens in the author list. We process the deltas in $D$ in reverse order, because thereby modifications are applied to $A(f, v_i)$ back-to-forth, which ensures that the starting positions of the deltas are not invalidated by previously processed modifications. If a deletion and an addition appear at the same token position (tokens have been replaced), the deletion is processed prior to the addition. In Figure 7.1 on the preceding page the author $b$ replaces the tokens 3 and 4 from author $a$ with the new tokens 7 to 9. The authorship for the removed tokens is also removed in the author list and $b$ is inserted three times as the author of the new tokens.

**Deletions** If $c$ is a deletion of a file $f$ that was present in $v_{i-1}$, its author list $A(f, v_{i-1})$ will not be resumed in $v_i$.

**File Copies** If $c$ copies a file $f$ that existed in $v_{i-1}$ to a file $f'$, then $f'$ will be handled as an added file according to the rules above.

**Unchanged Files and File Moves** If a file $f$ has no corresponding change $c$ in $v_i$, or if it was just moved to $f'$ in the file system, we copy the author information without changing it. That is, for unchanged files $A(f, v_i) = A(f, v_{i-1})$. For moved files we assign $A(f', v_i) = A(f, v_{i-1})$ and do not resume the old author list, that is, we maintain no $A(f, v_i)$.

## Code Authorship

The author information for tokens must now be aggregated for code fragments, which are sequences of tokens. A code fragment $cf = (f, v, s, l)$ is a continuous subsequence of the tokens from $T(f, v)$, where $f$ is the containing file, $v$ the version, $s$ is the start index in $T(f, v)$, and $l$ is the length of the sequence. Since $T(f, v)$ and $A(f, v)$ are isomorphic and we know $cf$'s position in the token stream we can also define the tokens of $cf$ in $v$ as $T(cf, v)$ and the authors of $cf$ in $v$ as $A(cf, v)$. The set of tokens of $cf$ authored by an author $a$ in version $v$ is defined as:

$$AT(cf, a, v) = \{t_i \in T(cf, v) | a_i \in A(cf, v) \wedge a = a_i\}$$

Each author contributes a share of the tokens in a fragment. An authors share of the tokens in a fragment in a specific version is defined as:

$$AS(cf, a, v) = \frac{|AT(cf, a, v)|}{|T(cf, v)|}$$

Knowing the author's share of tokens for each fragment allows us to determine the author who contributed most tokens to a fragment in a specific version. That is, the author $a$ with the highest $AS(cf, a, v)$. We call this the *main author* of $cf$ in $v$ and denote it as $MA(cf, v)$. If two or more authors contributed the same amount of tokens to $cf$ one of them is randomly chosen as $MA(cf, v)$. Figure 7.2 shows an example of the authorship in a code fragment. The author $a$ is the main author contributing seven of the twelve tokens in the fragment. The authors $b$ and $c$ contribute only three and two tokens, respectively.

| 0 | 1 | 2 | 3 | 4 | 5 | 6 | 7 | 8 | 9 | 10 | 11 |
|---|---|---|---|---|---|---|---|---|---|----|----|
| $a$ | $a$ | $a$ | $b$ | $b$ | $a$ | $c$ | $c$ | $b$ | $a$ | $a$ | $a$ |

**Figure 7.2** – Authorship information for a code fragment $cf$ of 12 tokens. The author $a$ has an author share of $\frac{7}{12}$, $b$'s author share is $\frac{3}{12}$ and $c$'s is $\frac{2}{12}$. This makes $a$ the *main author* of the code fragment $cf$.

Defining a main author may appear to be a too strong simplification of our accurate authorship tracking. Nevertheless, it is required to categorize clones according the number of authors. In the Section 7.4 we provide data how much of a fragment is authored by its main author on average. The vast majority of all fragments is predominantly authored by just one person. Even though we loose some accuracy by defining a main author we still benefit from the fact that the token-based approach is not extensively distorted by formatting and that it allows to track the authorship over the entire project history. Comparisons with subversion's annotate command have shown that these would strongly affect the results in some systems because all tokens in a line are assigned to the developer who last changed at least one token of that line.

## Clone Authorship

Our definition for code authorship, finally, needs to be transferred to code clones. In our study clones are exact copies of code fragments. Such a fragment may be copied one or more times. All equal fragments together form a *clone class*. Defining the author of clone fragments is straightforward because these are code fragments for which we defined authorship before. Hence, we can obtain the main author for each clone fragment. In our study we are interested in the distinction between clone classes that have just one author and such that have multiple authors. We now can separate the set of all clone classes $CC$ into such classes whose fragments have different main authors as $CC_{multi}$ and such classes whose fragments have the same main author as $CC_{single}$. That is, $CC_{single}$ are the single-author clone classes, whereas the multi-author clone classes are in $CC_{multi}$. The classification of one clone class is only meaningful for one version of the source code. The category of same class may change across versions as the token authorship changes.

Figure 7.3 on the next page shows an example of a $CC_{single}$ clone class with two fragments. The author $a$ is the main author of both fragments. While $frag_0$ contains tokens from other authors as well, $frag_1$ contains only tokens authored by $a$, for instance because $a$ created $frag_1$ as a copy of $frag_0$.

| | 0 | 1 | 2 | 3 | 4 | 5 | 6 | 7 | 8 | 9 | 10 | 11 |
|---|---|---|---|---|---|---|---|---|---|---|---|---|
| $frag_0$ | $a$ | $a$ | $a$ | $a$ | $a$ | $a$ | $b$ | $b$ | $a$ | $a$ | $a$ | $a$ |

| | 0 | 1 | 2 | 3 | 4 | 5 | 6 | 7 | 8 | 9 | 10 | 11 |
|---|---|---|---|---|---|---|---|---|---|---|---|---|
| $frag_1$ | $a$ | $a$ | $a$ | $a$ | $a$ | $a$ | $a$ | $a$ | $a$ | $a$ | $a$ | $a$ |

**Figure 7.3** – A $CC_{single}$ clone class with two fragments. Author $a$ is the main author of both fragments.

Figure 7.4 shows an example of a $CC_{multi}$ clone class with two fragments. The author $a$ is the main author of $frag_0$, whereas $frag_1$'s main author is $d$. The reason could be that $d$ copied $frag_0$ to create $frag_1$.

| | 0 | 1 | 2 | 3 | 4 | 5 | 6 | 7 | 8 | 9 | 10 | 11 |
|---|---|---|---|---|---|---|---|---|---|---|---|---|
| $frag_0$ | $a$ | $a$ | $a$ | $b$ | $b$ | $a$ | $c$ | $c$ | $b$ | $a$ | $a$ | $a$ |

| | 0 | 1 | 2 | 3 | 4 | 5 | 6 | 7 | 8 | 9 | 10 | 11 |
|---|---|---|---|---|---|---|---|---|---|---|---|---|
| $frag_1$ | $d$ | $d$ | $d$ | $d$ | $d$ | $d$ | $d$ | $d$ | $d$ | $d$ | $d$ | $d$ |

**Figure 7.4** – A $CC_{multi}$ clone class with two fragments. Author $a$ is the main author of $frag_0$, whereas $d$ is the main author of $frag_1$.

### Sensitivity to initial checkins

Because of its incremental nature, our approach needs not only to visit every version to provide accurate results, it also needs to begin with the very first version of the project's history. If the analysis starts with a version to which multiple developers contributed, it cannot decide who authored the tokens. Often, subversion repositories begin with an import of some existing code. To avoid wrong author assignments in such cases, we mark all tokens that were added in the very first version as unresolved. Such tokens will receive special handling. Clones that contain unresolved tokens over a certain threshold will be excluded from the analysis. We chose subject systems that have only small initial check-ins to limit the amount of unresolved clones. How many clones have been excluded per system will be reported in Section 7.4.

### Branches

Branches in subversion are effectively clones of the whole code base in the *trunk*. Nevertheless, they cannot be compared to clones created by copy-and-paste programming, because they are explicitly managed via subversion. Consequently, our approach analyzes only the trunk (the main branch) of each system. Another issue regarding branches is the possibility that new code is created by different developers in a branch and then merged into the trunk by one developer. Although newer versions of subversion record branching and merging in the meta data, earlier versions did not. Since we analyze time periods of at least three years, we cannot rely on this kind of information. The consequence is that changes incoming from other branches cannot be reconstructed from the data. In such cases our technique would assign the changes to the developer who makes the merge, although the changes may have been carried out by different authors in the branch. To eliminate the effect of such cases on our measurements, we choose subject systems where the development happens in the trunk and branches are used to propagate bug-fixes to previous releases but not for forward development. We will further discuss this in Section 7.3.

## 7.3  Study Setup

We use the approach described in Section 7.2.3 to detect the authors in five different software systems. In the following we describe how we detected clones and which systems have been analyzed.

### 7.3.1  Clone Detection

As in Chapter 6 we use Göde's incremental clone detector `iclones` to detect clones in all relevant versions [56]. We utilize and extend the incremental mechanism that reuses data structures from the previous version when the next version is analyzed. To update its data structures `iclones` calculates the difference between the token streams of the two versions using LCS. The detected differences are used to update the internal search structure, to track clone fragments, and to detect changes to clones. We extend this step with our authorship tracking approach. That is, we extend `iclones` to maintain the lists of authors for each version during clone detection.

Although token-based clone detection scales well compared with other techniques, the analysis of long project histories still comes with extensive hardware requirements. During the detection RAM is required to keep the token and tracking information. Our tracking approach further increases this demand. After the detection finished the data for all version must be stored which requires a large amount of disk space. Our approach adds the authorship information of all versions to this data. Although being created at the same time, we decided to map authorship and clone information in post-processing so that the RAM consumption of `iclones` does not increase significantly. This would have limited the number of versions we would be able to analyze. Consequently, the size stored data increases significantly, as does the time for the post-analysis.

We also use `iclones` detection of consistent and inconsistent changes to distinguish changes to clone classes into these categories. `Iclones` regards a change to a clone class as consistent if the changes to all fragments, as they are computed by LCS, are identical.

Similar to our previous study, described in Chapter 6, we removed generated code, excluded array initializers and imports, and separated methods in the token stream to circumvent common shortcomings of token-based clone detection. These properties of our clone detection approach are discussed in detail in Section 3.3.

**Degree of Similarity**

The high hardware requirements for our study forced us to use more restrictive settings for the clone detector. We chose to detect exact clones only for our case study.

| System | Domain | Language | max. KLOC | max. clone ratio [%] |
|---|---|---|---|---|
| Ant | Build System | Java | 215.0 | 2.1 |
| FindBugs | Static Analyzer | Java | 264.3 | 14.9 |
| FreeCol | Game | Java | 184.8 | 4.0 |
| Handbrake | Video Transcoder | C | 88.4 | 4.8 |
| swclones | Clone Detector | Java | 58.2 | 5.0 |

**Table 7.1** – Properties of the Subject Systems. *max KLOC* is the maximum size during the system's evolution in thousand lines. *Max. clone ratio* is the maximum clone ratio during the system's evolution in percent.

Another reason for detecting only exact clones is that we differentiate between consistent and inconsistent changes to clones. While change consistency can be exactly defined for exact clones it is more difficult to define for near-miss clones, in which the fragments have differences. An inconsistent change to a near-miss clone may make its fragments actually more similar by removing differences. This is not the kind of inconsistency we are interested in. Our research questions are directed to changes where different authors change clones inconsistently causing unintended inconsistencies.

Meanwhile, a technique to detect change patterns in near-miss clones has been presented by Bazrafshan [20]. Nevertheless, the more complex mapping mechanism requires more resources during detection. Saha and colleagues presented a similar approach, which, however, is based on code lines [158].

**Minimum Clone Length**

For the minimum length of a clone we first attempted to distinguish between 50, 100, and 150 tokens as we have done in our previous study in Chapter 6. Nevertheless, the analysis of small clones proved to be impractical with our long-lived subject systems because the higher amount of results increased the hardware requirements. A way to circumvent this problem is to shorten the analyzed time periods. This, however, would have provided too few cases where clones change, because these are rare. So we decided to analyze only the 100 token setting. As we have already discussed in Chapter 6, 100 tokens roughly correspond to 10 lines of code. For the smaller systems we compared the metrics for 50, 100, and 150 token settings, but did not found notable differences in the results.

## 7.3.2   Subject Systems

We analyzed the history of five software systems from different domains. We have chosen subject systems that satisfy three major requirements: First, a system needs to have a long history, which is completely documented in its Subversion repository from its beginning on. Second, a notable number of developers had to be involved in its development so that authorship effects can occur. Third, the development had to

| System | Versions | Begin | End | Years | Committers |
|--------|---------|-------|-----|-------|-----------|
| Ant | 8,774 | 2000-01-13 | 2011-08-19 | 11.6 | 46 |
| FindBugs | 10,339 | 2003-03-24 | 2012-07-26 | 9.4 | 28 |
| FreeCol | 10,930 | 2005-11-02 | 2013-01-30 | 7.3 | 35 |
| Handbrake | 1,970 | 2006-01-14 | 2013-04-01 | 7.2 | 25 |
| swclones | 1,378 | 2009-06-16 | 2012-03-21 | 2.8 | 18 |

**Table 7.2** – Evolution of the Subject Systems. *Versions* is the number of relevant versions that were analyzed in the time period between *begin* and *end*. The column *years* represents the time period in years. *Committers* is the number of developers who contributed to the source code in the analyzed period.

be focused on the trunk, while branches are only used to maintain old releases but not for forward development. Table 7.1 on the previous page shows general properties, such as application domain, programming language, size, and clone ratio. For the two latter we report the maximum that was reached in the time period we analyzed, to give an impression of the systems' scale.

Table 7.2 reports the time periods we analyzed per system, as well as the number of committers who contributed during these. The *Versions* column shows the number of relevant versions we analyzed. As can be seen from the *years* column, we analyzed project histories of considerable length. Where possible the whole available history was taken into account. For `Ant` and `FindBugs` the time periods had to be shortened, because of hardware limitations. Nevertheless for both systems roughly a decade of their history could be analyzed, which even exceeds the data we analyzed in our previous study in Chapter 6. For the clone detection tools from `softwareclones.org`, which we abbreviate as `swclones`, the analyzed time frame ends earlier because of an extensive reorganization of the `Subversion` repository, which would have distorted our measurement. We deliberately chose such long time periods, because changes to clones are rare and clones tend to survive long in the code as we have discussed in Chapter 4. In `Ant` we detected only 134 changes to clones although we analyzed more than a decade of its history.

The column labeled *committers* contains the number of unique users who committed at least one relevant version. Possible alias names, which are used by some users, have been merged as far as they could be reconstructed. To this end we manually searched for obvious aliases among the names of the contributors (such as 'johndoe' and 'doejohn'). We also used the social network *Open Hub*[1] where authors can claim contributions to open-source projects as their own and identified some cases where the same person used different aliases within one project.

All five systems either did not use branches at all or used them mainly to maintain old releases. If branches where used for other purposes we will describe these in the following.

---

[1] Website: `https://www.openhub.net` Previously known as *Ohloh*.

## Apache Ant

Ant[2] is an open-source build-automation system for Java development. For our study we analyzed its `core` component. Several proposals for a next-generation `Ant` have been made and developed in the *proposals* folder of the code repository, which can be regarded as a branch folder. Some proposals started with a clone of the code base that was heavily refactored and changed. Nevertheless, all proposals have been discarded eventually and no merges back to the trunk were applied. Consequently, we entirely excluded all proposals from our analysis.

## FindBugs

FindBugs[3] is an open-source static-analysis tool for Java source code. It searches the byte code for typical patterns that indicate potential programming errors. The high maximum clone coverage is caused by an outlier version. For most of the time it lay between 0.5% and 3.0%.

## FreeCol

FreeCol[4] is an open-source reimplementation of the commercial strategy game `Colonization`. It has been newly developed from scratch by a team of enthusiasts and is written in Java. It reaches its maximum clone coverage in the middle of the analyzed period. From there on, the coverage steadily declined to 0.7% in the last version.

## Handbrake

Handbrake[5] is an open-source multi-platform video transcoder written in C. It consists of a central library that performs the transcoding and three GUI applications for Linux, Mac and Windows. The Windows GUI was left out in this study, because it is written in C# and not in C as the remainder of the system.

## softwareclones.org

Our research group develops tools for clone detection and analysis in Java[6]. These are the tools that have been used to execute this study. Namely `iclones`, `cyclone`, `RCF`, and `RCFViewer`. For brevity we will refer to them as `swclones` in the remainder of this chapter. The whole code repository including tools for clone detection, analysis, visualization, and transformation was analyzed for this study. The code is developed by a team of 18 researchers and student assistants. Although the main focus of the tools are code clones, clone detection has only been used sporadically during the development process.

---

[2]Website: `http://ant.apache.org`
[3]Website: `http://findbugs.sourceforge.net`
[4]Website: `http://www.freecol.org`
[5]Website: `http://www.handbrake.fr`
[6]Website: `http://www.softwareclones.org`

It must be noted that `swclones` and `clones` from our stability study in Chapter 6 are different systems. Both are developed in the same group, but are different projects, written in different programming languages.

## 7.4   Results

Before we pursue our research questions, we take a look on the feasibility of our approach for the chosen subject systems. The idea of the main author is based on the assumption that code fragments are usually predominantly authored by one author. If this is not the case and different authors equally contribute to the fragments our classification would be inaccurate.

Consequently, we measure the average share the main author has over all clone fragments we detected in the analyzed systems. To this end we define the *average main author share* as $\overline{MAS}$. Let $CF_{all}(v)$ be the set of all clone fragments found in version $v$, then the average main author share for all fragments $\overline{MAS}_{all}$ is defined as:

$$\overline{MAS}_{all} = \frac{\sum\limits_{v \in V} \sum\limits_{cf \in CF_{all}(v)} |AT(cf, MA(cf, v), v)|}{\sum\limits_{v \in V} \sum\limits_{cf \in CF_{all}(v)} |T(cf, v)|} \times 100$$

The numerator summarizes the number of tokens added by the fragment's main author $MA(cf, v)$ for all clone fragments $cf \in CF_{all}(v)$ in all versions $v \in V$. We divide this by the total number of tokens in all fragments of all versions. The result is the fraction of cloned tokens that were authored by the respective fragment main authors.

Likewise, we also define the average main author share for all fragments that are part of $CC_{single}$ clone classes as $\overline{MAS}_{single}$. Let $CF_{single}(v)$ be the set of all fragments that are part of the $CC_{single}$ clone classes in version $v$, then $\overline{MAS}_{single}$ is defined as:

$$\overline{MAS}_{single} = \frac{\sum\limits_{v \in V} \sum\limits_{cf \in CF_{single}(v)} |AT(cf, MA(cf, v), v)|}{\sum\limits_{v \in V} \sum\limits_{cf \in CF_{single}(v)} |T(cf, v)|} \times 100$$

$\overline{MAS}_{all}$ gives an impression of how accurate our main author detection is in general. High values indicate that the main author indeed contributed the majority of the fragments. We also compute $\overline{MAS}_{single}$ to analyze whether this also holds for the clone classes we identified as $CC_{single}$, which would mean that $CC_{single}$ clone classes can indeed be regarded as being mainly authored by just one person.

The results are shown in Table 7.3 on the next page. Except for one case all $\overline{MAS}_{all}$ and $\overline{MAS}_{single}$ are above 90%, which means that on average the vast majority of tokens in a clone fragment are contributed by its main author. In `FreeCol` the $\overline{MAS}_{all}$ reaches only 80%, which, however, still means that the majority of the tokens of the cloned fragments are contributed by the main author. For $\overline{MAS}_{single}$ the values are even higher and lie between 95% and 99%. This means that our approach indeed provides an acceptable estimation of the fragment's main author.

| System | $\overline{MAS}_{all}$ | $\overline{MAS}_{single}$ | Excluded [%] |
|--------|------|---------|--------------|
| Ant | 90.7 | 95.0 | 3.245 |
| FindBugs | 98.7 | 99.0 | 0.000 |
| FreeCol | 80.1 | 94.9 | 13.767 |
| Handbrake | 94.9 | 98.1 | 0.004 |
| swclones | 96.5 | 96.0 | 0.000 |

**Table 7.3** – Average main author shares for all fragments ($\overline{MAS}_{all}$), the fragments of all $CC_{single}$ ($\overline{MAS}_{single}$), and the ratio of excluded clone classes for all subject systems.

For three of the systems, the `subversion` history started with the import of an existing code base. That is, for these systems all tokens of the initial version have been marked as unresolved. As soon as more than one percent of a fragment's tokens are marked as unknown, we excluded the fragment and its whole clone class from the analysis. We experimented with higher values of this threshold up to 5%, but the exclusion rate did not change to an considerable amount. Consequently, we went on with 1% unresolved tokens as exclusion criterion. The *excluded* column in Table 7.3 shows how many of all clone classes were excluded per system. The exclusion of clone classes is notable only for `Ant` and `FreeCol`. For the latter, 13.8% had to be excluded, because the first 600 versions in its repository seem to be corrupted[7] and were skipped.

### 7.4.1 Clone Authors

To answer Question B1, that is the question how often clones are authored by more than one developer, we first detect clones in every relevant version of each system. All detected clone classes are categorized into $CC_{single}$ and $CC_{multi}$ and counted. If a clone class appears in more than one version, each occurrence will be counted. The decision whether a clone class is $CC_{single}$ or $CC_{multi}$ is made for each occurrence. 7.4 shows the results which are also visualized in Figure 7.5 on the next page.

The answer for Question B1 is that for all systems, both $CC_{single}$ and $CC_{multi}$ do exist in a notable quantity. The number of $CC_{single}$ is always higher than the number of $CC_{multi}$ clone classes. That is, most of the clones we have found in the project histories are mainly authored by just a single developer. Nevertheless, 15 to 40% of the clone classes contain fragments that are mainly authored by different developers.

### 7.4.2 Change Frequency

To answer Question B2, that is whether changes occur more often, when multiple developers are involved, we analyze whether $CC_{single}$ and $CC_{multi}$ change differently by analyzing whether clone classes of the two categories have the same probability to change. For each clone class we detect in version $v_i$, we check whether its fragments are

---

[7]The `Subverison` client reported errors when we attempted to checkout these revisions. Our working copies did not contain all files that are stored in the revisions according to their version logs.

| System | All | $CC_{single}$ | % | $CC_{multi}$ | % |
|--------|-----|---------------|---|--------------|---|
| Ant | 138.1 | 96.1 | 69.6 | 42.0 | 30.4 |
| FindBugs | 421.0 | 353.9 | 84.1 | 67.1 | 15.9 |
| FreeCol | 413.3 | 247.6 | 59.9 | 165.8 | 40.1 |
| Handbrake | 72.7 | 53.3 | 73.3 | 19.4 | 26.7 |
| swclones | 28.4 | 18.2 | 64.1 | 10.2 | 35.9 |

**Table 7.4** – Absolute amount and relative frequency of $CC_{single}$ and $CC_{multi}$ clone classes. The column *all* lists the total number of clone classes in each system. All absolute numbers are displayed in thousand.

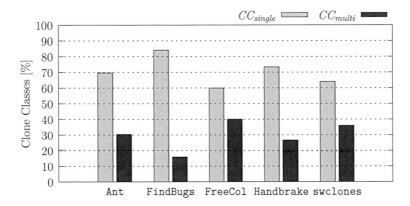

**Figure 7.5** – Relative frequency of $CC_{single}$ and $CC_{multi}$ clone classes in the subject systems.

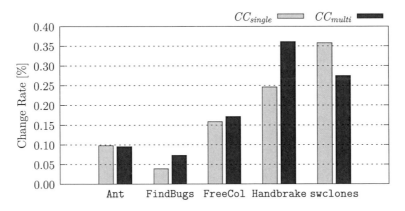

**Figure 7.6** – Change rate of $CC_{single}$ and $CC_{multi}$ clone classes in the subject systems.

| System | Sample | CR [%] | CC [%] | IC [%] |
|--------|--------|--------|--------|--------|
| Ant | $CC_{single}$ | 0.098 | 39.4 | 60.6 |
| | $CC_{multi}$ | 0.095 | 37.5 | 62.5 |
| | all | 0.097 | 38.8 | 61.2 |
| FindBugs | $CC_{single}$ | 0.039 | 15.9 | 84.1 |
| | $CC_{multi}$ | 0.073 | 18.4 | 81.6 |
| | all | 0.044 | 16.6 | 83.4 |
| FreeCol | $CC_{single}$ | 0.158 | 46.9 | 53.1 |
| | $CC_{multi}$ | 0.171 | 30.6 | 69.4 |
| | all | 0.164 | 40.1 | 59.9 |
| Handbrake | $CC_{single}$ | 0.246 | 49.6 | 50.4 |
| | $CC_{multi}$ | 0.361 | 57.1 | 42.9 |
| | all | 0.277 | 52.2 | 47.8 |
| swclones | $CC_{single}$ | 0.358 | 38.5 | 61.5 |
| | $CC_{multi}$ | 0.274 | 3.6 | 96.4 |
| | all | 0.328 | 28.0 | 72.0 |

**Table 7.5** – Change rates of clone classes in the subject systems. $CR$ is the overall change rate over all clone classes, $CC$ the rate of consistent changes, and $IC$ the rate of inconsistent changes.

changed in the transition to $v_{i+1}$. If the tokens of at least one fragment were changed, the clone class is marked as changed. The change rate of $CC_{single}$ clone classes can then be computed as the fraction of the changed $CC_{single}$ clone classes and the total number of $CC_{single}$ clone classes. The change rate of $CC_{multi}$ clone classes is computed accordingly. That is, these change rates reflect the probability that a clone class, found in one version, is changed in the next version.

Table 7.5 shows the results. The CR column represents the change rate of the respective clone classes. Figure 7.5 illustrates the change frequency of $CC_{single}$ and $CC_{multi}$ for each system in comparison. First of all, it is to be noted that clones do not change too often in general. In all systems less than 0.4% of all clone classes we detected during the system's evolution changed in the next version. For example, we detected 138,096 clone classes in all versions of Ant, but only 134 changes occurred to these within the 11.6 years we analyzed. These data support findings of a previous study on this topic [55]. The clones in Handbrake and swclones have a notably higher change rate compared with the clones in the other systems. Both systems have a much shorter history in terms of versions than the others. It is also these two systems whose change rates for $CC_{single}$ and $CC_{multi}$ expose the largest difference. In Handbrake the change probability of $CC_{multi}$ clone classes is 55,5% higher than the change probability of $CC_{single}$ clone classes. In swclones the opposite is the case and $CC_{single}$ clone classes change more frequently. The highest relative difference can be observed in FindBugs where the change rate of $CC_{multi}$ is twice as high as for $CC_{single}$. For Ant and FreeCol no notable difference was measured.

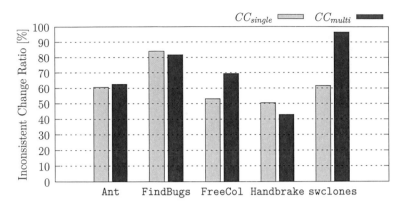

**Figure 7.7** – Rate of inconsistent changes for $CC_{single}$ and $CC_{multi}$ clone classes in the subject systems.

In summary, there is no systematic difference that indicates a general effect clone authorship has on the probability that a clone class changes. The effect seems to be system dependent.

### 7.4.3 Change Consistency

We further analyze the consistency of the changes to answer Question B3. That is the question whether inconsistent changes more likely if multiple developers are involved. If a clone class changed and all its fragments underwent identical changes, we consider the change to be consistent. If the fragments changed differently or some fragments did not change, while others in the same class did, we consider the change as inconsistent. Table 7.5 shows how often $CC_{single}$ and $CC_{multi}$ changed consistently or inconsistently. Figure 7.7 shows only the percentage of inconsistent changes in comparison for the subject systems. For most systems the rate of inconsistent changes does not differ notably for $CC_{single}$ and $CC_{multi}$. In FreeCol and swclones $CC_{multi}$ are changed more often inconsistently than $CC_{single}$. A possible explanation for the huge difference in swclones will be given in the next section where we inspect all changes manually. In Handbrake $CC_{single}$ has a slightly higher rate of inconsistent changes. Again, there is no systematic difference in the analyzed systems. That is, we cannot conclude that the authorship of clone fragments has a systematic effect on the consistency of changes to their clone classes.

### 7.4.4 Intentions and Bugs

To answer question B4 and to learn more about the intentions and possible defects connected to $CC_{single}$ and $CC_{multi}$ clone classes, we manually inspected a large part of the results. To this end, the clone evolution visualization tool cyclone[8] was used

---

[8]Website: http://www.softwareclones.org/cyclone.php

[56]. Cyclone visualizes clone histories, which eases the reconstruction of changes and intentions. For swclones and Ant we evaluated each change to clones on four levels: (1) For inconsistent changes, whether the inconsistency was intentional, (2) whether the inconsistency caused a bug or is an incomplete bug removal, (3) the rationale of the cloning and the changes to the clones, (4) whether the fragments of the changed clone class were located in the same or different files.

### swclones

We inspected all changes to the clones in swclones, because for this system we measured the largest difference in change consistency. Multi-author clones changed more often inconsistently than single-author clones. Furthermore, we have in-depth knowledge about the code which allows us to judge the intentions behind changes and whether an inconsistency is a bug.

The inconsistent changes to clones were mostly intentional for both single-author and multi-author clones. Among the multi-author clones only one out of 25 inconsistent changes was unintentionally inconsistent (4.0%). A bug-fix regarding the canonicalization of path names was applied only in the default input module of our clone detector, which reads source code from a local disk. A similar module for network input contains the same bug, which was not fixed. This module, however, has not been used since and became non-functional in general because it was not maintained. Hence, it should be regarded as unmaintained and dead code. We regard this case as rather unproblematic from a cloning perspective, as the general problem lies in the existence of the dead code that should be cleaned up. Surprisingly, 3 out of the 38 inconsistent changes to single-author clones (7.9%) were unintentional and caused actual bugs that still existed in the most recent version. They have in common that the bugs are located in complex algorithms and that their cloned occurrences lie closely together in the same file. In each case only one of two bug occurrences was fixed.

Regarding bugs we found that multi-author clones were less often subject to bug-fixing activity compared with single-author clones (7.7% vs. 20.6%). Most of these fixes, except the ones mentioned above, were applied consistently.

Single-author and multi-author clones differ in their rationale. Almost all multi-author clones (21 out of 27) are copies between two different viewer applications. One of these was started by copying existing GUI components from the other. The plan to reintegrate both applications at a later point of time was soon abandoned, because it was found that the different functional requirements could be better satisfied in separate tools. Consequently, the two GUIs were purposefully developed independently which caused the high volume of inconsistent changes to multi-author clones in swclones.

Not a single multi-author clone class had all its fragments in the same file. In contrast, the single-author clones lie in 57.7% of the cases in the same file. These often represent logic snippets that are difficult or impossible to unify. For instance, because the same logic is implemented for different primitive types.

To summarize, multi-author clones were mostly caused by file cloning, which was less often the case for single-author clones. Furthermore, the changes to multi-author clones contained less problematic cases, such as bug fixes, compared with single-authored ones.

**Apache Ant**

As second system, we inspected all 134 changes to clones in `Ant`. According to our statistics single-author and multi-author clones do not differ significantly regarding their change frequency and their change consistency. Since we are not familiar with the code, we cannot safely judge whether inconsistent changes were made intentionally. Nevertheless, we can analyze how single-author and multi-author clones differ in this system. We further inspected the commit messages to evaluate whether the changes were bug fixes.

We found bug-fixing activity to be more common in single-author than in multi-author clones (31.2% vs. 13.2%). Inconsistencies that were obviously unintended, because the missing changes were propagated to all fragments later, rather occurred in the single-authored clones. We clearly identified three such cases for single-author clones, one of which took three attempts over eight months to be fixed consistently. Among the changes to multi-author clones only one such late propagation was found. In this case the inconsistency was fixed in the following version where the clone was also removed.

The rationale of cloning is less discriminative than in `swclones`, the tendency, however, is the same. The changed multi-author clones lie to 25.64% within the same file. For single-author clones this is the case in 30.11%. This smaller difference may be caused by `Ant`'s highly generic architecture that decomposes the build-process into tasks, each of which are implemented in their own class. These tasks are often similar, especially when they implement similar functionality, such as different commands of the same source code management system.

More interesting is why the clones are changed. Most of the consistent changes to multi-author clones are directed to warnings from static defect checkers, which are usually issues of style, performance, program comprehensibility, or typical programming mistakes. These issues are automatically detected by tools. We did not consider them as bugs. If they are cloned, the tool will point out all locations to the user automatically. Hence, it does not come as a surprise that these issues are removed consistently. While 71.4% of the consistent changes to multi-author clones are directed to such issues, only 35.1% of the consistent changes to single-author clones fall into this category. Among the inconsistent changes, such issues are rarely the reason for the change (9.1% for multi-author clones vs. 5.6% for single-author clones).

To summarize, we did not find multi-author clones to be related to problematic changes more often than single-author clones. Most inconsistencies are intentional and the rare cases of clearly unintentional inconsistencies were rather found among the single-author clone classes. When multi-author clone classes changed consistently, the reason mostly were automatically detected warnings about coding conventions and style.

## 7.5   Discussion

Our analysis of code authorship was motivated by the conjecture that problems with clones may be caused when the copied fragments are authored by different developers. If this was the case, the authorship of clones could be used to prioritize clones in clone management and to develop measures to prevent such problems. Our results show that multi-author cloning is common in software, albeit most clones are created and mainly maintained by one developer. The analysis of the change frequency and consistency did not reveal a notable and systematic difference for the multi-author clones. To be a useful metric for clone management, multiple authors would need to have an effect of considerable size on the harmfulness of clones, which our data do not indicate. The small number of changes to clones in general, the relative differences we measured for the change rate and the consistency sum up to a very small absolute number of actual cases where multiple authors caused problems with clones. To be practically relevant the differences between single-author and multi-author clones had to be much larger and there had to be a clear tendency towards multi-author clones, which we did not observe.

Our manual inspection further contradicts our initial conjecture, as the few harmful clones we found were rather single-author than multi-author. Our results suggest that single-author clones could be more likely to cause harm. A possible explanation lies in the different rationales we observed for single-author and multi-author clones. As our manual inspection revealed, multi-author clones tend to be larger copies of whole structures across multiple files, whereas single-author clones were more often smaller copies within a method or file—often complex algorithmic parts. An inconsistency in the layout of two GUI dialogs, for example, should be less harmful than an inconsistency in some critical part of the application logic. We observed this tendency for both `swclones` and `Ant`.

In both systems, for which we did manual inspections, we observed that consistent changes were very often directed to style issues, while inconsistent ones rarely are. When multiple authors were involved in the cloning, the amount of style related changes was higher in `Ant`. This is also true for `swclones`, but this result is based on only one existing consistent change to multi-author clones.

Our study investigates the effect of multiple developers on clones from only one perspective. Besides the question whether it makes a difference if different developers create and maintain the copied fragments, it may also be asked, whether unwanted inconsistencies occur when a clone authored by one developer is changed by another. This, however, is another question that should be asked in broader context because changing someone else's code may cause problems in general and probably is not specific to clones.

## 7.6 Threats to Validity

There are certain threats to the validity of our study, which we describe in this section, ordered by threats to internal, construct, and external validity.

### 7.6.1 Internal Validity

The results of our study depend on the meta data provided by `subversion`. As any other SCM it can only provide what was explicitly inserted. Information may be lost if files are moved or copied without using `subversion`'s commands for this purpose. In such cases, the authorship may change incorrectly. If changes are proposed as patches by an external developer, the project member who commits the changes appears as their author. Our approach detects the committer as author in such cases, which is not the original author. Nevertheless, the committing author is still responsible for the correctness of the changes she or he makes. In some projects the same developer contributes under different user names. We merged different aliases to mitigate this threat.

Another possible threat, which also applied to our previous study in Chapter 6, is the Longest Common Subsequence (LCS) algorithm, which we use to analyze changes to the token stream. In practice, LCS is usually able to reconstruct the changes that were applied to a sequence correctly. Nevertheless, is not able to track code movements inside a file. If, for instance, a method is moved inside a file, our approach will regard this as a deletion and an addition that was authored by the developer who moved the method. Such cases may appear in refactorings. To evaluate whether such changes do largely affect the authorship detection, we analyzed how the amount of authored tokens changes over time for each developer. We did not find abrupt changes in authorship, which would be visible if such situations occurred frequently and affected the measurements thoroughly.

## 7.6.2   Construct Validity

Similar to our previous study in Chapter 6, the fact that state-of-the-art clone detectors are constructed to search for similarity in the code poses a possible thread to construct validity. Namely, the threat that something different from the thing that was to be measured was actually measured. As we have described before our clone detector finds code fragments that are similar, but not necessarily code clones that are of particular interest to someone who aims to achieve a specific maintenance task. Consequently, our study must be interpreted as an analysis of what state-of-the-art clone detectors provide and how this information can be interpreted and used in software maintenance.

Our analysis does only regard type-1 clones. This must be taken into account when our results on inconsistent changes are interpreted. An inconsistent change to a type-1 clone can have different results, including a change in the clone type. If for instance some tokens are inserted into one fragment of a clone class but not into the others, a type-1 clone may become a type-3 clone. Such a clone may only be detected partially (the remaining type-1 parts) or not at all by our approach. The effect on our results could be for example that clones stated as exact copies and are then continuously modified inconsistently disappear from our data set. Since we do not have data on such cases, we cannot assess the effect of such possible cases.

## 7.6.3   External Validity

Although we chose multiple long-lived systems from different domains, we cannot generalize our results to all other software systems. Most of the analyzed systems are written in Java and developed as open-source software. Systems written in other languages or in an industrial context may expose different properties. Furthermore, our results indicate that the relationship between developers and the effects of clones, may be system dependent.

We chose subject systems that use branching in the source code management system only to a very limited extent. While this decision improves the accuracy of our measurements, it also limits our observations to software systems that use branching only to maintain older releases, but not for parallelized new developments. We do not see reasons why the clone authorship should differ in such projects, but we cannot rule out that such differences exist.

The results of our study are valid for exact clones. We did not analyze clones with different variable names or gapped clones. Inconsistent changes may split previously found exact clones into multiple classes. In our manual inspection of all changes to the clones in `swclones` and `Ant`, in which we also analyzed clone genealogies, such cases did not appear frequently.

## 7.7  Conclusion

In this chapter we analyzed how multiple developers affect the evolution of exact code clones. We found that both single-author and multi-author clones do exist in real software systems. Most of the clone classes, however, are maintained by mainly one developer. We did not find a systematic relationship between the number of authors and the likelihood that clone classes change. Inconsistent changes were also not systematically related to the number of authors. Whether single-author or multi-author clones change more often or are more likely to change inconsistently varied between the systems. The differences were mostly small. From manual inspection of changes to clones we found that multi-author clones are not more likely to contain bug fixes. Indeed, changes single-author clones tend to be related to bugs more often.

We further learned that multi-authored clones differ from single-author clones as they are more often copies of larger structures. When a developer copies his own code the result seem to be rather small copies of business logic. When code is copied by other developers than the original author the reason is often related to reuse of larger existing structures. In some cases with the intent to develop something new as in the *replicate and specialize* pattern as Kapser and Godfrey describe it [94].

All these findings do not support our initial assumption that developers who copy from each other are a reason for clone related problems. Consequently, the number of authors cannot be recommended as a metric to prioritize clones for clone management activity. Or to put it simpler: it did not prove suitable to separate the 'good' from the 'bad' clones.

# Chapter 8

# Clones and Programmer Performance

The commonly used methods to analyze the relationship of clones and maintainability have a lot in common with archeology. They analyze what was left over from the past to reconstruct what happened back then. Instead of excavating bones and shards to reenact how our ancestors may have lived, we mine such archives as code repositories, issue tracking systems, or documentation to learn which kind of problems software developers had to face. Although software developers document their work more thoroughly than Neanderthals, the data we can analyze retrospectively are fragmentary.

Source code management systems, such as *Subversion*, store only the *result* of a code change. These snapshots do not provide information on how they were made. Every programmer knows a story how he had to search for a bug for hours and hours until he found a missing comma to be the cause. Retrospective analysis will find that just one character was changed and will assess the costs of the change to be small, while, indeed, the programmer spent half a day to get it right.

As we have learned in Chapter 4, developers tend to experiment and layout until they find a proper abstraction [97]. Often they will commit only the final result to the source code repository, hiding the actual work effort from the retrospective analysis of the revisions.

Other than our counterparts in archeology, we have the advantage, that software developers are not long gone. We have the opportunity to speak to them, to observe them while working, and even to ask them if they would participate in a controlled experiment. Surprisingly, researchers did not take much advantage of this situation, yet. This lead us to our third research focus in Chapter 4.

> **Research Perspective C:** *How do clones affect performance of programmers in real software engineering tasks?*

Maintenance tasks usually involve activities that are likely to be affected by clones but cannot be measured completely retrospectively. Among these are program comprehension, bug reproduction, code changes, and testing. Controlled experiments are an adequate means to observe such aspects of software development. Although there has been clone research for more than a decade, hardly any human-based studies have been carried out to evaluate the effect that clones have on maintenance.

In this chapter we report on a controlled experiment that evaluates how the programmer's performance is affected by clones in specific maintenance tasks with a total number of 81 participants. To the best of our knowledge, this is the first controlled experiment of this kind.

But why are controlled experiments so unpopular while mining software repositories is widely adopted? The main reason may be the simplicity of retrospective case studies: Download some open-source code repository from the Internet, write some analysis scripts, and publish the results—without having faced any actual developer. Controlled experiments, in contrast, require long preparation. Subjects must be found in a reasonable number, pre-studies must be performed to evaluate the set-up, data collection often requires manual effort, and there is low experimental expertise in general. It is also more difficult to acquire large amounts of data, which increases the risk that the results are not statistically significant. Indeed, it took us more than one and a half year to design and execute the experiment we report in this chapter in its final version.

Despite all the complications a controlled experiment brings, we believe that it adds important insights into how the performance of developers is affected by clones. First, it makes programmer behavior available to analysis, which retrospective studies miss altogether. Second, our previous studies have shown that the thorough manual inspection of changes and their discussion added as much insight as the bare numbers from the statistical analysis. In fact, many statistical findings appeared in an altogether different light when the underlying changes and their rationale have been understood. That is, besides the statistics, which are often problematic in human-based studies on software engineering, we expect to gather new insights from our detailed observations.

With our study we are the first to contribute data and insight on this new level of detail. We also lay the groundwork on how controlled experiments on clones can be performed. Already, others have continued our work providing further support for our findings. The contents of this chapter have been previously presented at the *20th International Conference on Program Comprehension* and were published in the conference proceedings [68]. We also provide data from a replication by Chatterji, Carver, Kraft, and Harder, to which we contributed setup and methodology, that was presented at the *20th Working Conference on Reverse Engineering* and published in the conference proceedings [32].[1] In this chapter we present additional data and evaluate the results for all participants together, which has not been published previously. We also revise some of the statistical results from our initial publication.

The organization of the remainder of this chapter is geared to the *Reporting Guidelines for Controlled Experiments in Software Engineering* from Jedlitschka and

---

[1]This publication also contains an extension of our study, which we will summarize briefly. The focus lies on the replication of our original experiment.

Pfahl [82]: Section 8.1 describes our research questions, which we derive from Research Focus C. The experimental design is described in Section 8.2, while its execution is documented in Section 8.3. Section 8.4 summarizes the results statistically and tests the hypotheses. The interpretation and discussion of the results can be found in Section 8.5. Threats to validity are discussed in Section 8.6. Section 8.7 concludes.

## 8.1   Research Questions

Software maintenance is a broad field that subsumes various activities—usually categorized into corrective, adaptive, and perfective maintenance. It is not possible to investigate the whole field at once. When we designed our experiment we aimed to address the two most common effects clones are believed to have. First, the increased effort required to maintain cloned code and, second, the alleged risk of bugs through inconsistent changes. Since human-based studies are costly to perform, we sought for a controlled environment in which both effects can be assessed for cloned and non-cloned scenarios. We found the removal of an existing bug to be a well suited maintenance task for this purpose. The most obvious relation between bugs and clones is that the bug itself is cloned. Consequently, we analyze how the removal of a bug is influenced by the fact that it is cloned or not. We define two research questions:

> **Question C1:** *Does the time needed for a bug removal increase when the bug is cloned?*

It seems obvious that it may take more time to make a change to a cloned concept than to a non-cloned one. By answering this question, we aim to provide empirical evidence as to whether this difference exists. If it exists, we also analyze to which extent it does. The second question is directed to the correctness of the bug removal:

> **Question C2:** *Does the probability of incorrect bug removals increase when the bug is cloned?*

A commonly stated threat of clones is that they may lead to inconsistent changes. In our study, such a change would cause an incomplete and, therefore, incorrect bug fix. By answering this question, we aim to provide empirical evidence on the extent of this risk.

## 8.2   Experimental Design

This section describes the experimental design we chose to obtain our results. First, we describe the hypotheses and variables measured followed by the design, the subjects and the objects of our study. Finally, we describe the instrumentation. All materials and instructions on how to replicate this study are available for research purposes. The printed materials are included in this thesis. The experimenter's manual is enclosed in Appendix B; the handout can be found in Appendix C. All further materials are available on the Internet.[2]

## 8.2.1   Hypotheses and Variables

Deriving the hypotheses for the experiment from the two research questions is straightforward. Table 8.1 shows how research question and hypotheses relate. Both alternative hypotheses represent the common expectations that the presence of clones does have negative effects. Consequently, they are 1-tailed.

|  | Null hypothesis | Alternative hypothesis |
|---|---|---|
| Question 1 | $H_0^{time}$: The time needed to remove a cloned bug is *shorter or equal* compared to the time needed to remove a non-cloned bug. | $H_1^{time}$: The time needed to remove a cloned bug is *longer* compared to the time needed to remove a non-cloned bug. |
| Question 2 | $H_0^{corr}$: The probability of a correct removal of a cloned bug is *higher or equal* compared to the probability of a correct removal of a non-cloned bug. | $H_1^{corr}$: The probability of a correct removal of a cloned bug is *lower* compared to the probability of a correct removal of a non-cloned bug. |

**Table 8.1** – Null and alternative hypotheses

The sole *independent variable* of our experiment is whether a bug is cloned or not. The *dependent variables* of our experiment are similar to those used in other empirical evaluations in software maintenance [80, 144, 174]: First, the *time* needed to complete a given task and, second, the *correctness* of the task solution. The variable *correctness* can be decomposed into three more precise factors:

1. *Addressed.* The bug report has been addressed with an action that corrected *at least one* occurrence of the bug.

2. *Complete.* The solution provided corrects *all* occurrences of the bug. The set of *complete* solutions is a subset of the set of *addressed* solutions.

3. *Incomplete.* The solution provided corrects one but not all occurrences of the bug. The set of *incomplete* solutions is a subset of the set of *addressed* solutions.

---

[2]Website with replication materials: http://www.softwareclones.org/experiment
Tarball with all materials (2.3 GB): http://www.softwareclones.org/download/experiment/experiment-replication-set.tar.bz2

Theoretically, there is a further category *failed*, in which non of the cloned bugs gets fixed. This, however, is not of particular interest for our study, because failing to fix any bug occurrence does not allow any conclusion on the effects of clones.

Each solution that falls into the *addressed* category is either *complete* or *incomplete*. The union of *complete* and *incomplete* equals *addressed*. If only one bug occurrence has to be fixed in a task—the bug is not cloned—*addressed* implies *complete*. *Complete* is the highest level a solution can reach. When we speak of the *correct* solutions in this chapter in general, we mean all *complete* ones, because we consider a solution to be correct only if all bug occurrences where fixed. We will use the distinction between *addressed* and *complete* not only to quantify the number of cases, but also to distinguish solution times for *addressed* and *correct* solutions.

## 8.2.2   Design

The experiment is based on the two small open-source games `FrozenBubble`[3] and `Pacman`[4]. For each system, we defined one maintenance task that requires fixing a bug: *tFB* for `FrozenBubble` and *tPM* for `Pacman`. For each of these tasks, we prepared two variations that differ only in the independent variable, which is whether the bug is cloned or not. Task $tFB_{nc}$ is the variant of `FrozenBubble` containing the non-cloned bug, while the variant containing the cloned bug will be referred to as $tFB_c$. Likewise, $tPM_{nc}$ and $tPM_c$ are the task variants for `Pacman`.

The subjects were separated into two groups $A$ and $B$. The participants of each group were assigned one variation per task. Table 8.2 shows how groups and tasks were assigned.

|        | $A$        | $B$        |
|--------|------------|------------|
| Task 1 | $tFB_{nc}$ | $tFB_c$    |
| Task 2 | $tPM_c$    | $tPM_{nc}$ |

**Table 8.2** – Assignment of groups to tasks

These decisions result in a $2 \times 2$ factorial within-subject design for the experiment [177]. The two variants of each task cannot be assigned to the same participant who would have learned the solution after solving the first variant. The design ensures that each participant is presented a cloned and a non-cloned task. That is, each participant will be exposed to both levels of our independent variable. With this design decision we aim to rule out the possible bias that one group may contain participants with better skills than the other. If that was the case and we chose a between-subjects design, the differences in measurement may be caused by the characteristics of the group and not by the independent variable.

The feasibility of the experiment was evaluated in pilot studies. Because of organizational constraints and to control possible fatigue effects, the experiment was

---

[3]Website: http://www.frozen-bubble.org/
[4]Website: http://code.google.com/p/pacman-rkant/

designed so that it can be executed within a two-hour time slot. In the following, we describe the resulting experiment setup in detail.

### 8.2.3  Subjects

A total of 80 Subjects from three distinct populations participated in the experiment. Table 8.3 shows the most important characteristics of these and a fourth group in which we joined all participants.

| Population | Participants | Java Skill (SD) | Expertise |
|---|---|---|---|
| Bremen | 22 | 56 (27.4) | students |
| Tuscaloosa | 47 | 45 (28.5) | students |
| Dagstuhl | 12 | 60 (31.4) | industrial & academic professionals |
| Joined | 81 | 50 (28.8) | mixed |

**Table 8.3** – Statistics on the subject groups. Java Skill is reported as arithmetic mean and standard deviation (in brackets).

The first group were computer science students from the University of Bremen in Germany. All of them learned Java as primary programming language in their classes. Besides Java skills, basic knowledge in using the Eclipse IDE for Java development was made a requirement for participation. In total, 21 students participated in the experiment. For motivational purposes, a prize was raffled among all participating students, regardless of their performance in the experiment. The participants were asked to self-assess their Java skills on a scale from 1 (low) to 100 (high), with an average skill value of 56 as result. As can be seen from the standard deviation, the variance in the Java skills is notable. All groups have similarly strong variances in their Java skills. This variance, however, may be caused by the subjectivity of the assessment and different confidence in the own skills. We will refer to this group as the *Bremen group*.

Students of three computer science classes at the University of Alabama in the City of Tuscaloosa, formed the second population. They participated in a replication of the original experiment by Chatterji, Carver, Kraft, and Harder [32]. These students attended the experiment in the context of a class assignment and received credit points for participation (regardless of their performance in the tasks). In total 47 students participated of which one third did not meet the requirement of Eclipse knowledge. The self-assessment of Java-Skills resulted in an average of 45. We will refer to this group as the *Tuscaloosa group*.

The third group consisted of participants of the Dagstuhl Seminar 12071: *Software Clone Management Towards Industrial Application* [106], who volunteered to partake. Only experts of the field of software clones from academia and industry were invited to the seminar. The same requirements were defined for this group. Nevertheless, one perquisite that holds for the student populations does not hold for this one: Although no participant was told that the experiment was directed to clones, the experts will have expected this as they where participating in a seminar on software clones. In total, 12 people from this population participated in the experiment. The self-assessed Java skill averages at 60 for this group to which we will refer as the *Dagstuhl group*.

All subjects were randomly assigned to the groups $A$ and $B$ with no further mechanism of blocking. It has to be noted that it would have been desirable to apply blocking using the self-assessed Java skills of the participants. This, however, was not possible, because multiple sessions were carried out over a longer period of time and not all participants were known to the experimenters when the first session took place. The main focus of our experiment lies on the student groups, which are larger and lack the bias of knowing the general theme of clones. We added the Dagstuhl group to use the opportunity to learn more about how the tasks are solved by more experienced professionals and experts to the field.

Reaching statistically significant results requires a sufficient number of participants. The three distinct groups are rather small for this goal and participants are difficult to acquire. We will report the results for all groups separately but also for a joined group that consists of all participants. We chose to merge the results for all participant in this group to provide overall results. At a first glance, it may seem plausible to join only the Bremen and Tuscaloosa groups, because both consist of students, whereas the Dagstuhl group has longer programming expertise. Nevertheless, the Bremen group is closer to the Dagstuhl group in terms of their self-assessed Java skills. Furthermore, as we will see, the Dagstuhl group provides surprising results. Leaving these out of the overall results for all participants would also mean to leave out particularly interesting results. The *joined group* sums up to 80 participants with an average self-assessed Java skill of 50.

## 8.2.4   Objects

The two tasks *tFB* and *tPM* where designed to emulate real bug-fixing tasks as close and thoroughly as possible. The subjects were asked to perform all activities that belong to a bug removal, including reading the bug report, making themselves familiar with the related feature, locating the defect, applying changes to the code, and testing the outcome (in our case by executing the program). This procedure allows us to measure the time needed for the whole process of removing a bug and to accurately evaluate the correctness of the solution. If the subjects would perform only some of these activities, we were not able to measure time and correctness. If, for instance, the task would require only to locate the defect without fixing and testing the solution, participants may overlook a clone of the defect they would have recognized if they had executed the program.

The emulation of a whole maintenance task, but also the limited time of an experiment like this and the variables that are to be analyzed, lead to two essential constraints that the systems used for the tasks must meet. First, they must not be too small so that the location of the defect is non-obvious; but at the same time not too big so that the participants do not get lost in the source code. `FrozenBubble` as well as `Pacman` satisfy this constraint with 3,000 respectively 2,400 SLOC. Second, the subjects must be able to understand and reproduce the bug easily and quickly. Games with simple and intuitive mechanics are well suited for this purpose.

The tasks were designed in a way that the bug will cause wrong program behavior, but not an entire crash. Both bugs had to be easy to spot and reproduce. Another important requirement for the design of the task variants was that the bug has to provoke two visible symptoms. For the non-cloned variant these had to be correctable by fixing a single location. The cloned variant contained two occurrences of the bug of which each caused one of the visible symptoms. Only if both locations were fixed, all symptoms would disappear. That is, incomplete solutions in the cloned task variants lead to remaining symptoms. We deliberately chose rather small and localized bugs, because our pilot studies showed that the participants will require too much time to solve more complex bug scenarios.

For both tasks, real clones that already existed in the programs could be used. That is, for the cloned variant we added a defect into the existing clone fragments. The non-cloned variants were prepared by removing the clones and implementing an abstraction. The defect was then inserted into the abstraction and, thus, only appearing once. In the following we describe the two tasks in detail.

**FrozenBubble Task (*tFB*)**

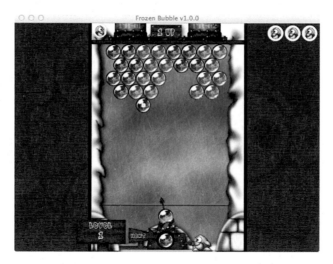

**Figure 8.1** – A screenshot of `FrozenBubble`.

The goal of the Tetris-like game `FrozenBubble` is to eliminate all colored bubbles that appear on top of the game screen. This is accomplished by subsequently shooting new bubbles from a launcher located at the bottom of the screen. A group of at least three identically colored bubbles is eliminated by a new bubble of the same color on collision. The bubble to be shot is displayed in front of the launcher and a preview of the subsequent bubble appears below it. Figure 8.1 shows a screen shot of the game.

The visual representations of the colored bubbles are stored as eight GIF image files. In the original version of the `FrozenBubble` code, their loading sequence is cloned in the classes *FrozenGame* and *LaunchBubbleSprite*. *FrozenGame* loads all bubbles except for the ones that are displayed in front of the launcher. These are loaded by almost identical code in *LaunchBubbleSprite*. The original code snippets are shown in Figure

8.2. The fragment in *LaunchBubbleSprite* is identical to the one in *FrozenGame*, with the exception that it does not contain the third array. We use pseudo code in the code listings to save space and to improve readability.

```
1 bubbles = Image[8]
2 bubblesBlind = Image[8]
3 frozenBubbles = Image[8]
4
5 for i in 0 .. 7 do
6   bubbles[i] = load("b-" + toString(i+1) + ".gif")
7   bBubbles[i] = load("bb-" + toString(i+1) + ".gif")
8   fBubbles[i] = load("fb-" + toString(i+1) + ".gif")
9 end for
```

**(a)** *FrozenGame*

```
1 bubbles = Image[8]
2 bubblesBlind = Image[8]
3
4 for i in 0 .. 7 do
5   bubbles[i] = load("b-" + toString(i+1) + ".gif")
6   bBubbles[i] = load("bb-" + toString(i+1) + ".gif")
7 end for
```

**(b)** *LaunchBubbleSprite*

**Figure 8.2** – Pseudo code of the original clone in `FrozenBubble`.

To prepare $tFB_c$, we inserted a bug in the existing clones by changing the $i + 1$ to 1 in lines 6–8 in *FrozenGame* and lines 5–6 in *LaunchBubbleSprite*. As result, only one bubble—the gray one—is loaded and, thus, only gray bubbles appear on the screen. The game uses the loaded images for both the display of the bubbles and the internal representation of the bubble color for the collision logic. Consequently, loading only the gray bubble image causes a complete elimination of all bubbles with only one single shot, because there are only gray bubbles in the game.

To prepare $tFB_{nc}$, the clone was removed. Figure 8.3 on the following page shows this variant as pseudo code. It was created by removing the code passage from *LaunchBubbleSprite*. The three bubble image arrays are loaded only by *FrozenGame* now. Two of the loaded arrays are passed to *LaunchBubbleSprite* upon its instantiation. We also removed the repeated assignments in the for loop by extracting the loading functionality to a new function. Hereby, the bug location appears only once in $tFB_{nc}$.

The following task description was prepared for the subjects. The pilot test showed that subjects may spend a long time seeking the defect in the wrong classes or fail to find the bug location altogether. Hence, we provided some hints where to look for the defect along with the task description.

*Project 1 implements a simple Tetris-like game written in Java. The implementation has a bug that is described in the following bug report. Your*

```
 1 bubbles = loadBubbles("b")
 2 bubblesBlind = loadBubbles("bb")
 3 frozenBubbles = loadBubbles("fb")
 4
 5 // ...
 6
 7 Image[] loadBubbles(String type)
 8 begin
 9   bubbles = Image[8]
10   for i in 0 .. 7 do
11     bubbles[i] = load(type + toString(1) + ".gif")
12   end for
13   return bubbles
14 end function
```

**Figure 8.3** – Pseudo code of the unified variant in FrozenBubble with the bug.

*task is to fix the described bug in the code. You may execute the program as often as you wish to analyze the problem and to verify that it has been solved. Please do not make any other changes to the code.*

**Bug Report:**
*There are eight differently colored bubbles in the game. When a level starts, only gray bubbles appear on top. The launcher at the bottom will also fire only gray bubbles. Obviously not all available bubbles are loaded.*

**Hints:**

- *The bug is located in the default package. You do not have to modify the packages lib, manager, or screens.*

- *The class BubbleSprite handles the top bubble area but does not load the bubbles itself. The constructor of the BubbleSprite class takes a BubbleManager as an argument and the BubbleManager takes the already loaded bubbles as an argument. So it may help to find out where the BubbleManager is initialized.*

## Pacman Task (*tPM*)

Pacman is the classic arcade game. The player navigates the main character Pacman through a right-angled maze and must collect all items. Up to four ghosts, controlled by the computer, also move through the maze and will kill Pacman on collision. When Pacman collects a special power-up item, he can chase the ghosts for a limited time. Figure 8.4 on the next page shows a screenshot of Pacman.

The game's implementation knows two kinds of game characters: Pacman and ghosts. Both are implemented as Java classes that extend the generic *Actor* class. Even

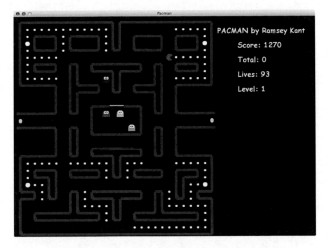

**Figure 8.4** – A screenshot of `Pacman`.

though they share a common parent class, their movement implementation is cloned in the classes *Player* (Pacman) and *Ghost*.

The game maintains two coordinates for each *Actor*. One is its position on a coarse grained and invisible grid that is used to check for actor collisions and possible movement directions (*gridX* and *gridY*). The other coordinate is the movement delta in pixels, relative to the center of the current grid cell (*deltaX* and *deltaY*). In each of its main loops, the game moves all actors some pixels in their current direction on the screen. If an actor moved enough pixels to reach the center of the next grid cell, it is assigned to this newly reached cell. Figure 8.5 on the following page shows simplified pseudo code of the movement function in the original version of *Player* without the defect. Note that the check whether a movement is possible (lines 3, 13, 23, and 33) is missing in *Ghost*. It is not needed there because ghosts move on pre-computed paths and therefore cannot collide with walls.

The defect was inserted by changing the grid movements for the directions up and left. While the actor's image still moves in the correct direction its grid position is changed in the opposite direction. When an actor reaches the next grid cell, it is assigned to the next cell in the opposite direction, to which it suddenly jumps. This causes a reversed movement in a flickering motion. It was realized by simply changing the subtractions in lines 8 and 38 to additions in Figure 8.5. By inserting this defect, we obtained the code for *tPM$_c$*.

To prepare *tPM$_{nc}$* we removed the clones. Note that there are two clone relations. The complete *switch* structure appears cloned in *Player* and *Ghost*, while each *case* block in both switches is a near-miss clone of all the other *case* blocks. We removed both clone relations by first pulling up the *switch* to the *Actor* class. We then removed the clones in the *case* statements as far as possible. The code for the actual movement on the grid was placed after the *switch* statement. The check whether movement in the current direction is possible is now a precondition to enter the movement functionality.

```
 1 switch currentDirection
 2   case up
 3     if canMoveTo(gridX, gridY - 1) then
 4       deltaX = 0
 5       deltaY = deltaY - speed
 6       if |deltaY| >= CELL_SIZE then
 7         deltaY = 0
 8         moveTo(gridX, gridY - 1)
 9       end
10     end
11     break
12   case right
13     if canMoveTo(gridX + 1, gridY) then
14       deltaX = deltaX + speed
15       deltaY = 0
16       if |deltaX| >= CELL_SIZE then
17         deltaX = 0
18         moveTo(gridX + 1, gridY)
19       end
20     end
21     break
22   case down
23     if canMoveTo(gridX, gridY + 1) then
24       deltaX = 0
25       deltaY = deltaY + speed
26       if |deltaY| >= CELL_SIZE then
27         deltaY = 0
28         moveTo(gridX, gridY + 1)
29       end
30     end
31     break
32   case left
33     if canMoveTo(gridX - 1, gridY) then
34       deltaX = deltaX - speed
35       deltaY = 0
36       if |deltaX| >= CELL_SIZE then
37         deltaX = 0
38         moveTo(gridX - 1, gridY)
39       end
40     end
41     break
42 end
```

**Figure 8.5** – Correct variant *tPM_c*, cloned in *Player* and *Ghost*

```
 1 if map.canMove(currentDirection) do
 2   switch currentDirection
 3       case up
 4           deltaX = 0
 5           deltaY -= speed
 6           break
 7       case right
 8           deltaX += speed
 9           deltaY = 0
10           break
11       case down
12           deltaX = 0
13           deltaY += speed
14           break
15       case left
16           deltaX -= speed
17           deltaY = 0
18           break
19       case none
20           deltaX = 0
21           deltaY = 0
22   end
23
24   if max(|deltaX|, |deltaY|) >= CELL_SIZE then
25       newX = gridX
26       newY = gridY
27
28       if (deltaX > 0) then
29           newX = newX + 1
30       elif (deltaX < 0) then
31           newX = newX - 1
32       elif (deltaY > 0) then
33           newY = newY + 1
34       elif (deltaY < 0) then
35           newY = newY - 1
36       end
37
38       deltaX = 0
39       deltaY = 0
40       moveTo(newX, newY)
41   end
42 end
```

**Figure 8.6** – Correct variant $tPM_{nc}$, only in *Actor*

The code without the defect is shown in Figure 8.6. In this task we added the defect by changing the subtractions in lines 31 and 35 to additions. The following task description was prepared for the subjects. We included some hints to guide the participants to the right places.

> *Project 2 implements a simple Pacman game written in Java. The implementation has a bug that is described in the following bug report. Your task is to fix the described bug in the code. You may execute the program as often as you wish to analyze the problem and to verify, that it has been solved. Please do not make any other changes to the code.*

> *Bug Report:*
> *For all game characters, the movement up and left does not work correctly. Instead of moving up or left the characters move in the opposite direction in a flickering motion. Moving down and right works fine for all characters.*

> *Hints:*
>
> - *To solve the problem, it is important to know how the movement works. The game has an underlying map grid, which is used to decide in which direction a character can currently move and to check whether two characters are at the same position. The cells are the same size as the characters and each character is assigned to one cell in the grid at a time. On every move, the characters move some pixels in one direction on the screen. When they have moved enough pixels to reach the next map cell, they will be assigned to that new cell.*
>
> - *The bug is located in the package 'pacman.actors', you should only search for it there.*

### 8.2.5 Instrumentation

We chose an entirely automated approach to data collection. This allowed us to run sessions with many participants at once and prevents observation bias. It also ensures that each participant was presented exactly the same information. Errors in measurement, as they may occur when the data is collected manually, are avoided. Once the working environment is set up, the participants can act autonomously by following automated instructions. All recordings, such as time measurements were made automatically in the background.

These functions were implemented in a custom plug-in for the Eclipse IDE that has been used in a previous experiment by Quante [144]. After the IDE is started, the plug-in displays step-by-step text information that guides the participant through the experiment. Whenever the participant finishes a step, the next step can be accessed by clicking a *next* button.

Information required from the participant are gathered through automated surveys that appear in pre-configured steps of the experiment. All data entered in the forms are saved automatically to be collected later. The plug-in also allows the participant to start a bug-free version of the games in pre-configured steps. Each time the participant advances to the next step, the current time is recorded in the background. We use these data to measure the time needed for each task.

Further data are collected, but were not used for analysis. One of the additional measurements is the tracking of specific actions within the IDE, such as switching between files, saving files, typing in the code, running the program, or using the debugger. This information, however, proved to be fragmentary because the used Eclipse mechanism records in different detail depending on the machine. The other information we acquired, but did not use, is the assessment of the perceived workload using the *NASA Task Load Index* (TLX) [69]. It was designed to assess the perceived workload of pilots on six scales when using different cockpit layouts. The answers to the TLX scheme showed such high deviation that no meaningful information could be extracted. TLX has previously been used in another software engineering experiment [1].

## 8.3   Execution

The experiment had to be executed several times with different subjects because it was not possible to bring all participants together at one time and place. Hence, a repeatable work flow that ensured identical conditions for all participants was defined. It was executed with small groups of participants as well as in individual appointments. In the following, we describe this work flow that consists of four phases: introduction, installation, execution, and data collection.

### Introduction

First, the participants were given an introduction containing the experiment schedule, information on how to use the materials, short videos of the two games (without the bugs), and some organizational details. No information on software clones was provided in any way—the subjects were not informed that the experiment focused on clones. The introduction was given as a slide presentation along with a previously scripted talk. The participants were assigned to the groups by alternating between $A$ and $B$ in the seating order.[5]

### Installation

All participants received a prepared copy of the Eclipse IDE as well as an Eclipse workspace containing the two tasks for their respective group. Furthermore, a handout with instructions was provided.

### Execution

The participants were instructed to use the provided Eclipse IDE. This included the aforementioned plug-in. No time limit was defined for the execution of each task. Time

---

[5]The participants were free to choose a seat at the beginning of the session.

limits bare the risk that subjects fail to complete a task, although they would have accomplished it after more time. In such a case neither the timing, nor the correctness can be compared to those subjects who succeeded within the time limit. In our pilot studies, this turned out to be a major mortality threat we had to obviate because of the limited number of subjects available. Nevertheless, subjects were allowed to give up.

Before each task, the subjects were allowed to play each game in its original and bug-free version for three minutes at most. After this familiarization phase, the task itself started with the presentation of the bug report. The subjects were allowed—and encouraged—to execute the program at any time to inspect the bug and the effect of their changes to the code. No restrictions were made on the use of the debugger or other standard Eclipse features. Nevertheless, we forbade the use of any other tools or commands outside the Eclipse environment, which would have invalidated our measurements.

## Data Collection

Finally, the workspaces with all sources and recordings were collected from each participant.

## 8.4   Analysis

The data for the four subject groups will be analyzed separately, because they meet the experiments requirements to different extent and we must assume significant differences in their skills. Consequently, we will report our results on four levels: First, for the Bremen group only, second, for the Tuscaloosa group only, third, for the Dagstuhl group only and, forth, for all three groups combined. We excluded the results from some participants who gave up on both tasks they were given. Such aborted tasks where the subjects specified that they failed to find a solution cannot be compared to finished tasks regarding time and correctness in a meaningful way. We also excluded data from the evaluation when the solution was not *addressed*, that is, the participant failed completely to solve the task. Timing information for such tasks is useless because the participant did not actually show the behavior we want to measure. For the correctness evaluation it is not of our interest when a participant did not find any solution, because no relation to the independent variable exists.[6] In total we excluded one participant from the Bremen group and 17 participants from the Tuscaloosa group. The higher drop-out rate for the Tuscaloosa group may be caused by the fact that all members of a software engineering class were assigned to the tasks—even those who do not meet the requirements of Java and Eclipse knowledge. These had to be excluded. The participants of the other groups volunteered.

---

[6]The replication by Chatterji and colleagues did not exclude non-*addressed* solutions from the time analysis [32]. We excluded these in our revised evaluation. Although our results differ slightly we come to the same overall conclusions as Chatterji and colleagues.

## 8.4.1   Descriptive Statistics

To pursue research Question C1, we analyze the recorded times statistically. To pursue research question Question C2 on page 141, we manually inspected the results of each subject. To assess completeness, the programs were executed to test whether the bug was removed. Furthermore, the changes applied by the subjects were inspected using the Unix *diff* tool. The results will be presented in the following.

### Bremen Group

Table Table 8.4 on the following page shows the average time needed by the Bremen group to solve the tasks. Figure Figure 8.7 on the next page visualizes the distribution of the timing data using box plots. The box represents the data between the lower and upper quartiles. That is, it represents the middle 50% of the data. The dashed lines— the whiskers— indicate how far all data points spread. Outliers are shown as small circles. The median value is represented by a vertical bar, whereas the arithmetic mean is denoted by the $*$ symbol.

In all cases, the students from Bremen were faster on average when the bug was not cloned. This difference is most distinctive for *tFB*, where the group with the clone needed nearly twice as much time on average. The average time for $tFB_{nc}$ and $tFB_c$ differs by 803 seconds—more than 13 minutes. The respective box-and-whisker plots in Figure Figure 8.7a on the following page indicate that the difference in the mean is not caused by outliers, but rather by a shift of the distributions.

The difference in the time measures is much smaller when *incomplete* solutions are excluded from the analysis. Correcting the cloned bug took only 122 seconds—about two minutes—longer on average than fixing the non-cloned bug. That is, the time difference we measured among all subjects is mainly caused by those subjects who failed to provide a *complete* solution. Among the subjects with *complete* solutions, the cloning of the bug had smaller effect on the time measured. In relative proportions, the clone increased the average time by 98.9% for the *addressed* solutions, but only by 15.0% for the subjects with *complete* solutions.

For the *tPM* tasks, the students likewise required more time to finish the task when the bug was cloned. The time difference for these tasks is less distinctive than for *tFB*. The average time required for the *addressed* solutions differs by 230 seconds, which is an increase by 46.9% from the non-cloned to the cloned variant. When *incomplete* solutions are excluded, the difference raises to 352 seconds, which is an increase by 71.8%. Figure 8.7b on the next page shows that these figures are influenced by an outlier. When the outlier is removed, the difference shrinks to merely 15 seconds (3.0%) for the subjects with *addressed* solutions and 50 seconds (10.2%) for subjects with *complete* solutions. Figure 8.7b on the following page also shows that, although the averages differ, no clear shift in the distributions is visible. The deviation is much larger for the non-cloned task variants.

Table 8.5 on the next page shows the correctness of the solutions in the Bremen group. All participants succeeded in finding and fixing at least one of the bug locations. That is, all solutions *addressed* the problem. Nevertheless, when the bug was cloned several subjects failed to fix both occurrences. In *tFB*, less than half of the subjects

|  | $tFB_c$ | | $tFB_{nc}$ | p-value | $tPM_c$ | | $tPM_{nc}$ | p-value |
|---|---|---|---|---|---|---|---|---|
| addressed | 1,615 | > | 812 | **0.0079** | 720 | > | 490 | 0.1747 |
| complete | 934 | > | 812 | 0.2198 | 842 | > | 490 | 0.0754 |

**Table 8.4** – Bremen group: Average solution times for each task in seconds and p-values according to Mann-Whitney U-Test.

| Solutions | $tFB_c$ | | $tFB_{nc}$ | | $tPM_c$ | | $tPM_{nc}$ | |
|---|---|---|---|---|---|---|---|---|
| Addressed | 11 | (100.0 %) | 10 | (100.0 %) | 10 | (100.0 %) | 11 | (100.0 %) |
| Complete | 5 | (45.5 %) | 10 | (100.0 %) | 7 | (70.0 %) | 11 | (100.0 %) |
| Incomplete | 6 | (54.5 %) | 0 | (0.0 %) | 3 | (30.0 %) | 0 | (0.0 %) |
| p-value | **0.0038** | | | | **0.0375** | | | |

**Table 8.5** – Bremen group: Correctness of the addressed solutions in absolute numbers and percent. The p-values are given for Barnard's test.

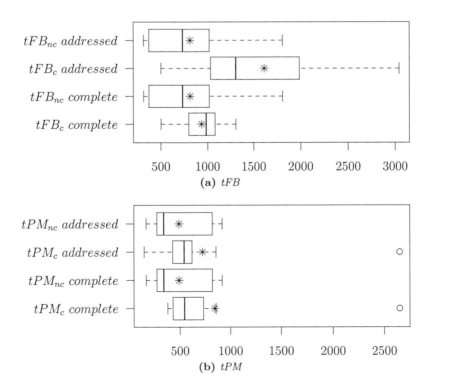

**Figure 8.7** – Bremen group: Distribution of solution times in seconds as box plot

| | $tFB_c$ | | $tFB_{nc}$ | p-value | $tPM_c$ | | $tPM_{nc}$ | p-value |
|---|---|---|---|---|---|---|---|---|
| addressed | 1222 | > | 817 | **0.0234** | 523 | > | 494 | 0.1826 |
| complete | 1223 | > | 817 | 0.0576 | 484 | < | 494 | 0.2588 |

**Table 8.6** – Tuscaloosa group: average solution times for each task in seconds and p-values according to Mann-Whitney U-Test.

| Solutions | $tFB_c$ | | $tFB_{no}$ | | $tPM_c$ | | $tPM_{nc}$ | |
|---|---|---|---|---|---|---|---|---|
| Addressed | 15 | (100.0 %) | 12 | (100.0 %) | 16 | (100.0 %) | 18 | (100.0 %) |
| Complete | 8 | (53.3 %) | 12 | (100.0 %) | 12 | (75.0 %) | 18 | (100.0 %) |
| Incomplete | 7 | (46.7 %) | 0 | (0.0 %) | 4 | (25.0 %) | 0 | (0.0 %) |
| p-value | **0.0054** | | | | **0.0497** | | | |

**Table 8.7** – Tuscaloosa group: Correctness of the addressed solutions in absolute numbers and percent. The p-values are given for Barnard's test.

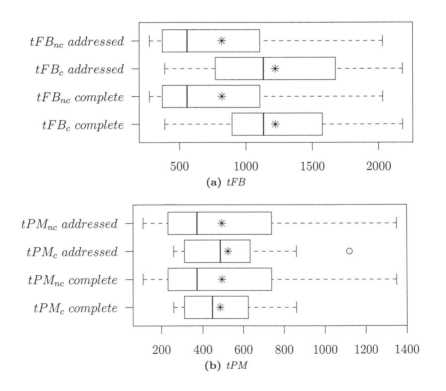

**(a)** $tFB$

**(b)** $tPM$

**Figure 8.8** – Tuscaloosa group: Distribution of solution times in seconds as box plot

who were presented the cloned variant fixed both bug occurrences. For *tPM* nearly one third handed in *incomplete* solutions. All partial solutions have in common that either the bug in *LaunchBubbleSprite* for *tFB* or the bug in *Ghost* for *tPM* was overlooked.

The results for the Bremen group can be summarized as follows. In both tasks the subjects required more time to fix the bug when it was cloned. If the bug was cloned, the required time increased between 3% and 98%. While all subjects succeeded in finding and fixing one occurrence of the bug, 30% to 54% failed to fix both occurrences when the bug was cloned.

## Tuscaloosa Group

The results for the students from Alabama are presented in Table 8.6 on the preceding page. Both the *addressed* and *complete* solutions for *tFB$_c$* required about 400 seconds more time than the non-cloned variant—an additional six minutes and 40 seconds or an increase of nearly 50%. For *tPM* the difference is comparatively low. The *addressed* solutions were prolonged by only 29 seconds by the clone, which is an increase by 5.9%. For the *complete* solutions the cloned variant was fixed faster than the non-cloned variant, but only by 10 seconds, which is a decrease by 2.0%. The box plots in Figure 8.8 on the previous page show that this result does only hold for the average values. If the medians are compared, *tPM* was solved faster when the bug was not cloned.

The correctness of the solutions is shown in Table 8.7 on the preceding page. Other than in the Bremen group about one third of the participants failed to solve the tasks completely. The other two thirds of the participants provided *addressed* but often *incomplete* solutions. For *tFB* only 53.3% of the *addressed* solutions are *complete*. For *tPM* 75.0% of the *addressed* solutions are *complete*. All but one subject with *incomplete* solutions missed the bug occurrence in *LaunchBubbleSprite* in *tFB*. In *tPM* all *incomplete* solutions overlooked the bug occurrence in *Ghost*.

In summary the results for the Tuscaloosa group show that the non-cloned bugs were fixed notably faster on average for *tFB*. For the *tPM* tasks the clone caused only minimal differences. The *complete* solutions with the clone were fixed slightly faster. If the bug was cloned 25.0% to 46.7% of the solutions were *incomplete*.

## Dagstuhl Group

The Dagstuhl group yields results that differ from those of the two other groups as can be seen in Table 8.8 on page 160. These participants fixed the cloned bug in *tFB* faster than the non-cloned bug. Both *addressed* and *complete* solutions were created in about 760 seconds less time when the bug was cloned. This is twelve minutes and 40 second less or an decrease by almost 60%.

The opposite is the case for the *tPM* tasks where the clone increased the required average time by 65.0% for the *addressed* solutions and by 62.4% for the *complete* ones. This is 330 or 317 seconds more, respectively—roughly five and a half minutes. Figure 8.9 on page 160 shows that the *tPM$_{nc}$* is heavily effected by an outlier. If it is removed from the data the non-cloned variant is fixed up to 524 seconds slower, which corresponds to

8 minutes and 44 seconds or an time increase by 66.9%. Nevertheless, results obtained by removing outliers from a set of only six data points should certainly not be overrated.

Table 8.9 on the next page shows the correctness for the Dagstuhl group. Surprisingly, some of these subjects also failed to fix both occurrences of the cloned bug. Among the *addressed* solutions for *tFB*, one was *incomplete*, which corresponds to 20% of all *addressed* solutions. For *tPM* one of the experts fixed only one occurrence of the bug, which makes 17.7% of the *addressed* solutions *incomplete*. Like in the student groups, all *incomplete* solutions missed the occurrence in *LaunchBubbleSprite* for *tFB* or *Ghost* for *tPM*.

To summarize, the Dagstuhl group solved the bug in *tFB* notably faster when it was cloned, but also needed notably more time to fix the cloned bug in *tPM*. All but one subject succeeded in fixing at least one bug occurrence. One bug occurrence was overlooked by 17.7% to 20.0% of the subjects when the bug was cloned.

## Joined Group

The results for the previous three groups are diverse. One reason could be that the populations are affected by the clone in different ways. It could also be the case that the groups have too few subjects to provide reliable results. Consequently, we also report the results for all participants in one joined group.

For the joined group the average required time is always higher when the bug is cloned. The *addressed* solutions for *tFB* required 334 additional seconds on average, which roughly corresponds to 5 and a half minutes or an increase by 36.5%. The time difference is much smaller with 32 seconds when only the *complete* solutions are regarded. With an increase by only 3.5% the difference is negligible. As can be seen from Figure 8.10a on page 161 one outlier affects the average for *tFB$_c$ complete*. If it is removed the average value drops from 914 to 874 seconds, which is faster than the solution time for the non-cloned bug. If the medians are compared, the non-cloned variant was still fixed faster.

For *tPM* the clone caused an additional time of 149 seconds for the *addressed* solutions and 165 seconds for the *complete* ones—roughly 2 and a half minutes. This is an increase of 30.1% or 33.3%. Again, some outliers affect the average for *tPM$_c$* as shown in Figure 8.10b on page 161. Removing the outliers from the data has only minor effect on the results, as the average time decreases from 495 to 485 seconds.

Table 8.11 on page 161 shows the correctness for the joined group. With 45.2% a large number of the participants with *addressed* solutions fixed only one occurrence of the cloned bug. For *tPM* one quarter of the solutions for the task with the cloned bug were *incomplete*.

The combined results for all participants can be summarized as follows. On average the non-cloned task variants were fixed in less time. The clone increased the required time between 3.5% and 36.5%. Among the *addressed* solutions 25.0% to 45.2% were *incomplete*.

|            | $tFB_c$ |     | $tFB_{nc}$ | p-value | $tPM_c$ |     | $tPM_{nc}$ | p-value |
|------------|---------|-----|-----------|---------|---------|-----|-----------|---------|
| addressed  | 517     | <   | 1,276     | 0.9848  | 838     | >   | 508       | 0.1201  |
| complete   | 516     | <   | 1,276     | 0.9848  | 825     | >   | 508       | 0.1645  |

**Table 8.8** – Dagstuhl group: average solution times for each task in seconds and p-values according to Mann-Whitney U-Test.

| Solutions  | $tFB_c$ |            | $tFB_{nc}$ |            | $tPM_c$ |            | $tPM_{nc}$ |            |
|------------|---------|------------|-----------|------------|---------|------------|-----------|------------|
| Addressed  | 5       | (100.0 %)  | 6         | (100.0 %)  | 6       | (100.0 %)  | 6         | (100.0 %)  |
| Complete   | 4       | (80.0 %)   | 6         | (100.0 %)  | 5       | (83.3 %)   | 6         | (100.0 %)  |
| Incomplete | 1       | (20.0 %)   | 0         | (0.0 %)    | 1       | (17.7 %)   | 0         | (0.0 %)    |
| p-value    |         | 0.0985     |           |            |         | 0.2590     |           |            |

**Table 8.9** – Dagstuhl group: Correctness of the addressed solutions in absolute numbers and percent. The p-values are given for Barnard's test.

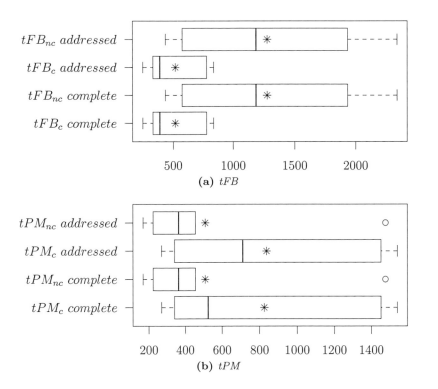

**Figure 8.9** – Dagstuhl group: Distribution of solution times in seconds as box plot

| | $tFB_c$ | | $tFB_{nc}$ | p-value | $tPM_c$ | | $tPM_{nc}$ | p-value |
|---|---|---|---|---|---|---|---|---|
| addressed | 1248 | > | 914 | **0.0253** | 644 | > | 495 | **0.0303** |
| complete | 946 | > | 914 | 0.2848 | 660 | > | 495 | **0.0361** |

**Table 8.10** – Joined group: average solution times for each task in seconds and p-values according to Mann-Whitney U-Test.

| Solutions | $tFB_c$ | | $tFB_{nc}$ | | $tPM_c$ | | $tPM_{nc}$ | |
|---|---|---|---|---|---|---|---|---|
| Addressed | 31 | (100.0 %) | 28 | (100.0 %) | 32 | (100.0 %) | 35 | (100.0 %) |
| Complete | 17 | (54.8 %) | 28 | (100.0 %) | 24 | (75.0 %) | 35 | (100.0 %) |
| Incomplete | 14 | (45.2 %) | 0 | (0.0 %) | 8 | (25.0 %) | 0 | (0.0 %) |
| p-value | **0.0052** | | | | **0.0002** | | | |

**Table 8.11** – Joined group: Correctness of the addressed solutions in absolute numbers and percent. The p-values are given for Barnard's test.

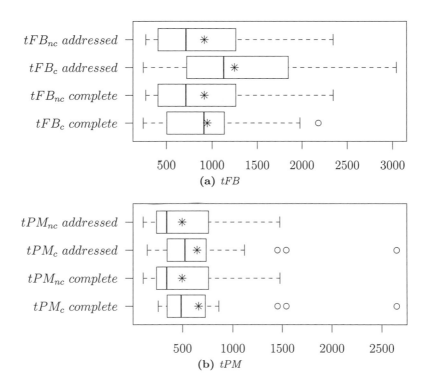

(a) $tFB$

(b) $tPM$

**Figure 8.10** – Joined group: Distribution of solution times in seconds as box plot

## Summary

The different groups provided different results, which we summarize in this section. Table 8.12 shows how much the average solution time was increased by the clone for the different groups. The strength of the effect differs. While the increase is strong in Bremen, it is less in Tuscaloosa, especially for *tPM*. In Dagstuhl the effect for *tFB* is turned around—fixing the clone went faster than fixing the non-cloned variant. Nevertheless, for *tPM* the prolonging effect of the clone is rather strong. For all groups joined we observed an increase of 3.5% to 36.5%.

| Group | *tFB* addressed | complete | *tPM* addressed | complete |
|---|---|---|---|---|
| Bremen | +98.9% | +15.0% | +46.9% | +71.8% |
| Tuscaloosa | +49.6% | +49.7% | +5.9% | -2.0% |
| Dagstuhl | -59.5% | -59.6% | +65.0% | +62.4% |
| Joined | +36.5% | +3.5% | +30.1% | +33.3% |

**Table 8.12** – Relative increase of the required time for a task when the bug is cloned in percent.

Table 8.13 shows the time increase through the clone in seconds. For the joined group the absolute increase ranges between 32 and 334 seconds. That is, fixing the cloned bug took up to five minutes and 34 seconds longer.

| Group | *tFB* addressed | complete | *tPM* addressed | complete |
|---|---|---|---|---|
| Bremen | +803 | +122 | +230 | +352 |
| Tuscaloosa | +405 | +406 | +29 | -10 |
| Dagstuhl | -759 | -760 | +330 | +317 |
| Joined | +334 | +32 | +149 | +165 |

**Table 8.13** – Absolute increase of the required time for a task when the bug is cloned in seconds.

Finally, Table 8.15 on the next page summarizes the effect of the clone on the correctness of the solutions. It shows the percentage of incomplete solutions. In FrozenBubble the participants had more problems fixing the cloned variant than in Pacman. The group that performed best still provided 17.7% incomplete solutions, the worst result is 54.5%.

Finally, Table 8.14 on the facing page shows the effect size using Rosenthal's estimation $r$ [150]. By convention 0.1 is regarded as a small effect, 0.3 as a medium effect and 0.5 as a large effect [48]. The effect size measure estimates whether the size of the difference is large compared to the size of the observations. All effect sizes we measured lie above the 0.5 threshold for a large effect, except two cases: First, for the complete solutions for *tPM* in the Tuscaloosa group the effect is medium to large. Second the effect for the complete solutions to *tFB* in the joined group is also in the medium to large region.

| Group | $tFB$ | | $tPM$ | |
|---|---|---|---|---|
| | addressed | complete | addressed | complete |
| Bremen | 1.705 | 0.5465 | 0.6617 | 1.0157 |
| Tuscaloosa | 1.405 | 1.1137 | 0.6402 | 0.4575 |
| Dagstuhl | 1.532 | 1.5317 | 0.8304 | 0.6902 |
| Joined | 1.382 | 0.4020 | 1.3270 | 1.2711 |

**Table 8.14** – Estimated effect size $r$ according to Rosenthal [150].

| Group | $tFB_c$ | $tPM_c$ |
|---|---|---|
| Bremen | 54.5 % | 30.0 % |
| Tuscaloosa | 46.7 % | 25.0 % |
| Dagstuhl | 20.0 % | 17.7 % |
| Joined | 45.2 % | 25.0 % |

**Table 8.15** – Relative amount of *incorrect* solutions for the cloned tasks for all groups.

## 8.4.2   Hypothesis Testing

To support $H_1^{time}$, the null hypothesis $H_0^{time}$ has to be rejected. We use the non-parametric Mann-Whitney U-test for independent samples on the time data. The alternative hypothesis $H_1^{time}$ postulates that the time needed to correct the cloned variants is larger, which makes it a 1-tailed hypothesis. Hence, we use the 1-tailed variant of the statistical test. The results were already shown in Tables 8.4, 8.6, 8.8, and 8.10. Table 8.16 summarizes these values for a better overview. Values below the commonly used threshold for statistical significance $p < 0.05$ are printed bold.

| Population | addressed | | complete | |
|---|---|---|---|---|
| | $tFB$ | $tPM$ | $tFB$ | $tPM$ |
| Bremen | **0.0079** | 0.1747 | 0.2198 | 0.0754 |
| Tuscaloosa | **0.0234** | 0.1826 | 0.0576 | 0.2588 |
| Dagstuhl | 0.9848 | 0.1201 | 0.9848 | 0.1645 |
| Joined | **0.0253** | **0.0303** | 0.2848 | **0.0361** |

**Table 8.16** – Mann-Whitney U-test for times (p-values)

For the Bremen, Tuscaloosa and Dagstuhl groups, statistical significance is not reached. The measured times for the *addressed* solutions to *tFB* in Bremen and Tuscaloosa are the only ones with a significant difference. For the three separated groups $H_0^{time}$ cannot be rejected. For the joined group, however, significance is reached for all differences with the exception of the *complete* solutions to *tFB*. Here the measured time difference is very small, which is probably the reason. In summary we can reject $H_0^{time}$ and, hence, formally support $H_1^{time}$ for the *addressed* solutions for the joined group, but not for the *complete* ones.

To support $H_1^{corr}$, the null hypothesis $H_0^{corr}$ must be rejected. Testing the hypothesis requires a different statistical test, because the data is represented as $2 \times 2$ contingency tables. Table 8.17 shows an exemplary table for the results the Dagstuhl group provided for $tPM$.

| Outcome | Treatment non-cloned | cloned | Combined Response |
|---------|:---:|:---:|:---:|
| Complete | 6 | 5 | 11 |
| Incomplete | 0 | 1 | 1 |
| Totals | 6 | 6 | 12 |

**Table 8.17** – $2 \times 2$ contingency table on the correctness for the Dagstuhl group and task $tPM$.

Since more than 20% of the cells in the table may contain values $< 5$ the commonly used chi-squared test may be inaccurate. Consequently, we use the exact, but more conservative, tests from Fisher [49] and Barnard [16], which can deal with small sample sizes as ours. While Fisher's test is more popular, Barnard's test is said to have greater power when the cell values are small [130]. Since some of our tables contain very small values (such as the Dagstuhl group), others contain values where Fisher's test may be more accurate (such as the joined group). Consequently, we will present the results for both tests. $H_1^{corr}$ is a 1-tailed hypothesis, so the respective variants of the two tests are used. Table 8.18 shows the results.[7]

| Population | Fisher (1-tailed) $tFB$ | $tPM$ | Barnard (1-tailed) $tFB$ | $tPM$ |
|-----------|:---:|:---:|:---:|:---:|
| Bremen | **0.0085** | 0.0902 | **0.0038** | **0.0375** |
| Tuscaloosa | **0.0072** | **0.0392** | **0.0054** | **0.0479** |
| Dagstuhl | 0.2273 | 0.5000 | 0.0985 | 0.2590 |
| Joined | **< 0.0001** | **0.0016** | **0.0052** | **0.0002** |

**Table 8.18** – Statistical significance of correctness evaluation (p-values)

According to Barnard's test the difference in correctness is statistically significant for the Bremen, Tuscaloosa, and joined groups, but not for the Dagstuhl group, which is the smallest group. Fisher's test does not establish significance for $tPM$ in the Bremen group, which may be caused by the small number of observations. For the larger Tuscaloosa and joined groups it also establishes significance for $tPM$.

This means that $H_0^{corr}$ is rejected for the Tuscaloosa and joined groups. According to Barnard also for the Bremen group. For these groups $H_1^{corr}$ is supported, which means that we can indeed assume that the cloned bug caused more incorrect answers.

---

[7]In the original paper [68] we incorrectly reported higher p-values for Barnard's test because the contingency tables were accidentally turned when passed to the statistics tool R. This has been corrected in this publication. The corrected computation causes lower p-values.

## 8.5  Interpretation & Discussion

So far we have reported the results from a statistical perspective. In this section we will discuss how these results can be interpreted in the context of our research questions.

### 8.5.1  Time

Our results for Research Question C1 show a tendency towards our hypothesis $H_1^{time}$. In many cases we observed that fixing the cloned task variant required more time. Altogether, the results do not suffice to entirely support $H_1^{time}$, because some results are not statistically significant. Nevertheless, a tendency that clones increase the time to fix a bug is visible.

The size of the effect is an important aspect of Research question C1. Besides the 59.5% decrease in time for the Dagstuhl group we have measured an increase of up to 98.9% when the bug is cloned. As Table 8.14 on page 163 shows, the effect differs among the groups, but is at least of medium size. When all groups are joined we find the clone to either increase the required time by 3.5% for *tFB complete*, which is still a medium to large effect according the statistics, or make a difference between 30.1% and 36.5%, which is a large effect according to the test statistics. Higher time demand causes additional costs. Nevertheless, the absolute difference in minutes does not exceed 5 minutes and 34 seconds for the joined group. In general such extra effort should be avoided. Nevertheless, such a difference should only matter in maintenance if cloned bugs occur often. Our results only illustrate what happens if a cloned bug needs to be changed. They must be seen in the context of the frequency in which such changes actually take place. Consequently, it would be premature to conclude that clones need to be removed or counteracted because of the effects we measured.

Our results do not tell which part of the maintenance task is prolonged by the clone. The additional effort may lie in the program comprehension, bug fixing, or testing phases. We have to assume that this depends highly on the task, the source code, the type of cloning, and the strategy the developer uses.

The reason why the professionals in the Dagstuhl group performed faster with the cloned variant of *tFB* is not clear. We cannot assume that this group is more effective in changing clones in general, because in the other task *tPM* it was faster fixing the non-cloned variant. We found no difference in the tasks that would explain why the group was more effective fixing the cloned bug in *tFB*. Both tasks have in common that the clones are located in different classes. Clone information was provided in neither of the two tasks. Explanations for the differing results could be the small size of the Dagstuhl group with twelve participants and the uneven distribution of Java skills between the subgroups *A* and *B*. *A* self-assessed their Java skills with an average of 54.2, whereas *B* averages at 66.0—a difference of 11.8 points. This difference is only 1.2 for the Bremen group and 5.04 for the Tuscaloosa group. Another difference between the groups is their prior knowledge of clones and the expectation that the experiment is directed to clones in some way. Nevertheless, it seems unlikely that the measured difference is caused by the fact that the Dagstuhl group may have been looking for a clone in $tFB_{nc}$, which was presented as the first task. If that was the case, the other group, which was presented with $tPM_{nc}$ as their second task, would have had the same problem, which they did not.

An unexpected finding is the reason behind the time difference for $tFB$ among the Bremen group. The higher time consumption of the participants with the cloned variant seems not to be caused by the additional effort needed to find and fix the clone. The subjects who required most time were also the ones who failed in fixing the cloned bug. All six subjects with incomplete solutions are among the group of the seven subjects with the highest time measures. Logs of the Eclipse usage of these subjects reveal a high rate of focus switches between files. Often files that are unrelated to the bug were visited. The logs further indicate that these subjects struggled to find the first bug occurrence and did not search for the other occurrence after the first was fixed.

We tried to use the logs that report the Eclipse usage to further investigate the reasons for the differences in the time measurement. We also asked every participant to write down his bug-fixing strategy in his own words after each task. Both information sources did not reveal recurring patterns, but rather completely different strategies with different usage of search and debugging functionality.

Apart from the fact that our results do not allow to entirely support $H_1^{time}$, the results indicate that cloned bugs cause a medium to large increase of time needed to fix a bug. A relevance for maintenance costs, however, should only be assumed when such situations occur often.

## 8.5.2 Correctness

A surprisingly large number of subjects failed to fix the bug completely if it was cloned. As Table 8.15 on page 163 shows that with 45.2% almost half of the participants who found one bug occurrence in $tFB_c$ overlooked the other one. Most of these subjects, however, believed that they were successful. For $tPM$ the rate of incomplete solutions is lower, but a 25.0% chance of an incomplete bug fix should also not be acceptable in practice. The results of our hypothesis testing in Section 8.4.2 shows that these observations are not coincidental. We can assume that cloned bugs indeed pose a high risk of incomplete fixes.

We expect incomplete bug fixes to have a notable effect on maintenance costs, because—depending on the processes in an organization—it may be necessary to repeat the whole bug-fixing process when the incomplete fix is revealed. Incomplete changes may also cause damage when the still defective software is deployed to its production environment.

Even among the professionals in the Dagstuhl group, we observed single cases where the clone was not fixed. This is surprising because these subjects participated in the context of a seminar that was dedicated solely to code clones, so that they should have expected clones. Nevertheless, the Dagstuhl group failed less often to fix both occurrences of the cloned bug than the others. This can be seen as an indication that awareness of cloning risks could help to avoid such mistakes.

The main reason for the incomplete bug-fixes seems to be insufficient testing of the solution. Both tasks were designed in a way that incomplete changes lead to misbehavior that should be striking to the subjects. In `FrozenBubble`, an incomplete fix will make it practically impossible to complete a level because the player cannot see which bubble she will shoot next. Figure 8.11 shows such an incomplete fix. While the bubbles on the top appear in the correct colors, the bubble on the launcher is always displayed in gray. When a new bubble is shot from the launcher it will appear in its actual color. In this situation the player will not be able to decide in which direction the bubble should be played. The colored bubble on the bottom serves as a preview for the bubble after the next bubble that lies on the launcher.

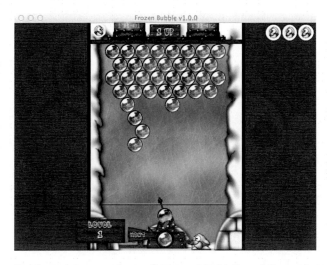

**Figure 8.11** – A screenshot of `FrozenBubble` with an incomplete solution. The bubble at the launcher appears gray, but will be colored when shot.

In `Pacman`, the ghosts will get stuck quickly in the game and quiver without moving around. Conversations with participants revealed that some of them actually believed that they fixed the bug as soon as they noticed that some of the behavior changed. One subject even stated in his strategy description that he or she did not run the game after one fix was applied, because the fix seemed to be obviously right. Indeed, all but one of the incomplete fixes changed only the more apparent bug symptom—the colors of the bubbles on the top of `FrozenBubble` or the movement of `Pacman`. One participant from Tuscaloosa fixed the launcher in `FrozenBubble`, but not the Bubbles at the top.

While the clones in our experiment had only two fragments, real clones may have more. For such clones, the chance of complete bug fixes should be even lower than in our experiment. Furthermore, we use bug removals as exemplary maintenance tasks in our study. In such tasks, the system will remain defective if the developer fails to change all redundant occurrences of the bug. But maintenance tasks may also be of adaptive or perfective nature. When such changes affect cloned code and are carried out in only some but not all clone fragments, inconsistent behavior and new bugs may be the consequence. Our experiment shows that clones can be easily overlooked, even when hints about the different locations are given. Such hints may be missing in many real maintenance tasks, which would further raise the risk of inconsistent changes. The tasks in our experiment are rather simple and easy to fix. In more complex scenarios the risk for inconsistent changes may be even higher.

Chatterji and colleagues have extended our experiment to pursue the question whether clone information helps to reduce the risk of incomplete solutions [32]. They have shown that the rate of incomplete solutions is reduced significantly when a clone report is available and the participants were trained to use it. The overall rate of complete solutions improved from 59% to 83%. While this is a better result, a 17% probability of incomplete solutions still remains. Bazrafshan and Koschke further investigated whether clone information helps to avoid clone related problems in a study based on ours [21]. They found that developers perform faster in the tasks when clone information is provided. Their results also indicate that proper testing helps to avoid bugs.

## 8.6   Threats to Validity

Controlled experiments are subject to various threats to validity. In this section, we describe how we mitigate common threats and which threats may affect the results.

### 8.6.1   Internal validity

The following influencing factors may have an effect on the internal validity of our experiment.

**Selection**

The subjects from Bremen and Dagstuhl volunteered to participate in the experiment. In Tuscaloosa all students of three classes participated in the context of their computer science classes. The participants were assigned to groups $A$ and $B$ using simple randomized sampling. Due to organizational constraints, no blocking could be applied. Because of the low number of participants, the subjects may be unequally distributed over the groups according to their skills. As we already mentioned in Section 8.4, this could be the case especially for the expert groups.

To rule out that existing knowledge on specific libraries affects the results, we designed the tasks in a way that no knowledge beyond the standard Java Class Library was required. Nevertheless subjects that are familiar with the concepts of game programming (such as sprites) may have a small advantage over participants that have only little knowledge of game programming.

Our subjects were drawn from two different populations. The groups differ in their academic and professional backgrounds. We report the results for each group and the joined results separately to exhibit possible differences between the groups. The subjects from the Dagstuhl population must be regarded as a special group because they participated in the context of a cloning seminar. No group was informed that clones were the independent variable, but the Dagstuhl group certainly expected that the experiment was related to clones somehow.

## Maturation

During the experiment subjects learn details about the software they are working on. To rule out learning effects on the systems, we used another system for each task. The groups $A$ and $B$ differ in the order in which they were presented the cloned and the non-cloned variant. This order could possibly cause different expectations for the second task presented. Participants who were presented with a cloned task first may look for clones in the second and vice versa. The possible effects would be that the cloned bug in $tPM_c$ was overlooked because the first task had no clone and that solving $tPM_{nc}$ took longer because the first task contained a clone and the participants may have looked for one. We found, however, that $tPM_c$ had less incorrect solutions than $tFB_c$ and that $tPM_{nc}$ was solved faster than $tPM_c$.

## Mortality

Pilot studies revealed a high risk of unfinished tasks when a time limit is set. Unfinished tasks cannot be analyzed because the time at which a subject gave up cannot be compared to the time where another subject completed the task. The same problem exists for the correctness rating, because an incomplete solution cannot be treated the same as a non-solution from a subject who gave up on the task. Hence, tasks from subjects that gave up were not included in the analysis. The risk of aborted tasks because of too strict time limits was averted by not defining a time limit for the Bremen and Dagstuhl groups. Subjects of these groups were explicitly informed that they can use as much time as they needed. In Tuscaloosa the class hours restricted the available time. Nevertheless, this was the last of the three groups that performed the experiment so that we could assess the available class hours to be suitable for the experiment before it took place.

Subjects who failed on both tasks were excluded from the analysis because they cannot be analyzed in a meaningful way.

## Instrumentality

All subjects were forced to use the Eclipse IDE the experimenters provided. Experience with Eclipse was made mandatory for participation in Bremen and Dagstuhl. In Tuscaloosa one third of the subjects participated although they were not familiar with Eclipse. A brief introduction how to use Eclipse was given to all groups. Some subjects may be familiar with Eclipse but use another editor primarily, which could cause some differences in their performance. The recording of times and activity was performed invisibly by our Eclipse plug-in so that the subject's behavior were not altered.

## Repeats

The subjects of our pilot studies were not allowed to participate in the main experiment and no subject was allowed to participate twice. Therefore, no subject could benefit from earlier participation.

**Diffusion**

Subjects were not allowed to communicate during the experiment sessions, which were supervised by the experimenters. Because of organizational constraints, multiple sessions with different subjects were held. All subjects were asked not to tell others about details of the experiment, but we cannot guarantee that no information has been exchanged.

**Compensatory rivalry**

The subjects had no opportunity to compensate their treatment in any way, because they did not know about the independent and dependent variables. Furthermore, members of each group received both treatments and were not aware which treatment they were exposed to in which task.

**Experimenter bias**

Despite from the introduction, which was given to all subjects of a session at once, there was no interaction between the experimenters and the subjects. The experiment was guided by the Eclipse plug-in, which was identical for all subjects. It gave step-by-step instructions, which were the same for all subjects, regardless of the treatment. The evaluation is based on objective measurements as timing and correctness and their statistical evaluation. Both do not leave room for different handling of the subjects by the experimenters.

## 8.6.2   Construct Validity

Fixing a bug requires different kinds of activities: such as reading the report, reproducing the fault, locating the bug, applying and testing changes. These activities may also occur in iterations. Our set-up does not allow conclusions on which of these activities takes more or less time when a bug is cloned. Nevertheless, we deliberately constructed the tasks in a way that they emulate complete maintenance tasks, because we were interested in the overall time needed to solve the task and the outcome at the moment when the subjects regard their task as finished.

The code containing the bug in the non-cloned variant of *tPM* differs from the respective cloned code fragments in the cloned task variant. This is due to the two overlapping clone relations. It is possible that differences in the subject performance were not only caused by the fact that the code appears only in one file and not two, but also by the restructuring of the whole *switch* statement whose *case* blocks were also cloned in the original version. Both the removal of the clone in the two different files and the refactoring of the *case* blocks are clone removals, but we cannot decide which of these removals caused the differences we measured.

A difference between the tasks is that the logic that contains the bug is shorter and less complex for *tFB*. This could cause differences in the overall time needed to fix the bugs. The code that needs to be changed to fix the bug, however, does not differ in size.

## 8.6.3   External Validity

We cannot assert that our results can be generalized to other subject populations, systems, cloning scenarios, bugs or other kinds of maintenance tasks, because these were not part of our controlled environment. The following factors may affect the results.

Clones are diverse and can vary in their individual size, their spreading, and their similarity. We chose near-miss clones because we often observe these in the systems we analyze. We expect these clones to be harder to understand than exact ones. The clones in our experiment had only two occurrences. Real clones may be copied to more locations, which may make complete changes more difficult.

Likewise, there are many different kinds of maintenance tasks. We chose corrective tasks because bugs can be prepared so that they appear within the clones. This ensures that the subjects have to actually deal with the clones. This would be more difficult for adaptive and corrective tasks, where numerous different solutions may exist and it would be difficult to ensure that the solution chosen by the subject does actually intersect with the cloned code. The tasks in this experiment are rather simple and small as many real maintenance tasks. The results may differ for more complicated tasks, especially for such ones that require changes in many different locations.

Both systems we used are games, which have been chosen because of pragmatic considerations. Choosing software of different size or from other application domains may have an effect on the results. This may also be the case for systems written in other languages than Java.

We also cannot assert that the same experiment with different populations would produce the same results. The executions with the student and expert populations revealed that both groups have different preconditions. While the students from Bremen all learned to use Java and Eclipse in their studies, the professionals from Dagstuhl have different backgrounds and form a more heterogeneous group. The Tuscaloosa group has less Java skills on average and one third was not familiar with Eclipse.

A peculiarity of our experiment design is the fact that the participants had to fix foreign code they have never seen before. As we have seen in Chapter 7, clones are often maintained by their author. Consequently, the risk of incomplete solutions may be lower when programmers change their own code.

Our experimental design compares fixing one defect location (non-cloned) with fixing two locations (cloned). The results may be different when all task variants required the participant to fix two defect locations. We chose the presented design to analyze the fact that a bug is cloned as independent variable. As a bug, we understand unintended program behavior that affects the correctness or capabilities the software in some way and that is apparent to the end user. That is, a bug is defined by program behavior, but not necessarily by a single code location. The difference of being cloned or not naturally translates into one and respectively two code locations that need to be fixed. In our design the bug symptoms are identical for both tasks variants. The difference in the two variants lie in the locations of the symptoms. They are all located in one location for the non-cloned variant. For the cloned variant they appear in two locations. This resembles the case where the same behavior is needed for different functionalities of the application, which can be achieved with cloning. Consequently, our results indicate how such cloning affects the solution time and correctness for some logical error. Our observations do not allow any conclusions how the solution time for one defect location differences between the non-cloned and cloned variants. It would be possible to design an alternative experiment that compares two non-cloned defect locations with two cloned defect locations. Such an experiment, however, would not be suited to answer our research questions.

Finally, the lack of time constraints for the tasks may affect how the results can be generalized. The lack of a time limit may differ from real situations in industry where time pressure is common. Under such conditions, we would expect even more incorrect solutions.

## 8.7 Conclusion

In this chapter we analyzed what happens between the snapshots retrospective studies on the effects of clones usually analyze. With 80 participants from different populations we created 160 cases where cloned bugs had to be fixed and compared these with identical tasks where the only difference was that the bug was not cloned. We asked the questions whether the cloned bug requires more time to be fixed (Research Question C1) and whether the correctness of the solutions is reduced when the bug is cloned (Research Question C2).

We found the results for the groups to differ, but when all participants are joined into a single group we observed a strong tendency towards longer solution times for the cloned bugs. We found that the required time is increased by up to 36.5% for all participants. In one case an increase of 98.9% was measured. For a single population we also observed that one of the cloned bugs was fixed in 59.6% less time, which, however, is an exception in the results. The increase we found for all participants does not exceed six minutes per task. We measured medium to large effect sizes in the time difference between the cloned and non-cloned bug-fixing tasks. These results indicate that cloned bugs may increase the solution time when they occur and have to be fixed. It does not express the overall increase of maintenance costs, though. This depends on the frequency of such changes, which we could not analyze in this study. These results add important insights to the retrospective studies which did not reveal additional effort caused by clones. Our results show that this effort may well be hidden in the *creation* of the snapshots that other studies analyze.

We also found that the risk of incomplete bug fixes is high when the bug is cloned. For the FrozenBubble task 45.2% of our participants failed to fix both occurrences of the cloned bug. In contrast all participants who managed to find one bug occurrence fixed the bug correctly when it was not cloned. For the other task Pacman the participants performed better, but still 25.0% of them failed to fix both occurrences. A main reason for this bad performance of the participants was insufficient testing of the solution. Many subjects did not notice that some of the erroneous behavior was still present although it was explicitly noted in the bug description they were given. Again, this high risk must be seen in the context of the frequency of such changes before systematic countermeasures against clones are taken.

# Part IV

# Finale

# Chapter 9

# Conclusion

Code clones have a notoriously bad reputation. Beck and Fowler are prominent advocates of the accusations [50], but they are not the only ones. Hunt and Thomas dedicate a whole section of their book *The Pragmatic Programmer* to "The Evils of Duplications" [79]. There they formulate the *DRY* principle, which stands for *Don't Repeat Yourself*. Martin picks up the matter in his book *Clean Code*, adding that "duplication may be the root of all evil" [125]. Echoes can be found in many places. For example on Blogs with such promising names as *Coding Horror* where duplicated code is called "the bane of software development".[1] At the time of this writing the English version of the Wikipedia has entries for *Redundant Code*[2], *Duplicated Code*[3], *Copy and Paste Programming*[4], and of course the *Don't repeat yourself*[5] principle.

All the prosecutors have a strong voice but no evidence to exhibit. In this thesis we have learned that there are good reasons to be skeptical. Research, such as Krinke's evaluation of code stability, cast doubt on the negative judgment. In this thesis we have analyzed different aspects from different perspectives to deepen the understanding of the effects clones have on software. Neither did we prove the innocence of clones nor did we support the fierce allegations from the programmer's text books. The results of our three research perspectives indicate that the answer may lie somewhere in the middle.

**Research Perspective A:** *How do clones affect the instability and, therefore, changeability of source code?*

Our in-depth analysis of clone stability in Chapter 6 has shown that cloned code does not change more than non-cloned code in large-scale software systems with different characteristics. We analyzed up to five years of history per system and did not find

---

[1]https://blog.codinghorror.com/code-smells/
[2]https://en.wikipedia.org/wiki/Redundant_code
[3]https://en.wikipedia.org/wiki/Duplicate_code
[4]https://en.wikipedia.org/wiki/Copy_and_paste_programming
[5]https://de.wikipedia.org/wiki/Don\%27t_repeat_yourself

that cloned code indeed has a higher change rate than non-cloned code. Like Krinke [112] and Hotta [74] we observed that clones do change even less. Nevertheless, Mondal and colleagues [131] have found that the change rate of clones may be higher in smaller systems. Altogether, these insights do not support the strong accusations against clones, because we cannot find evidence for the existence of the alleged effect.

> **Research Perspective B:** *How do multiple developers affect the evolution of clones? Are different authors a key reason why clones are changed inconsistently and cause bugs?*

While the evidence against an increased maintenance effort becomes more frequent, other studies have shown that clones do indeed cause bugs [6, 24, 61, 90, 120]. This cannot be denied because actual cases have been documented. In Chapter 7 we analyzed a possible cause for these bugs by analyzing the authorship of clones. The hypothesis that bugs with clones occur because different programmers are changing cloned code, is not supported by our findings. We found that most clone classes are maintained by just one programmer and we did not find a systematic relationship between the consistency of changes and the number of developers involved in these. Clone classes also do not change more often when multiple programmers are involved. Single and multi-author clones differ in the characteristics, though. When programmers copy their own code, they tend to copy smaller pieces of logic, whereas multi-author clone classes are often copies of larger structures. Nevertheless, if there is a factor that causes bugs through clones, then our results indicate that it is probably not the number of developers involved.

> **Research Perspective C:** *How do clones affect performance of programmers in real software engineering tasks?*

In our controlled experiment in Chapter 8 we chose a new perspective to look at the problem. We observed programmers in a controlled environment to evaluate the effects clones have *during* the development process. We are the first to analyze the phase between the repository snapshots that retrospective analyses use. With a total of 81 participants from different populations we have found that the time needed to fix a bug increased by up to 36% when the bug is cloned. With 25% to 45%, many participants failed to fix the bug completely when it was cloned. In this part of our work we found indication that clones indeed can have harmful effects. We encountered both prolonged solution times as well as a higher risk of incomplete bug fixes. These results, however, do only describe what happens when programmers face bug-fixing tasks in the presence of clones. The do not tell whether this situation occurs often. Others have shown that this does not seem to be the case [61, 145].

Altogether our findings do not summarize in a clear result pro or contra clones. On the one hand our controlled experiment shows that clones can be problematic. The high failure rates on the cloned bug are alarming. The dominant reason rather seems to lie in improper testing when programmers, who did not write the code in the first place, make the changes. On the other hand, the investigations on the stability indicate that the maintenance effect of clones that can be measured in real systems seems to be small. Together with the findings of other researchers these results tell the story that clones rarely change and that cloned code does not contain more bugs than non-cloned code.

These results are not an acquittal for clones. Nevertheless, the headless crusade against clones also does not withstand the empirical evidence we and others have collected. Clones *can cause harm*, but this does *not seem to happen often*.

One possible explanation is that the programmers avoid changing clones when they encounter them and prefer workarounds. This seems unlikely, because reports of such cases are rare and such behavior would cause a strong increase in the clone rates over time. We have not observed such cases and it does not seem plausible that avoidance is the reason why clones change so rarely.

Another explanation, which seems more plausible given our results, is that software developers may be smarter than we thought. What if most programmers are well aware of the risks of cloning? Maybe they are responsible enough to remove clones when they do become a problem. This would mean that we do not find many cases where clones cause problems, because developers are aware and able to manage them without additional tool support. The warnings of authors like Beck, Fowler, Hunt, Thomas, and Martin may be effective and help developers to prevent the problems, which clones undoubtedly can cause, most of the time.

Cloning cannot be avoided. And software development without the text editing command of copy and paste seems to be impracticable. As with most things in life, the right amount of copy and paste is probably beneficial. The dose makes the poison. We should consider it possible that many developers are able to choose the right amount on their own.

Despite all plausibility our results do not prove these theories, which are only possible interpretations. Nonetheless, these perspectives illustrate how difficult it is to derive advice for practitioners from our findings. Certainly, we cannot recommend the aggressive removal of clones, because we did not find the existing clones to cause frequent harm. At the same time, we cannot mark clones as unproblematic, because we have shown that they are not. We even cannot refute the strong statements against clones, such as Beck's and Fowler's, because these may be a reason why programmers are aware enough to prevent actual harm.

A reasonable attitude for a programmer is probably awareness of the possible causes of clones, but at the same time a prudent approach to existing clones. In our manual inspections we have seen cases where programmers removed clones to improve future maintenance. If a clone needs to change repeatedly, the developer will probably notice the problem. Chances are good, that the same developer will can take notice because most clones are maintained by the same person, as we have shown. Timely countermeasures against repeatedly changing clones will then also reduce the risk of bugs because of inconsistent changes.

Considering all the facts we have collected we would suggest that the case of software clones should be resolved in a settlement in the above sense.

# Future Work

Although, today, clones are probably the best analyzed anti-pattern in software engineering, research did not conclude in clear advice for practitioners. There is still more research required to assess the harmfulness of clones and to infer advice for practitioners. Our work, presented in this thesis, has opened new research questions that are worthwhile future research endeavors.

## Characteristics of Harmful Clones

Although we found many clones not to be as harmful as expected, some are. Our study on clone authorship was an attempt to find one factor that causes clones to become problematic. Clone detection will only be helpful to practitioners if we find a way to discriminate the many irrelevant clones from those that cause harm. Future research should aim to find such factors that can be used to prioritize clones for clone management activity.

## Code Clones and Software Processes

The results of our experiment indicate that the lack of testing caused incorrect solutions when the bug is cloned. This raises the question whether and how proper software development processes can help to mitigate clone related effects. Besides testing, code reviews could help to avoid clones. A possible explanation for our results is that problem awareness exists among developers. Code reviews could help it to spread. It would certainly be interesting to investigate whether certain processes or the level to which they are adhered help to reduce or prevent negative effects of clones.

## Reasons for the low Change Frequency of Clones

The results of our clone stability study show that cloned code changes less than non-cloned code. One explanation could be that this code is so mature and has proven correct that is has to change rarely. It could be the case that developers use cloning as a tool for the reuse of trusted code. Another explanation, however, could be that developers are aware of the cloning relationship and refrain to change the clones to avoid extra effort or risking bugs. Cordy reported that this may especially be the case in environments where correctness is crucial, such as in banks [34]. Future research should be directed to the question whether developers actually are afraid of changing clones.

## Costs and Benefits of Cloning

Our research focused exclusively on the costs of cloning. The benefits, that could exist, have not been investigated yet. Cloning accelerates software development in the beginning and not every abstraction may be easier to understand than the original. Analyzing such positive effects probably requires human-based studies as we applied with our controlled experiment. It would be interesting to learn what effect the inability to copy and paste has on developers to gain insight on the positive aspects of cloning.

## Replication and Meta Studies

The empirical knowledge we have gathered about clones helps us to understand how clones affect maintainability. To gather a comprehensive overview, single studies on a question are not enough. Other fields, such as medical sciences, are more mature in performing and interpreting such results and require replication and meta studies before final conclusions are drawn. With our study on clone stability we followed this idea by replicating a previous one. Others followed us so that now four studies can be compared. Their results vary, indeed. Replication will be of continuous importance as clone detection approaches evolve and the significance of their results must be evaluated.

Our controlled experiment was the first of its kind in code clone research, but was deliberately designed for replication with all materials made available. Indeed it was replicated once [32] and reused twice, so far [21, 32]. In general more replications would help us to mitigate the problem of generalizability all case studies have. When enough results are available, meta studies could help to provide inside at a higher level.

# Closing Words

I spent most of my scientific work with the effects of software clones. I was driven by my personal doubt that clones are as harmful as they are said to be. During my scientific journey of the past years I learned how diverse the answer to this question is. Indeed, I was able to present some negative effects myself in our controlled experiment. Probably we will never be able to prove clones good or bad. Empirical evidence, however, helps us find a reasonable attitude towards clones.

Since more than three years I work as Head of Development and Team Leader in a software company. I am concerned with software quality every day. Surprisingly, it never occurred to me that clones are a key reason for the problems we face. Instead I experienced that developers in my company, regardless of their age and experience level, do deeply care about the code they write. They try to avoid clones as they see fit. They remove clones when they are annoyed about them. Together we feel that extensive testing and code reviews help best to make good software.

With this thesis I hope to contribute to a reasonable attitude towards clones. They do matter, but we could not support the fierce allegations, which have been voiced frequently.

# Appendices

# Appendix A

# Clone Stability Charts

In Chapter 6 we presented time series charts for the clone instability for the different systems and settings. Since the charts are very similar only some represenative ones are discussed in detail. This appendix contains all time series charts that were collected in the study. The charts that were already included in Chapter 6 are also repeated here in larger scale.

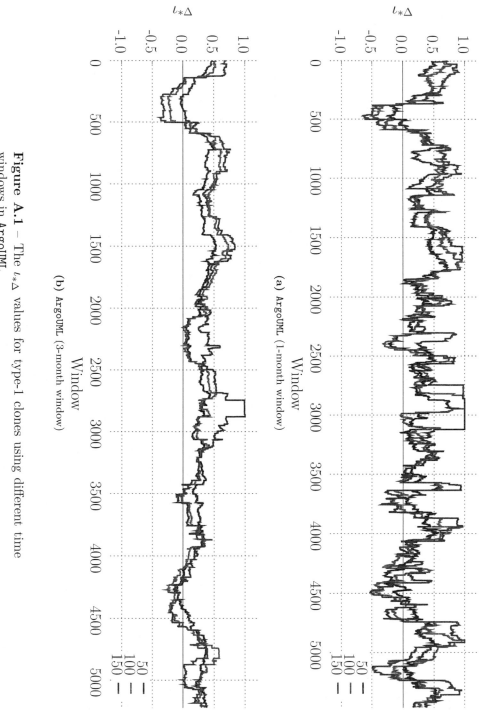

**Figure A.1** – The $\iota_{*\Delta}$ values for type-1 clones using different time windows in ArgoUML

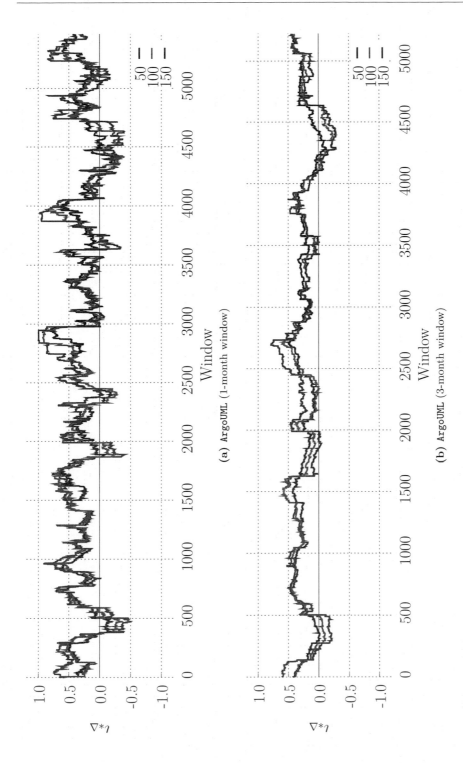

**Figure A.2** – The $\iota_{*\Delta}$ values for type-1, type-2, and type-3 clones using different time windows in ArgoUML

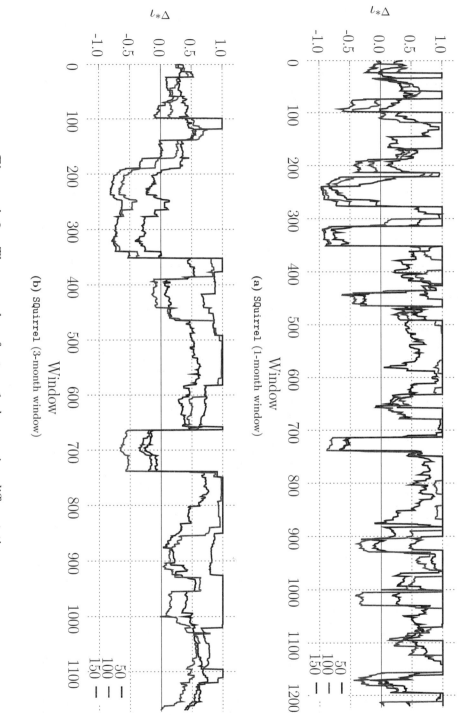

**Figure A.3** – The $\iota_{*\Delta}$ values for type-1 clones using different time windows in Squirrel

187

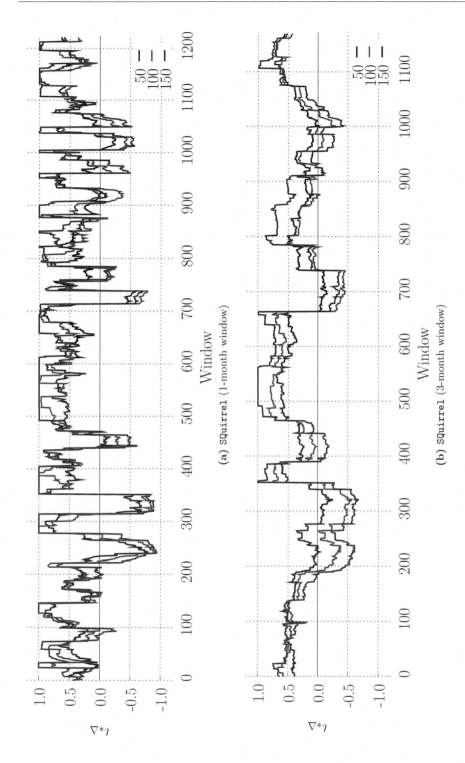

**Figure A.4** – The $\iota_{*\Delta}$ values for type-1, type-2, and type-3 clones using different time windows in SQuirrel

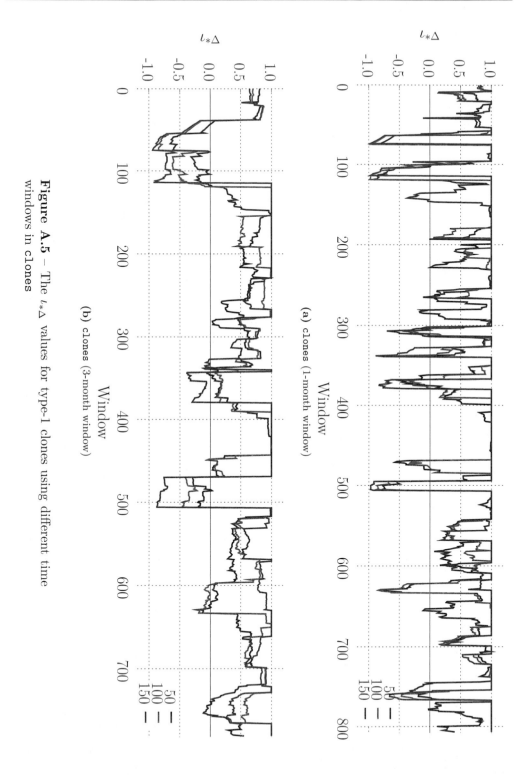

**Figure A.5** – The $\iota_{*\Delta}$ values for type-1 clones using different time windows in clones

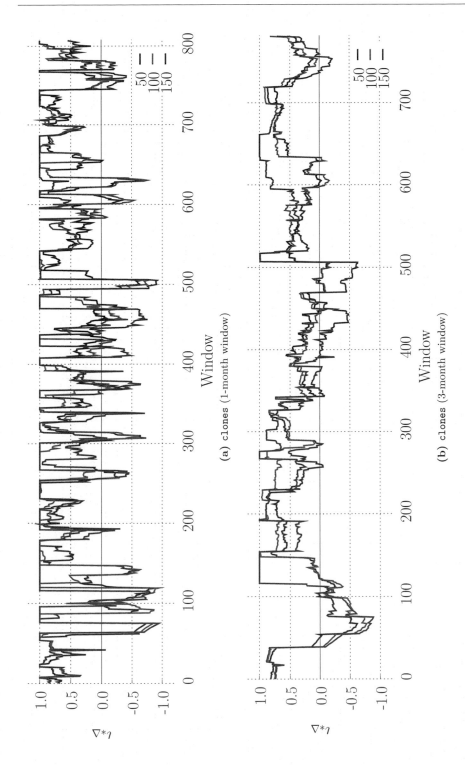

**Figure A.6** – The $\iota_{*\Delta}$ values for type-1, type-2, and type-3 clones using different time windows in clones

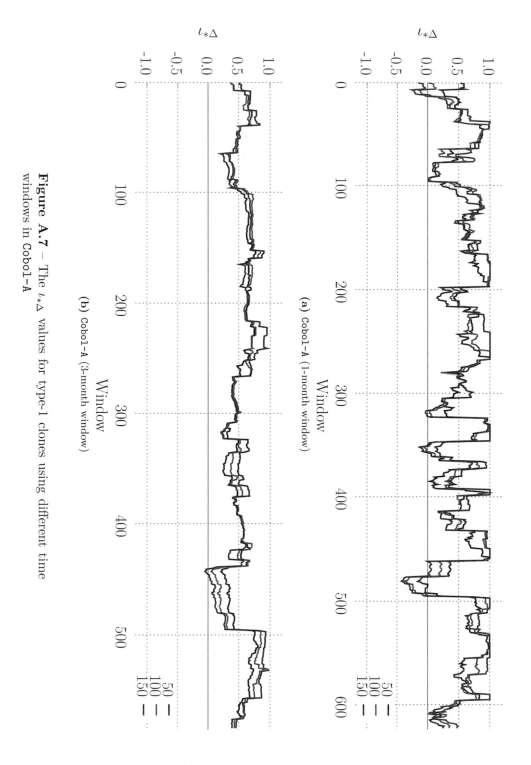

**Figure A.7** – The $\iota_{*\Delta}$ values for type-1 clones using different time windows in Cobol-A

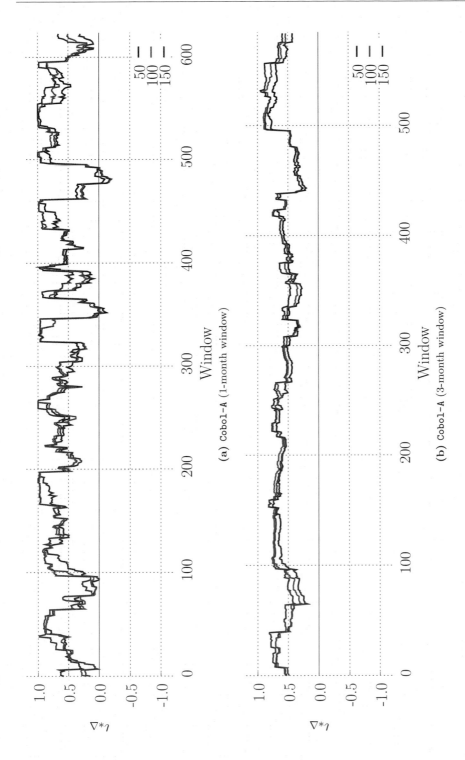

**Figure A.8** – The $\iota_{*\triangle}$ values for type-1, type-2, and type-3 clones using different time windows in Cobol-A

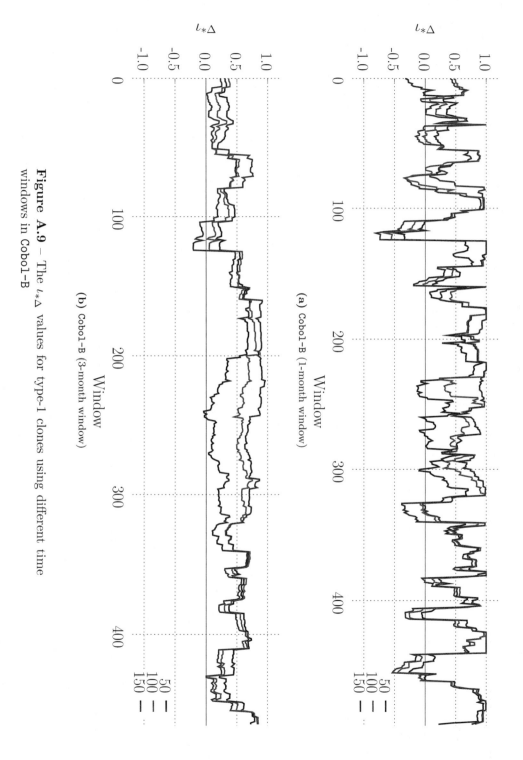

**Figure A.9** – The $\iota_{*\Delta}$ values for type-1 clones using different time windows in Cobo1-B

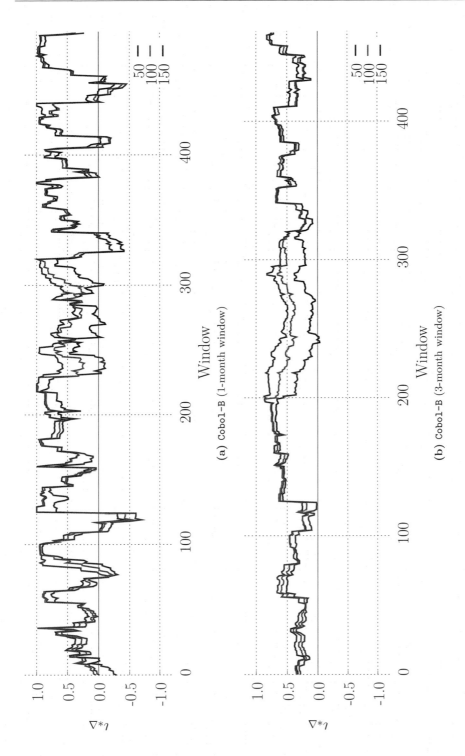

**Figure A.10** – The $\iota_{*\Delta}$ values for type-1, type-2, and type-3 clones using different time windows in Cobol-B

# Appendix B

# Experiment Replication Manual

To ease replications of our controlled experiment on software clones, which is discussed in Chapter 8, we made all materials available needed for a replication[1]. We also provided an experimenter's manual that contains additional information how to use the replication set to repeat our experiment. This experimenter's manual is enclosed in this appendix.

## B.1 Introduction

In the time from 2010 to 2012 we designed and conducted a controlled experiment on software clones. More precisely, we evaluated for two bug-fixing tasks how the required time and the correctness of the solution are affected when the bug is cloned. Our results did not reach statistical significance, but give first insights into the effects of cloning. This has not been evaluated in controlled experiments like ours before.

We found that the clone of the bug was often overlooked, even though faulty program behavior gave striking indications that the bug fix was incomplete. We did not observe strong indications for decisive differences in the time needed to solve cloned bugs compared with fixing non-cloned bugs.

The experiment has been conducted with a total number of 33 participants from two different populations: computer science students of the University of Bremen and clone experts who participated in the Dagstuhl seminar 12071 on software clones. The rather limited number of participants is likely to be the main reason why we did not achieve statistical significance.

A detailed report on the experiment, named *A Controlled Experiment on Software Clones* has been published at the International Conference of Program Comprehension

---

[1]Website with replication materials: http://www.softwareclones.org/experiment
Tarball with all materials (2.3 GB): http://www.softwareclones.org/download/experiment/experiment-replication-set.tar.bz2

2012 (ICPC'12). Please refer to this publication for details on the experiment. A copy of the paper is included in this replication set.

**Call for Replications**  The major problem of our study is the limited number of subjects we could call upon. We would like to replicate the study with more subjects from different contexts. The experiment was designed to be easy to replicate and we invite interested researchers to perform a replication. We are happy to help with the experiment executions and would be pleased to work together with other researchers on further publications on this experiment. Please contact Jan Harder (mail@jan-harder.de) if you are interested. If you join us in our empirical work we can also help you using our tools for data analysis.

## B.2  Contents of the Replication Set

The replication set, this manual belongs to, contains all material required for a replication of our experiment. All materials are prepared to minimize the effort required for a replication. This set has been designed to work out-of-the-box.

**Experimenter's Manual**  This document contains all information you need to replicate the experiment. The materials are pre-packaged for execution. This document contains instructions how to prepare experiment sessions, which requirements participants must meet, how the materials and tools work, how the experiment is executed, and what may go wrong during an execution.

**Paper**  The ICPC'2012 paper is included in this set. If you have not read it yet, please do so before reading this manual. This manual builds up on the paper, to avoid redundancy.

**Presentation & Script**  At the beginning of each experiment session the experimenters give an introduction. For comparability reasons it is important that all participants get the same information at the beginning of the experiment. Consequently, we added the slides for this presentation and a script with all information that must be given in the talk. All material for the presentation is located in the folder *introduction*. There you will find the slides, slides annotated with the talk, and two videos that are part of the presentation.

**Handout**  All participants receive a handout that recaps the instructions from the introduction. This handout is included as a PDF document.

**The DVD Images**  All digital material, the participants need, are packaged in DVD images. There is one DVD image for participants of group $A$ and one for participants of group $B$ (see the paper). These are identical except for the tasks. The images also contain prepared Eclipse packages for different platforms and a workspace with the tasks. You will find them in the folder *disk-images*. Besides the DVD images there is also a tarball that can be used for USB keys that work for both groups (it contains both workspaces).

**Analysis Tools**  This set includes a set of python scripts that can be used to analyze the data of an execution semi-automatically. The correctness has to be evaluated manually, but everything else is automated. The scripts are located in the folder *analysis*.

These scripts require Python in a version $> 2.7$ and $< 3.0$, the R tools for statistical computing, the python biding for R *Rpy*, and some other common python libraries. We have used them on Linux and Mac (with MacPorts for R). Nevertheless, they have not been tested on different platforms and require some background knowledge to be used properly.

If you want to evaluate results please contact Jan (mail@jan-harder.de). We will try to help you using these scripts.

## B.3  Shopping List

You will need to organize some materials, we could not include in the set.

1. **Blank DVDs:** As many as you expect participants.

2. **Envelopes:** One per participant; will hold handout and a DVD.

3. **USB-Keys:** For those participants whose laptop computers do not have a DVD drive and to collect the results in the end.

4. **Laptop & Projector:** For the introduction.

5. **A colleague:** Organizing the sessions may be stressful. You should get someone who knows this manual, can answer questions, and helps you to collect the results. Our experience shows that one experimenter should not supervise more than five participants at once.

## B.4  Preparing an Execution

### B.4.1  Requirements for Participation

When the experiment was designed, the expected subject population were computer science students from the University of Bremen. Consequently, the requirements for participation were aligned to this group. For the sake of comparability the same requirements should be used for replications of our study. All requirements are described in the following.

**Basic Java Knowledge**    Participants must have basic Java knowledge. The tasks
were chosen so that besides the Java Class library no knowledge on any specific library is
required. The participants should be familiar with the Java syntax, its execution model,
and object oriented programming. They should also be able to work with projects that
are some thousand lines of code in size.

**Basic Eclipse Knowledge**    Participants must be familiar with the Eclipse IDE, which
has to be used during the experiment. They should at least know how to browse files,
how to execute programs, and how to use the search. Our execution at the Dagstuhl
seminar showed that participants without Eclipse experience may waste most of the
time to figure out how Eclipse works, which will distort their results. Knowing some
IDE does not suffice. The participants need to know Eclipse.

**A Computer to work with**    We asked all participants to bring their own laptop
computer. The set up of the experiment proved to be very robust against technical
difficulties—no participant dropped out because something did not work on his machine.
Such problems rather occurred in the few cases where participants had to use other
hardware. The experiment was tested and successfully executed on Windows (XP or
newer), current Linux distributions, and Mac OSX. For comparability to our study it
would be best to let the participants use their own computer.

The sole requirement for the participant's computer is the presence of a Sun or Oracle
Java Development Kit (JDK) 1.6.x. If missing, it can be installed on the machine during
the experiment session. The experimenter should have installers ready. We could not
include JDKs in the disk images because of licensing issues. Please see also the remarks
on Java issues in section B.10. Newer JDK versions probably work as well, but have not
been tested.

## B.4.2   Preparing the materials

Prepare one envelope per participant which contains the required materials and has
the participant id written on it. Copying the materials to a computer takes some time
so that every participant should have his own disk. Otherwise, a lot of time will be
wasted for passing DVDs around. Passing around DVDs proved to be error-prone in
preliminary studies, because the participants may accidentally use the DVD for the
wrong group an execute the wrong tasks. Prepare the following:

**Envelopes**

- Burn $n$ DVDs for $n$ expected participants. Burn ISO image $A$ on one half and
  ISO image $B$ on the other half. Mark the DVDs with $A$ or $B$ to avoid confusion.

- Print out $n$ handouts.

- Get $n$ envelopes, split them into two stacks and enumerate each stack's envelopes
  with $A1$ to $\frac{An}{2}$ and $B1$ to $\frac{Bn}{2}$. These labels are the unique ID each participant
  will be assigned to. So every participant will need his own envelope.

- Put the DVDs labeled *A* into the *A* envelopes and the DVDs labeled *B* into the *B* envelopes.

- Put a handout in each envelope.

**Important!** If you replicate our study, do not make changes to the ISO images or the archives for the USB keys. The risk that something gets disarranged is high as we had to experience in our preliminary studies.

**USB Keys**   You will need USB keys for two reasons. First, you will need to collect the results somehow. Second, some participants will not have a DVD drive in their computer. Prepare the following.

- Some USB keys to collect the results. For a group of 10 Participants you should have at least two.

- Some USB keys containing the USB key data image we provide. This contains all data for both groups. If a participant uses the USB key you must tell her which workspace to copy. There will be a *workspace-a* and a *workspace-b*.

## B.5   What data are collected

In some organizations you may need approval from an ethics commission before you can execute the experiment. You may need to specify which data are collected during the experiment and how this is done. The following gives an overview of the measurements.

All data analysis is done anonymously. The participants will be assigned a unique id that is composed of their group code (A or B) and a number. The participants can provide their e-mail address voluntarily.

All measurements are performed automatically in the background. The participant is not informed about recordings in process. Most measurements are done by our Eclipse plug-in. We also collect the log files created by the *EPP Usage Data Collector*.[2] For all recorded events that we explain in the following the time of the event is recorded. This allows to reconstruct the actions afterwards without observing the participant during the experiment.

- Timing: The current time is recorded each time the participant advances to the next step in the experiment by clicking the *next* button in the experiment view. Furthermore, the current time is recorded when a survey is opened and closed.

- Eclipse IDE Usage: The Eclipse IDE is organized into different views. Focus changes between these views as well as opening and closing a view will be recorded for any view.

- Debugging: Usage of the Eclipse Debugger, such as breakpoint halts, stepping, resuming, etc., is recorded.

---

[2]http://www.eclipse.org/epp/usagedata/

- Program Executions: All executions of the programs, the participants have to modify in the tasks, are recorded. Before each task an error-free version of the program can be executed. These executions are also logged. Actions within the programs are not logged.

- Keystrokes: All keystrokes performed in an Eclipse editor view will be recorded. For each keystroke it is recorded when the key is pressed and also when the the the key is released.

- File Operations: It is recoded whenever a participant opens, closes, or saves a file. Focus changes between opened files are recorded as well.

- Searches: Searches in the source code using the Eclipse search features will be recorded.

- Source Code: The whole source code with all changes the participant has made is collected in the end of the experiment.

## B.6   Recorded Data not Analyzed in the Paper

In the paper we use the dependent variables time and correctness. The Eclipse plug-in we use for instrumentation collects more data. First, it records many interactions in the IDE, such as keystrokes, file operations, debugging, and program execution. These data were not analyzes in the paper because the recordings were not detailed enough to draw conclusions from them. For some participants the recording failed.

Second, an assessment of the NASA Task Load Index (TLX) is collected with surveys. TLX is an evaluation scheme for the subjective work load impression of human-machine interfaces. It was designed to measure the subjective workload experienced by the users. Our plug-in presents forms to collect the data that are required to compute the TLX.

Basically, the TLX collects ratings for 6 factors on a scale from 0 to 100. The user weights the scales afterwards and a summarized workload index is calculated form the weighted sums of the ratings. The data we collected, however, expose high variances and no clear tendencies. The results were far from being statistically significant.

We decided to leave the TLX forms in the plug-in because they require only small effort and may lead to more meaningful results if more subjects participate. We have changed the original TLX by removing ratings that do not apply to our experiment. Namely, we removed *Time Pressure*, because there is no time limit and, therefore, no time pressure. The other factor that was removed is *Physical Demand*. There should be no difference in physical demand for solving the tasks, because the independent variable does not change the physical interface. Furthermore, the TLX presents the factors pairwise and asks the participant which one had the bigger impact on the experienced workload. We removed *Performance* from this rating, because it is not possible to compare this factor to the others, as for instance the frustration level.

# B.7 Executing the Experiment

## B.7.1 Sessions

The experiment does not require all participants to come together at one time and place. You may set up several sessions. We executed the experiment with up to 20 people at once but we also had sessions with just one participant. Make sure that every participant will experience the same procedure, which is described in the following.

None of our sessions took longer than 90 minutes in total. Nevertheless, you should be prepared for more time, because there is no time limit for the tasks. The participants are allowed to take as much time as they want.

We strongly suggest that the experimenters should try out the experiment themselves in the role of an participant beforehand to be aware of everything that happens during a session.

## B.7.2 Phase 1: Arrival

Wait for everyone to appear. Late arrivers should not be allowed to join the experiment as they will not have the same prerequisites because they have missed parts of the introduction.

## B.7.3 Phase 2: Introduction

When all participants have arrived, give the introductory talk by using the prepared slides and the corresponding script. Allow the participants to ask clarification questions at the end of the talk.

## B.7.4 Phase 3: Distribution of Material

Hand out the material to the participants. Make sure that you alternate the groups A and B, meaning you start by handing out an envelope for group A followed by an envelope for group B and so on.

Hand the USB keys to the participants who do not have a DVD drive. Tell them to copy the workspace that corresponds to the group they were assigned to. When a DVD is used this is foolproof, because the DVD images are group specific and do not contain material for the other group. The USB key image contains all material. There will be a zip and a tarball archive of the workspace. The participant should use the archive he is comfortable with.

Let the participants install the material and provide help if needed. When the freshly installed Eclipse is started the participants have to choose the workspace directory. This should be the extracted workspace (the archives will extract a directory named *workspace*).

## B.7.5   Phase 4: Programming Tasks

After the participant opens the Eclipse IDE that was installed in the previous step a 'Task View' will appear at the bottom. This view contains instructions which allow the participant to proceed autonomously. Whenever the participant finished the instructions displayed in the 'Task View', the next button must be pressed. It is not possible to go back one this button has been pressed.

In the following we describe the steps the participant will be guided through by the task view.

Prior to the programming tasks, a survey that collects general information will be displayed. It asks for a *number*. The participants id from the envelope must be entered here. The e-mail field is optional. The intended use is to ask participants questions after the experiment.

Before a task starts, the participants are given the opportunity to run a bug-free version of the game to familiarize. A *run* button appears in the Task View which will execute the bug-free version.

After the familiarization the task itself begins with the bug report. There will be some hints on how to fix the bug. You should encourage the participants to actually read them. Fore some reason some of them are resistant to any help they are offered. During the task the participants should execute the code they are working on to reproduce the bug and to test their fix. The workspace is pre-configured so that the game will start when the Eclipse's green play button is pressed while the project has focus in the package explorer.

After each task another survey will be presented. Here the participants must self-assess the workload they experienced in the task on four scales (this is the first part of the NASA TLX assessment). They are also asked whether they believe that they have successfully finished the task. This is important for the evaluation of correct and incorrect solutions. It has a different quality when a participant believes that he was successful, when he actually failed. Furthermore there will be a free text field where the participant is asked to specify the strategy he used to find and fix the bug.

After both tasks have been finished a last survey will be presented. Here the the TLX scales will be weighted in pairwise comparisons. The participant must choose the factor that had the higher impact on the workload he experienced.

## B.7.6   Phase 5: Result Collection

At the end, the Task View will ask the participant to close Eclipse. On termination the complete workspace will be archived automatically. You will find a zip archived that is named after the participants id (the one he entered in the first survey). The archive will be located in the directory that contains the workspace. The experimenters must collect this workspace.

We recommend to copy all results from the USB keys to your computer as soon as possible for safety reasons. We found the USB keys break surprisingly often, when the are passed around during the experiment. Make sure participants do not leave before you have copied their data to your computer.

### B.7.7   Phase 6: End

After the has been collected, the participant may leave.

## B.8   Data Analysis

The workspace that have been collected after the experiment contain all data that are needed to evaluate the results.

### B.8.1   Logs

The following data can be found in the workspace archive of each participant:

**Interaction Log**   The file *interaction.log* contains all data recorded from the Task View. It contains logs of each click on the *next* button and each opening and closing of a survey. Timing information can be inferred from this data. This log file also contains log events for each execution of the programs.

**Workspace Log**   The file *workspace.log* contains all recorded data on the usage of the Eclipse workspace. That is, all context switches between views and perspectives. Among other events this includes context switches between files, to the search, or the debugger.

**Keys Log**   The file *keys.log* contains all recorded key events. It can be used to reconstruct typing in the editors. For each keystroke down and up events are logged.

**Survey Responses**   The files *General_Questions.xml*, *Task1.xml*, *Task2.xml*, and *Sources_of_Workload.xml* contain the data the participant entered in the surveys as XML.

**Eclipse EPP Usage Data**   Eclipse has a default usage recording facility that stores its data in the following hidden directory. There may be multiple CSV files, which have to be concatenated for analysis.

*.metadata/.plugins/org.eclipse.epp.usagedata.recording*

### B.8.2   Correctness

The correctness of the solution must be evaluated manually. To do this we ran the programs to check the behavior and we inspected the changes applied by the participant using diff. All versions of the source code—including the bug-free game—are available for download on the experiment's website `http://www.softwareclones.org/experiment`.

### B.8.3   Analysis Scripts

To gather all the data we reported in our publication, the aforementioned logs and the correctness evaluation must be combined. This is a very cumbersome task because some of the logs difficult to parse and a model of all the events of one participant must be built.

We included our analysis scripts in the set. Nevertheless, we strongly recommend to contact us (mail@jan-harder.de) before you use them, because they are not self-explanatory, not documented, may contain bugs, may contain hard coded stuff for our experiment, and require quite some background knowledge.

## B.9   How to keep the experiment sound

- Do not tell the participants anything about clones. They are not allowed to know what the experiment is about.

- Do not allow the participants to communicate during the experiment sessions.

- If you plan more than one session, ask the participants not to tell others about the experiment.

- Do not give any instructions or hints besides the information on the handout, in the introductory presentations and in the task descriptions!

- Do not set any time limits!

- Stick to the script for the talk!

- Do not allow the participants to use any other tool than Eclipse.

- Do not allow the participants to use another Eclipse than the one from the DVD.

- Do not allow anyone to participate twice.

## B.10   Known Issues & Questions Frequently Asked by Participants

**I pressed the next button too soon, what should I do?**   It happens that participants advance by pressing *next* before they finished all instructions in the experiment view. If this happens *before the participant has started to work on the first task*, you should instruct him to close Eclipse, delete the workspace, get a new copy from the DVD or USB key and start over (and not to click *next* too soon again). If the participant has started working on the first task, then timing will be wrong in the end. Unfortunately, there is no way of getting this fixed. In such cases the participant should be excluded from the analysis. This problem occurs more often than the others. Nevertheless, we only observed cases where participants read the first task description and directly pressed next without starting to work on the task. In this case a freshly extracted workspace and a restart works well. The workspace must be renewed to remove the logs created so far.

**I closed Eclipse in the middle of the experiment, what should I do?**    Again, it depends when Eclipse was closed. If the subject *did not start to work on the first task*, proceed as in the previous issue. If it happened later, the data for the task is falsified.

**The program does not start when I press the *run* button.**    This is a rare Windows-related issue. It only occurs when the participant tries to execute the bug-free version of the game before the task starts. Use this workaround: Open the Windows Explorer and navigate to the workspace directory. There you will find a *frozenbubble-bugfree.jar* and a *pacman-bugfree.jar*. A double click on the respective file will have exactly the same effect as pressing the corresponding *run* button.

**I can't control the game!**    Both games are controlled with keys. In FrozenBubble the *shift* key is the fire button. The direction in which the bubble launcher shoots can be adjusted with the arrow keys. Pacman is controlled with the arrow keys. To activate menu items press the *return* key. Both games start in new windows. You will need to click on the window once to give it focus, before the key controls will work.

**Eclipse asks for usage data upload.**    During the first few minutes there may appear a dialog asking whether the Eclipse may upload usage data. Tell the participants to cancel this dialog. Otherwise the usage data may be deleted by Eclipse in the end.

**Supported Java implementations & blank game screens.**    There are different Java variants available. The best choice for the experiment is an official JDK from Oracle in version 1.6 or newer. Others may work, but in some rare cases we encountered problems with them. These were characterized by blank game screens. If there are any problems that may be related to the JVM or JDK please check which one is installed and used. We observed problems with the GNU Java (GCJ) and OpenJDK. After installing another Java you may need to adjust the Eclipse configuration to use the newly installed version.

Currently, none of the supported operating systems comes with a pre-installed Oracle Java.

- Windows: No pre-installed Java. Have installers ready (32 & 64 bit).

- Linux: These often come with a free Java pre-installed. You may come across GCJ or OpenJDK. As said, both may cause problems with the Java programs used in the experiment. Our experience is that most people who use their machine to compile Java Programs will have installed the official JDK because of such problems. If you encounter blank game screens, this is likely to be such an JVM/JDK issue. You should have the binary installers for Linux ready to install an Oracle JDK during the experiment (32 & 64 bit).

- Mac: These do not have Java pre-installed. Today, Java for OSX can be downloaded from the Internet. Have installers ready (all current Mac computers are 64 bit). In older versions of OSX Java had to be installed as a software update. This process can be triggered by entering the *java* command on the command line.

**Choosing the right Eclipse.**    The ISO images contain Eclipse for different platforms. Whether 32 or 64 bit should be chosen does not depend on the system architecture but rather on the installed Java version. If the operating system is 64 bits, but a 32 bit Java is installed, the 32 bit Eclipse should be used.

# Appendix C

# Experiment Handout

The participants of our controlled experiment on software clones, which we describe in Chapter 8, where provided a handout with instructions. This appendix contains the original handout.

# EXPERIMENT INSTRUCTIONS

Jan Harder, Rebecca Tiarks

### Set Up

- Insert the DVD from the envelope into your computer's DVD drive. If your computer does not have a DVD drive, please ask for a USB key.
- Copy the following files to your computer:
  - Choose one of **workspace.zip** or **workspace.tar.gz**. Their contents are identical.
  - Choose the right Eclipse version for your platform. Whether you need 32 or 64 bits, depends on the Java VM you have installed.
- If no Java VM is installed on your computer, please ask the experimenters for one.
- Decompress both Eclipse and the workspace.
- Run Eclipse:
  - Double-click **eclipse** or **eclipse.exe** in the Eclipse directory.
  - Linux shell: **./eclipse** in the Eclipse directory.
  - Eclipse will ask for a workspace to load. Enter the path to the extracted workspace.

- Eclipse starts.

### Main part

The usual Eclipse workbench is displayed. Down to the right appears a ‚Task View'. From now on, this view will guide you through the experiment. Please follow the instructions displayed. You may need to scroll to read all instructions. When you finished the displayed instructions, click the ‚next' button. You cannot go back once you proceeded to the next step.

Please turn!

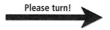 Universität Bremen  Arbeitsgruppe Softwaretechnik
Software Engineering Group

**Figure C.1** – Handout for experiment participants first page.

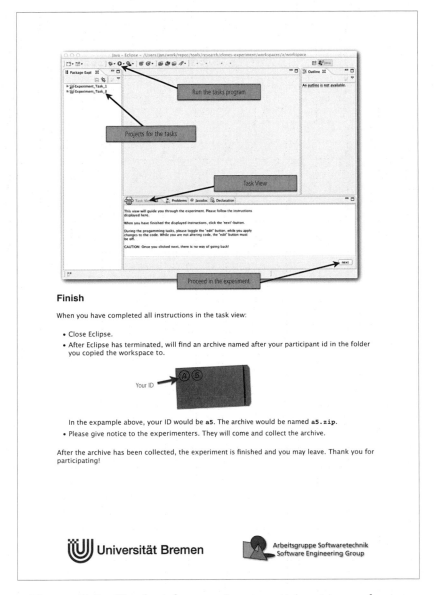

**Finish**

When you have completed all instructions in the task view:

- Close Eclipse.
- After Eclipse has terminated, will find an archive named after your participant id in the folder you copied the workspace to.

In the expample above, your ID would be **a5**. The archive would be named **a5.zip**.

- Please give notice to the experimenters. They will come and collect the archive.

After the archive has been collected, the experiment is finished and you may leave. Thank you for participating!

**Figure C.2** – Handout for experiment participants second page.

# TASK LOAD INDEX
# QUICK REFERENCE

During the experiment you will be asked to assess the workload you experienced on four scales. These scales are:

**Mental Demand:**
How mentally demanding was the task?

**Performance:**
How successful were you in accomplishing what you were asked to do?

**Effort:**
How hard did you have to work to accomplish your level of performance?

**Frustration:**
How insecure, discouraged, irritated, stressed and annoyed were you?

At the end, an automated survey will ask you, which of the four sources of workload mentioned above had the biggest impact on the workload you experienced. You will be presented pairs of the sources of workload. Please choose the source, which had the bigger impact of both.

**Figure C.3** – Handout for experiment participants thrid page.

# List of Figures

# List of Tables

# Bibliography

[1] M. Abbes, F. Komh, Y.-G. Gueheneuc, and G. Antoniol. An empirical study of the impact of two antipatterns, blob and spaghetti code, on program comprehension. In *Proceedings of the 15th European Conference on Software Maintenance and Reengineering*, pages 181–190. IEEE, 2011.

[2] E. Adar and M. Kim. SoftGUESS: Visualization and exploration of code clones in context. In *Proceedings of the 29th International Conference on Software Engineering*, pages 762–766. ACM, 2007.

[3] A.V. Aho, M.S. Lam, R. Sethi, and J.D. Ullman. *Compilers: Principles, Techniques, and Tools.* Pearson Education, 1986.

[4] M.H. Alafi, J.R. Cordy, T.R. Dean, M. Stephan, and A. Stephenson. Models are code too: Near-miss clone detection for simulink models. In *Proceedings of the 28th International Conference on Software Maintenance*, pages 295–304. IEEE Computer Society, 2012.

[5] G. Antoniol, U. Villano, E. Merlo, and M. Di Penta. Analyzing cloning evolution in the linux kernel. *Information and Software Technology*, 44(13):755–765, 2002.

[6] L. Aversano, L. Cerulo, and M. Di Penta. How clones are maintained: An empirical study. In *Proceedings of the 11th European Conference on Software Maintenance and Reengineering*, pages 81–90. IEEE Computer Society, 2007.

[7] B.S. Baker. On finding duplication and near-duplication in large software systems. In *Proceedings of the 2nd Working Conference on Reverse Engineering*, pages 86–95. IEEE Computer Society Press, 1995.

[8] B.S. Baker. Parameterized duplication in strings: Algorithms and an application to software maintenance. *SIAM Journal of Computing*, 26(5):1343–1362, 1997.

[9] T. Bakota. Tracking the evolution of code clones. In I. C, T. Gyimothy, J. Hromkovic, K. Jefferey, R. Kralovic, M. Vukolic, and S. Wolf, editors, *SOFSEM 2011: Theory and Practice of Computer Science*, volume 6543 of *Lecture Notes in Computer Science*, pages 86–98. Springer Berlin Heidelberg, 2011.

[10] T. Bakota, R. Ferenc, and T. Gyimothy. Clone smells in software evolution. In *Proceedings of the 23rd IEEE International Conference on Software Maintenance*, pages 24–33. IEEE, 2007.

[11] M. Balazinska, E. Merlo, M. Dagenais, B. Laguë, and K. Kontogannis. Measuring clone based reengineering opportunities. In *Proceedings of the 6th International Symposium on Software Metrics*, pages 292–303. IEEE, 1999.

[12] M. Balazinska, E. Merlo, M. Dagenais, B. Laguë, and K. Kontogannis. Partial redesign of java software systems based on clone analysis. In *Proceedings of the 14th International Conference on Program Comprehension*, pages 323–336. IEEE, 1999.

[13] M. Balint, R. Marinescu, and T. Girba. How developers copy. In *Proceedings of the 14th International Conference on Program Comprehension*, pages 56–68. IEEE, June 2006.

[14] L. Barbour, F. Khomh, and Y. Zou. A technique for just-in-time clone detection in large scale systems. In *Proceedings of the 18th International Conference on Program Comprehension*, pages 76–79. IEEE, 2010.

[15] L. Barbour, F. Khomh, and Y. Zou. Late propagation in software clones. In *Proceedings of the 27th International Conference on Software Maintenance*, pages 273–282. IEEE, 2011.

[16] G.A. Barnard. A new test for $2 \times 2$ tables. *Nature*, 156(3954):177, 1945.

[17] H.A. Basit, S.J. Puglisi, W.F. Smyth, A. Turpin, and S. Jarzabek. Efficient token based clone detection with flexible tokenization. In *The 6th Joint Meeting on European Software Engineering Conference and the ACM SIGSOFT Symposium on the Foundations of Software Engineering: Companion Papers*, pages 513–516. ACM, 2007.

[18] H.A. Basit, D.C. Rajapakse, and S. Jarzabek. An empirical study on limits of clone unification using generics. In *Proceedings of the 17th International Conference on Software Engineering and Knowledge Engineering*, pages 109–114, 2005.

[19] I.D. Baxter, A. Yahin, L. Moura, M. Sant'Anna, and L. Bier. Clone detection using abstract syntax trees. In *Proceedings of the International Conference on Software Maintenance*, pages 368–377. IEEE Computer Society, 1998.

[20] S. Bazrafshan. Evolution of near-miss clones. In *Proceedings of the 12th International Conference on Source Code Analysis and Manipulation*, pages 74–83. IEEE, 2012.

[21] S. Bazrafshan and R. Koschke. Effect of clone information on the performance of developers fixing cloned bugs. In *Proceedings of the 14th International Conference on Source Code Analysis and Manipulation*, pages 1–10. IEEE, 2014.

[22] K. Beck. *Test-Driven Development: by example*. Addison Wesley, 2003.

[23] S. Bellon, R. Koschke, G. Antoniol, J. Krinke, and E. Merlo. Comparison and evaluation of clone detection tools. *IEEE Transactions on Software Engineering*, 33(9):577–591, 2007.

[24] N. Bettenburg, W Shang, W.M. Ibrahim, B. Adams, Y. Zou, and A.E. Hassan. An empirical study on inconsistent changes to code clones at the release level. *Science of Computer Programming*, 77(6):760–776, 2012.

[25] C. Bird, N. Nagappan, B. Murphy, H. Gall, and P. Devanbu. Don't touch my code! examining the effects of ownership on software quality. In *Proceedings of the 19th ACM SIGSOFT Symposium and the 13th European Conference on Foundations of Software Engineering*, pages 4–14. ACM, 2011.

[26] B.W. Boehm and P.N. Papaccio. Understanding and controlling software costs. *IEEE Transactions on Software Engineering*, 14(10):1462–1477, 1988.

[27] P. Bulychev and M. Minea. Duplicate code detection using anti-unification. In *Proceedings of the 2nd Spring Young Researchers' Colloquium on Software Engineering*, pages 51–54. IEEE Computer Society, 2008.

[28] D. Cai and M. Kim. An empirical study of long-lived code clones. In *Proceedings of the 14th international conference on Fundamental approaches to software engineering: part of the joint European conferences on theory and practice of software*, pages 432–446. Springer-Verlag, 2011.

[29] F. Calefato, F. Lanubile, and T. Mallardo. Function clone detection in web applications: A semiautomated approach. *Jorurnal of Web Engineering*, 3(1):3–21, May 2004.

[30] J.C. Carver, D. Chatterji, and N.A. Kraft. On the need for human-based empirical validation of techniques and tools for code clone analysis. In *Proceedings of the 5th International Workshop on Software Clones*, pages 61–62. ACM, 2011.

[31] D. Chatterji, J.C. Carver, and N.A. Kraft. Code clones and developer behavior: results of two surveys of the clone research community. *Empirical Software Engineering*, pages 1–33, 2015.

[32] D. Chatterji, J.C. Carver, N.A. Kraft, and J. Harder. Effects of cloned code on software maintainability: A replicated developer study. In *Proceedings of the 20th Working Conference on Reverse Engineering*, pages 112–121. IEEE, 2013.

[33] D. Chatterji, B. Massengill, J. Oslin, J.C. Carver, and N. A. Kraft. Measuring the efficacy of code clone information: an empirical study. In *Proceedings of the 5th International Symposium on Empirical Software Engineering and Measurement*, pages 20–29. IEEE Computer Society, 2011.

[34] J.R. Cordy. Comprehending reality – practical barriers to industrial adoption of software maintenance automation. In *Proceedings of the 11th IEEE International Workshop on Program Comprehension*, pages 196–205. IEEE, 2003.

[35] J.R. Cordy, T.R. Dean, and N. Synytskyy. Practical language-independent detection of near-miss clones. In *Proceedings of the 2004 Conference for Advances Studies on Collaborative Research*, pages 1–12. IEEE, 2004.

[36] J.R. Cordy and C.K. Roy. The NiCad clone detector. In *Proceedings of the 19th International Conference on Program Comprehension*, pages 219–220. IEEE Computer Society, 2011.

[37] M. Dagenais, E. Merlo, B. Laguë, and D. Proulx. Clones occurence in large object oriented software packages. In *Proceedings of the Conference of the Centre for Advanced Studies on Collaborative Research*. IBM Press, 1998.

[38] N. Davey, P. Barson, S. Field, and R. Frank. The development of a software clone detector. *International Journal of Applied Software Technology*, 1(3/4):219–236, 1995.

[39] I.J. Davis and M.W. Godfrey. Clone detection by exploiting assembler. In *Proceedings of the 4th International Workshop on Software Clones*, pages 77–78. ACM, 2010.

[40] M. de Wit, A. Zaidman, and A. van Deursen. Managing code clones using dynamic change tracking and resolution. In *Proceedings of the 25th IEEE International Conference on Software Maintenance*, pages 169–178. IEEE, 2009.

[41] G.A. Di Lucca, M. Di Penta, and A.R. Fasolino. An approach to identify duplicated web pages. In *Proceedings of the 26th Annual International Conference on Computer Software and Applications*, pages 481–486. IEEE, 2002.

[42] E. Duala-Ekoko and M.P. Robillard. Tracking code clones in evolving software. In *Proceedings of the 29th International Conference on Software Engineering*, pages 158–167. IEEE, 2007.

[43] E. Duala-Ekoko and M.P. Robillard. Clone region descriptors: Representing and tracking duplication in source code. *Transcations on Software Engineering*, 20(1):3:1–3:31, 2010.

[44] S. Ducasse, M. Rieger, and S. Demeyer. A language independent approach for detecting duplicated code. In *Proceedings of the 15th International Conference on Software Maintenance*, pages 109–118, 1999.

[45] W.S. Evans, C.W. Fraser, and F. Ma. Clone detection via structural abstraction. In *Proceedings of the 15th Working Conference on Reverse Engineering*, pages 150–159. IEEE, 2007.

[46] R. Falke, P. Frenzel, and R. Koschke. Empirical evaluation of clone detection using syntax suffix trees. *Journal of Empirical Software Engineering*, 13(6):601–643, 2008.

[47] R. Fanta and V. Rajlich. Removing clones from the code. *Journal on Software Maintenance and Evolution*, 11(4):223–243, 1999.

[48] A. Field. *Discovering Statistics using SPSS*. Sage Publications, 3rd edition, 2003.

[49] R.A. Fisher. On the interpretation of from $\chi^2$ contingency tables, and the calculation of p. *Journal of the Royal Statistical Society*, 85(1):87–94, 1922.

[50] M. Fowler. *Refactoring: Improving the Design of Existing Code*. Addison Wesley, 1999.

[51] E. Gamma, R. Helm, R. Johnson, and J. Vlissides. *Disign Patterns: Elements of Reusable Object-Oriented Software*. Addison Wesley, 1995.

[52] R. Geiger, B. Fluri, H.C. Gall, and M. Pinzger. Relation of code clones and change couplings. In *Proceedings of the 9th International Conference on Fundamental Approaches to Software Engineering*, pages 411–425. Springer, 2006.

[53] S. Giesecke. Clone-based Reengineering für Java auf der Eclipse-Plattform. diploma thesis, Carl von Ossietzky Universität Oldenburg, Department of Computing Science, Software Engineering Group, Germany, 2003.

[54] T. Gîrba, A. Kuhn, M. Seeberger, and S. Ducasse. How developers drive software evolution. In *Proceedings of the 8th International Workshop on Principles of Software Evolution*, pages 113–122. IEEE Computer Society, 2005.

[55] N. Göde. Evolution of type-1 clones. In *Proceedings of the 9th IEEE International Working Conference on Source Code Analysis and Manipulation*, pages 77–86. IEEE Computer Society, 2009.

[56] N. Göde. *Clone Evolution*. PhD thesis, University of Bremen, Faculty of Mathematics and Computer Science, Bremen, Germany, 2011.

[57] N. Göde and J. Harder. Clone stability. In *Proceedings of the 15th European Conference on Software Maintenance and Reengineering*, pages 65–74. IEEE, 2011.

[58] N. Göde and J. Harder. Oops!... I changed it again. In *Proceedings of the 5th International Workshop on Software Clones*, pages 14–20. ACM, 2011.

[59] N. Göde and R. Koschke. Incremental clone detection. In *Proceedings of the 13th European Conference on Software Maintenance and Reengineering*, pages 219–228. IEEE, 2009.

[60] N. Göde and R. Koschke. Studying clone evolution using incremental clone detection. *Journal of Software Maintenance and Evolution: Research and Practice*, 2010. Published online. DOI: 10.1002/smr.520.

[61] N. Göde and R. Koschke. Frequency and risks of changes to clones. In *Proceedings of the 33rd International Conference on Software Engineering*, pages 311–320. ACM, 2011.

[62] D. Gusfield, G.M. Landau, and B. Schieber. An efficient algorithm for the all pairs suffix-prefix problem. *Information Processing Letters*, 41(4):181–185, 1992.

[63] J. Harder. How multiple developers affect the evolution of code clones. In *Proceedings of the 29th International Conference on Software Maintenance*, pages 30–39. IEEE, 2013.

[64] J. Harder and N. Göde. Modeling clone evolution. In *Workshop Proceedings of the 13th European Conference on Software Maintenance and Reengineering*, pages 17–21, 2009.

[65] J. Harder and N. Göde. Quo vadis, clone management? In *Proceedings of the 4th International Workshop on Software Clones*, pages 85–86. ACM, 2010.

[66] J. Harder and N. Göde. Efficiently handling clone data: RCF and Cyclone. In *Proceedings of the 5th International Workshop on Software Clones*, pages 81–82. ACM, 2011.

[67] J. Harder and N. Göde. Cloned code: stable code. *Journal of Software: Evolution and Process*, 25:1063–1088, 2012.

[68] J. Harder and R. Tiarks. A controlled experiment on software clones. In *Proceedings of the 20th International Conference on Program Comprehension*, pages 219–228. IEEE, 2012.

[69] S.G. Hart and L.E. Staveland. Development of NASA-TLX (task load index): Results of empirical and theoretical research. *Advances in Psychology*, 52:139–183, 1988. Elsevier.

[70] A. Hemel and R. Koschke. Reverse engineering variability in source code using clone detection: A case study for linux variants of consumer electronic devices. In *Proceedings of the 19th Working Conference on Reverse Engineering*, pages 357–366. IEEE, 2012.

[71] Y. Higo and S. Kusumoto. Enhancing quality of code clone detection with program dependency graph. In *Proceedings of the 16th Working Conference on Reverse Engineering*, pages 315–316. IEEE, 2009.

[72] Y. Higo, U. Yasushi, M. Nishino, and S. Kusumoto. Incremental code clone detection: A PDG-based approach. In *Proceedings of the 18th Working Conference on Reverse Engineering*, pages 3–12. IEEE, 2011.

[73] W. Hordijk, M.L. Ponisio, and R. Wieringa. Harmfulness of code duplication – a structured review of the evidence. In *Proceedings of the 13th International Conference on evaluation and Assessment in Software Engineering*, 2009.

[74] K. Hotta, Y. Sano, Y. Higo, and S. Kusumoto. Is duplicate code more frequently modified than non-duplicate code in software evolution?: an empirical study on open source software. In *Proceedings of the Joint ERCIM Workshop on Software Evolution and International Workshop on Principles of Software Evolution*, pages 73–82. ACM, 2010.

[75] D. Hou, P. Jablonski, and F. Jacob. CnP: Towards an environment for the proactive management of copy-and-paste programming. In *Proceedings of the 17th International Conference on Program Comprehension*, pages 238–242. IEEE, 2009.

[76] D. Hou, F. Jacob, and P. Jablonski. Exploring the design space of proactive tool support for copy-and-paste programming. In *Proceedings of the 2009 Conference of the Center for Advanced Studies on Collaborative Research*, pages 188–202. IBM Corporation, 2009.

[77] B. Hummel, E. Juergens, L. Heinemann, and M. Conradt. Index-based code clone detection: Incremental, distributed, scalable. In *Proceedings of the 26th IEEE International Conference on Software Maintenance*, pages 1–9. IEEE Computer Society, 2010.

[78] B. Hummel, E. Juergens, and D. Steidl. Index-based model clone detection. In *Proceedings of the 5th International Workshop on Software Clones*, 2011.

[79] A. Hunt and D. Thomas. *The Pragmatic Programmer: from journeyman to master*. Addison Wesley, 1999.

[80] P. Jablonski and D. Hou. Aiding software maintenance with copy-and-paste clone-awareness. In *Proceedings of the 18th IEEE International Conference on Program Comprehension*, pages 170–179. IEEE Computer Society, 2010.

[81] S. Jarzabek and S. Li. Unifying clones with a generative programming technique: A case study. *Jornal of Software Maintenance and Evolution*, 18(4):267–292, 2002.

[82] A. Jedlitschka and D. Pfahl. Reporting guidelines for controlled experiments in software engineering. In *Proceedings of the International Symposium on Empirical Software Engineering*, pages 95–104. IEEE Computer Society, 2005.

[83] L. Jiang, G. Misherghi, Z. Su, and S. Glondu. DECKARD: Scalable and accurate tree-based detection of code clones. In *Proceedings of the 29th International Conference on Software Engineering*, pages 96–105. IEEE Computer Society, 2007.

[84] J.H. Johnson. Identifying redundancy in source code using fingerprints. In *Proceedings of the 1993 Conference of the Centre for Advanced Studies on Collaborative Research*, pages 171–183. IBM Press, 1993.

[85] J.H. Johnson. Visualizing textual redundancy in legacy source. In *Proceedings of the 1994 Conference of the Centre for Advanced Studies on Collaborative Research*, pages 9–18. IBM Press, 1994.

[86] E. Juergens and F. Deissenboeck. How much is a clone? In *Proceedings of the 4th International Workshop on Software Quality and Maintainability*, 2010.

[87] E. Juergens, F. Deissenboeck, M. Feilkas, B. Hummel, B. Schaetz, S. Wagner, C Domann, and J. Streit. Can clone detection support quality assessments of requirements specifications? In *Proceedings of the 32nd International Conference on Software Engineering*, pages 79–88. IEEE Computer Society, 2010.

[88] E. Juergens, F. Deissenboeck, and B. Hummel. Clone detection beyond copy&paste. In *Workshop Proceedings of the 13th European Conference on Software Maintenance and Reengineering*, 2009.

[89] E. Juergens, F. Deissenboeck, and B. Hummel. Clonedetective – a workbench for clone detection research. In *Proceedings of the 31st International Conference on Software Engineering*, pages 603–606. IEEE Computer Society, 2009.

[90] E. Juergens, F. Deissenboeck, B. Hummel, and S. Wagner. Do code clones matter? In *Proceedings of the 31st International Conference on Software Engineering*, pages 485–495. IEEE Computer Society, 2009.

[91] Y. Kamei, H. Sato, A. Monden, S. Kawaguchi, H. Uwano, M. Nagura, K.I. Matsumoto, and N. Ubayashi. An empirical study of fault prediction with code clone metrics. In *Proceedings of the Joint Conference of the 21st International Workshop on Software Measurement and the 6th International Conference on Software Process and Product Measurement*. IEEE, 2011.

[92] T. Kamiya, S. Kusumoto, and K. Inoue. CCFinder: A multilinguistic token-based code clone detection system for large scale source code. *IEEE Transactions on Software Engineering*, 28(7):654–670, 2002.

[93] C. Kapser, P. Anderson, M. Godfrey, R. Koschke, M. Rieger, F. van Rysselberghe, and P. Weißgerber. Subjectivity in clone judgment: Can we ever agree? In R. Koschke, E. Merlo, and A. Walenstein, editors, *Duplication, Redundancy, and Similarity in Software*, number 06301 in Dagstuhl Seminar Proceedings, Dagstuhl, Germany, 2007. Internationales Begegnungs- und Forschungszentrum für Informatik (IBFI), Schloss Dagstuhl, Germany.

[94] C. Kapser and M.W. Godfrey. "Cloning considered harmful" considered harmful: patterns of cloning in software. *Empirical Software Engineering*, 13(6):645–692, 2008.

[95] S. Kawaguchi, T. Yamashina, H. Uwano, K. Fushida, Y. Kamei, M. Nagura, and H. Iida. SHINOBI: A tool for automatic code clone detection in the IDE. In *Proceedings of the 16th Working Conference on Reverse Engineering*, pages 313–314. IEEE, 2009.

[96] H. Kim, Y. Jung, S. Kim, and K. Yi. MeCC: Memory comparison-based clone detector. In *Proceedings of the Joint 33rd International Conference on Software Engineering*, pages 301–310. IEEE, 2011.

[97] M. Kim, L. Bergman, T. Lau, and D. Notkin. An ethnographic study of copy and paste programming practices in OOPL. In *Proceedings of the ACM-IEEE International Symposium on Empirical Software Engineering*, pages 83–92. ACM, 2004.

[98] M. Kim and D. Notkin. Using a clone genealogy extractor for understanding and supporting evolution of code clones. In *Proceedings of the 2005 International Workshop on Mining Software Repositories*, pages 1–5. ACM, 2005.

[99] M. Kim, V. Sazawal, D. Notkin, and G.C. Murphy. An empirical study of code clone genealogies. In *Proceedings of the Joint 10th European Software Engineering Conference and the 13th ACM SIGSOFT Symposium on the Foundations of Software Engineering*, pages 187–196. ACM, 2005.

[100] B.R. Kirkwood and J.A.C. Sterne. *Essential Medical Statistics*. John Wiley & Sons, 2003.

[101] R.V. Komondoor and S. Horwitz. Using slicing to identify duplication in source code. In *Proceedings of the 8th International Symposium on Static Analysis*, pages 40–56. Springer-Verlag, 2001.

[102] R.V. Komondoor and S. Horwitz. Eliminating duplication in source code via procedure extraction. Technical report 1461, University of Wisconsin–Madison Department of Computer Sciences, December 2002.

[103] K.A. Kontogiannis, R. Demori, E. Merlo, M. Galler, and M. Bernstein. Pattern matching for clone and concept detection. *Automated Software Engineering*, 3(1–2):77–108, 2012.

[104] R. Koschke. Survey of research on software clones. In R. Koschke, E. Merlo, and A. Walenstein, editors, *Duplication, Redundancy, and Similarity in Software*, number 06301 in Dagstuhl Seminar Proceedings, Dagstuhl, Germany, 2007. Internationales Begegnungs- und Forschungszentrum für Informatik (IBFI), Schloss Dagstuhl, Germany.

[105] R. Koschke. Large-scale inter-system clone detection using suffix trees and hashing. *Journal of Software: Evolution and Process*, 26(8):747–769, 2013.

[106] R. Koschke, I.D. Baxter, M. Conradt, and J.R. Cordy. Software clone management towards industrial application (dagstuhl seminar 12071). *Dagstuhl Reports*, 2(2):21–57, 2012.

[107] R. Koschke and S. Bazrafshan. A large-scale statistical analysis of software clone rates and localization in open-source programs written in c, c++, c#, or java. In *Proceedings of the 10th International Workshop on Software Clones*. IEEE Computer Society, 2016.

[108] R. Koschke, F. Falke, and P. Frenzel. Clone detection using abstract syntax suffix trees. In *Proceedings of the 13th Working Conference on Reverse Engineering*. IEEE, 2006.

[109] N. Kraft, B. Bonds, and R. Smith. Cross-language clone detection. In *Proceedings of the 20th International Conference on software Engineering and Knowledge Engineering*, pages 54–59. Knowledge Systems Institute Graduate School, 2008.

[110] J. Krinke. Identifying similar code with program dependence graphs. In *Proceedings of the 8th Working Conference on Reverse Engineering*, pages 301–309. IEEE Computer Society, 2001.

[111] J. Krinke. A study of consistent and inconsistent changes to code clones. In *Proceedings of the 14th Working Conference on Reverse Engineering*, pages 170–178. IEEE Computer Society, 2007.

[112] J. Krinke. Is cloned code more stable than non-cloned code. In *Proceedings of the 8th IEEE International Working Conference on Source Code Analysis and Manipulation*, pages 57–66. IEEE Computer Society, 2008.

[113] J. Krinke. Is cloned code older than non-cloned code? In *Proceedings of the 5th IEEE International Workshop on Software Clones*, pages 23–33. ACM, 2011.

[114] J. Krinke, N. Gold, Y. Jia, and D. Binkley. Distinguishing copies from originals in software clones. In *Proceedings of the 4th IEEE International Workshop on Software Clones*. ACM, 2010.

[115] B. Laguë, D. Proulx, J. Mayrand, E.M. Merlo, and J. Hudepohl. Assessing the benefits of incorporating function clone detection in a development process. In *Proceedings of the 13th IEEE International Conference on Software Maintenance*, pages 314–321, 1997.

[116] T.D. Latoza, G. Venolia, and R. DeLine. Maintaining mental models: A study of developer work habits. In *Proceedings of the 28th International Conference on Software Engineering*, pages 492–501. ACM, 2006.

[117] M.-W. Lee, J.-W. Roh, S.-W. Hwang, and S. Kim. Instant code clone search. In *Proceedings of the 18th International Symposium on Foundations of Software Engineering*, pages 167–176. ACM, 2013.

[118] A.M. Leitao. Detection of redundant code using R2D2. In *Proceedings of the 3rd International Workshop on Source Code Analysis and Manipulation*, pages 183–192. IEEE, 2003.

[119] H. Li and S. Thompson. Incremental clone detection and elimination for erlang programs. In *Fundamental Approaches to Software Engineering*, volume 6603 of *Lecture Notes in Computer Science*, pages 356–370. Springer, Berlin Heidelberg, 2011.

[120] Z. Li, S. Lu, S. Myagmar, and Y. Zhou. CP-Miner: finding copy-paste and related bugs in large-scale software code. *Transactions on Software Engineering*, 32(3), 2006.

[121] S. Livieri, Y. Higo, M. Matushita, and K. Inoue. Very-large scale code clone analysis and visualization of open source programs using distributed CCFinder: D-CCFinder. In *Proceedings of the 29th International Conference on Software Engineering*, pages 106–115. IEEE, 2007.

[122] A. Lozano and M. Wermelinger. Assessing the effect of clones on changeability. In *Proceedings of the 24th IEEE International Conference on Software Maintenance*, pages 227–236. IEEE, 2008.

[123] U. Manber. Finding similar files in a large file system. In *Proceedings of the Winter 1994 Usenix Technical Conference*, pages 1–10. USENIX Association, 1994.

[124] A. Marcus and J.I. Maletic. Identification of high-level concept clones in source code. In *Proceedings of the 16th International Conference on Automated Software Engineering*, pages 107–114. IEEE Computer Society, 2001.

[125] R.C. Martin. *Clean Code: A Handbook for Agile Software Craftmanship*. Prentice Hall, 2008.

[126] J. Mayrand, C. Leblanc, and E.M. Merlo. Experiment on the automatic detection of function clones in a software system using metrics. In *Proceedings of the 2nd International Conference on Software Maintenance*, pages 227–236. IEEE, 1996.

[127] E.M. McCreight. A space-economical suffix tree construction algorithm. *Journal of the ACM*, 23(2):262–272, 1976.

[128] T. Mende, R. Koschke, and F. Beckwermert. An evaluation of code similarity identification for the grow-and-prune model. *Journal of Software Maintenance and Evolution: Research and Practice*, 21(2):143–169, 2009.

[129] E. Merlo, G. Antoniol, M. Di Penta, and V.F. Rollo. Linear complexity object-oriented similarity for clone detection and software evolution analyses. In *Proceedings of the 20th International Conference on Software Maintenance*, pages 412–416. IEEE, 2004.

[130] C.R. Metha and P. Senchaudhuri. Conditional versus unconditional exact tests for comparing two binomials. Technical Report vol. 5, Cytel Software Corporation, 2003.

[131] M. Mondal, C.K. Roy, M.S. Rahman, R.K. Saha, J. Krinke, and K.A. Schneider. Comparative stability of cloned and non-cloned code: An empirical study. In *Proceedings of the 27th Symposium on Applied Computing*, pages 1227–1234. ACM, 2012.

[132] M. Mondal, C.K. Roy, and K.A. Schneider. Dispersion of changes in cloned and non-cloned code. In *Proceedings of the 6th International Workshop on Software Clones*, pages 29–35. IEEE, 2012.

[133] M. Mondal, C.K. Roy, and K.A. Schneider. An empirical study on clone stability. *SIGAPP Applied Computing Review*, 12(3):20–36, September 2012.

[134] A. Monden, D. Nakae, T. Kamiya, S. Sato, and K. Matsumoto. Software quality analysis by code clones in industrial legacy software. In *Proceedings of the 8th IEEE International Software Metrics Symposium*, pages 87–94. IEEE Computer Society, 2002.

[135] E.W. Myers. An O(ND) difference algorithm and its variations. *Algorithmica*, 1(1):251–266, 1986.

[136] H.A. Nguyen, T.T. Nguyen, N.H. Pham, J. Al-Kofahi, and T.N. Nguyen. Clone management for evolving software. *IEEE Transactions on Software Engineering*, 38(5):1008–1026, 2012.

[137] T.T. Nguyen, H.A. Nguyen, J.M. Al-Kofahi, N.H. Pham, and T.N. Nguyen. Scalable and incremental clone detection for evolving software. In *Proceedings of the 25th IEEE International Conference on Software Maintenance*, pages 491–494. IEEE, 2009.

[138] T.T. Nguyen, H.A. Nguyen, N.H. Pham, J.M. Al-Kofahi, and T.N. Nguyen. Clone-aware configuration management. In *Proceedings of the 24th ACM/IEEE International Conference on Automated Software Engineering*, pages 123–134. IEEE, 2009.

[139] D.L. Parnas. On the criteria to be used in decomposing systems into modules. *Communications of the ACM*, 15(12):1053–1058, 1972.

[140] J.R. Pate, R. Tairas, and N.A. Kraft. Clone evolution: a systematic review. *Journal of Software: Evolution and Process*, 25(3):261–283, 2013.

[141] J.-F. Patenaude, E. Merlo, M. Dagenais, and B. Laguë. Extending software quality assessment techniques to java systems. In *Proceedings of the 7th International Workshop on Program Comprehension*, pages 49–56. IEEE, 1999.

[142] K. Pearson. On the criterion that a given system of deviations from the probable in the case of a correlated system of variables is such that it can be reasonably supposed to have arisen from random sampling. *Philosophical Magazine Series 5*, 50(302):157–175, 1900.

[143] N.H. Pham, H.A. Nguyen, T.T. Nguyen, J.M. Al-Kohafi, and T.N. Nguyen. Complete and accurate clone detection in graph-based models. In *Proceedings of the 31st International Conference on Software Engineering*. IEEE, 2009.

[144] J. Quante. Do dynamic object process graphs support program understanding? – a controlled experiment. In *Proceedings of the 16th IEEE International Conference on Program Comprehension*, pages 73–82. IEEE Computer Society, 2008.

[145] F. Rahman, C. Bird, and P. Devanbu. Clones: What is that smell? In *Proceedings of the 7th IEEE Working Conference on Mining Software Repositories*, pages 72–81. IEEE, 2010.

[146] F. Rahman and P. Devanbu. Ownership, experience and defects: a fine-grained study of authorship. In *Proceedings of the 33rd International Conference on Software Engineering*, pages 491–500. ACM, 2011.

[147] D. Rattan, R. Bhatia, and M. Singh. Software clone detection: A systematic review. *Information and Software Technology*, 55(7):1165–1199, 2013.

[148] O.J.L. Riemann and R. Koschke. Robust parsing of cloned token sequences. In *Proceedings of the 8th International Workshop on Software Clones*. European Association of Software Science and Technology, 2014.

[149] T. Roehm, R. Tiarks, R. Koschke, and W. Maalej. How do professional developers comprehend software? In *Proceedings of the 34th International Conference on Software Engineering*, pages 255–265. IEEE, 2012.

[150] R. Rosenthal. *Meta-analytic procedures for social research*. Sage Publications, 2nd edition, 1991.

[151] C.K. Roy and J.R. Cordy. An empirical study of function clones in open source software. In *Proceedings of the 15th Working Conference on Reverse Engineering*, pages 81–90. IEEE, 2008.

[152] C.K. Roy and J.R. Cordy. NICAD: Accurate detection of near-miss intentional clones using flexible pretty-printing and code normalization. In *Proceedings of the 16th International Conference on Program Comprehension*, pages 172–181. IEEE, 2008.

[153] C.K. Roy, J.R. Cordy, and R. Koschke. Comparison and evaluation of code clone detection techniques and tools: A qualitative approach. *Science of Computer Programming*, 74(7):470–495, 2009.

[154] C.K. Roy, M.F. Zibran, and R. Koschke. The vision of software clone management: Past, present, and future. In *Proceedings of the IEEE Conference on Software Maintenance, Reengineering and Reverse Engineering*, pages 18–33. IEEE, 2014.

[155] T. Sager, A. Bernstein, M. Pinzger, and C. Kiefer. Detecting similar java classes using tree algorithms. In *Proceedings of the 2006 International Workshop on Mining Software Repositories*, pages 65–71. ACM, 2006.

[156] R.K. Saha, M. Asaduzzaman, M.F. Zibran, C.K. Roy, and K.A. Schneider. Evaluating code clone genealogies at release level: An empirical study. In *Proceedings of the 10th IEEE Working Conference on Source Code Manipulation*, pages 87–96. IEEE, 2010.

[157] R.K. Saha, C.K. Roy, and K.A. Schneider. An automatic framework for extracting and classifying near-miss clone genealogies. In *Proceedings of the 27th IEEE International Conference on Software Maintenance*, pages 293–302. IEEE, 2011.

[158] R.K. Saha, C.K. Roy, and K.A. Schneider. gCad: A near-miss clone genealogy extractor to support clone evolution analysis. In *Proceedings of the 29th IEEE International Conference on Software Maintenance*, pages 488–491. IEEE, 2013.

[159] S. Schulze, M. Kuhlemann, and M. Rosenmüller. Towards a refactoring guideline using code clone classification. In *Proceedings of the 2nd Workshop on Refactoring Tools*, pages 1–4. ACM, 2008.

[160] G.M.K. Selim, L. Barbour, S. Weiyi, B. Adams, and A.E. Hassan. Studying the impact of clones on software defects. In *Proceedings of the 17th Working Conference on Reverse Engineering*, pages 13–21. IEEE, 2010.

[161] D.M. Shawky and A.F. Ali. An approach for assessing similarity metrics used in metric-based clone detection techniques. In *Proceedings of the 3rd International Conference on Computer Science and Information Technology*, pages 580–584. IEEE, 2010.

[162] D. Steidl and N. Göde. Feature-based detection of bugs in clones. In *Proceedings of the 7th International Workshop on Software Clones*, pages 76–82. IEEE, 2013.

[163] H. Störrle. Towards clone detection in uml domain models. *Software & Systems Modeling*, 12(2):307–329, 2013.

[164] R. Tairas and J. Gray. Phoenix-based clone detection using suffix trees. In *Proceedings of the 44th Annual Southeast Regional Conference*, pages 679–684. ACM, 2006.

[165] S. Thummalapenta, L. Cerulo, L. Aversano, and M. Di Penta. An empirical study on the maintenance of source code clones. *Empirical Software Engineering*, 15(1):1–34, 2010.

[166] M. Toomim, A. Begel, and S.L. Graham. Managing duplicated code with linked editing. In *Proceedings of the 2004 Symposium on Visual Languages and Human Centric Computing*, pages 173–180. IEEE, 2004.

[167] Y. Ueda, T. Kamiya, S. Kusumoto, and K. Inoue. On detection of gapped code clones using gap locations. In *Proceedings of the 9th Asia-Pacific Software Engineering Conference*, pages 327–336. IEEE, 2002.

[168] E. Ukkonen. On-line construction of suffix trees. *Algorithmica*, 14(3):249–260, 1995.

[169] V. Wagler, D. Seipel, J. Wolff, and G. Fischer. Clone detection in source code by frequent itemset techniques. In *Proceedings of the 4th International Workshop on Source Code Analysis and Manipulation*, pages 128–135. IEEE, 2011.

[170] S. Wagner, A. Abdulkhaleq, K. Kaya, and A. Paar. On the relationship of inconsistent software clones and faults: An empirical study. In *Proceedings of the 23rd International Conference on Software Analysis, Evolution, and Reengineering*. IEEE, 2016.

[171] T. Wang, M. Harman, Y. Jia, and J. Krinke. Searching for better configurations: A rigorous approach to clone evaluation. In *Proceedings of the 9th Joint Meeting on Foundations of Software Engineering*, pages 455–465. ACM, 2013.

[172] W. Wang and M.W. Godfrey. A study of cloning in the linux SCSI drivers. In *Proceedings of the 11th International Working Conference on Source Code Analysis and Manipulation*, pages 95–104. IEEE, 2011.

[173] X. Wang, Y. Dang, L. Zhang, D. Zhang, E. Lan, and H. Mei. Can I clone this piece of code here? In *Proceedings of the 27th International Conference on Automated Software Engineering*, pages 170–179. ACM, 2009.

[174] R. Wettel. *Software Systems as Cities*. PhD thesis, Università della Svizzera italiana, Faculty of Informatics, Lugano, Switzerland, 2010.

[175] R. Wettel and R. Marinescu. Archeology of code duplication: recovering duplication chains from small duplication fragments. In *Proceedings of the 7th International Symposium on Symbolic and Numeric Algorithms for Scientific Computing*, pages 8–16. IEEE, 2005.

[176] E.J. Weyuker, T.J. Ostrand, and R.M. Bell. Do too many cooks spoil the broth? using the number of developers to enhance defect prediction models. *Empirical Software Engineering*, 13(5):539–559, October 2008.

[177] C. Wohlin, P. Runeson, M. Höst, C. Ohlsson, B. Regnell, and A. Wesslén. *Experimentation in Software Engineering – An Introduction*. Kluver Academic Publishers, 2000.

[178] S. Xie, F. Khomh, and Y. Zou. An empirical study of the fault-proneness of clone mutation and clone migration. In *Proceedings of the 10th Working Conference on Mining Software Repositories*, pages 149–158. IEEE, 2013.

[179] W. Yang. Identifying syntactic differences between two programs. *Journal of Software—Practice & Experience*, 21(7):739–755, June 1991.

[180] G.U. Yule. On the association of attributes in statistics. *Philosophical Transactions of the Royal Society*, Series A(75):257–319, 1900.

[181] G. Zhang, X. Peng, Z. Xing, S. Jiang, H. Wang, and W. Zhao. Towards contextual and on-demand code clone management by continuous monitoring. In *Proceedings of the 28th International Conference on Automated Software Engineering*, pages 497–507. IEEE Computer Society, 2013.

[182] G. Zhang, X. Peng, Z. Xing, and W. Zhao. Cloning practices: Why developers clone and what can be changed. In *Proceedings of the 28th International Conference on Software Maintenance*, pages 285–294. IEEE Computer Society, 2012.

[183] Y. Zhang, H.A. Basit, S. Jarzabek, D. Anh, and M. Low.    Query-based filtering and graphical viwe generation for clone analysis. In *Proceedings of the 24th International Conference on Software Maintenance*, pages 376–385. IEEE Computer Society, 2008.

[184] M.F. Zibran and C.K. Roy.   IDE-based real-time focused search for near-miss clones. In *Proceedings of the 27th Annual ACM Symposium on Applied Computing*, pages 1235–1242. ACM, 2012.